THE CONSERVATIVE REFORMERS

German-American Catholics and the Social Order

THE CONSERVATIVE

REFORMERS

GERMAN-AMERICAN CATHOLICS AND THE SOCIAL ORDER

PHILIP GLEASON

UNIVERSITY OF NOTRE DAME PRESS
Notre Dame – *London*

For Ann, Danny, Margaret, and Philip Michael
and all their immigrant ancestors

PREFACE

In the course of working on this book I came to envy historians who deal with subjects like the Civil War or the New Deal. If scholars in these areas are asked what they are doing, they do not ordinarily have to persuade the inquirer that their subjects exist and are worth studying. Experience has taught me that such is not the case when one says he is devoting his attention to the interest of the German-American Catholics in social reform. For that reason I hope it will not seem presumptuous for me to indicate briefly what this book is about and why it was worth undertaking.

The book is a case study in the assimilation of a Catholic immigrant group. All such groups, and the Catholic Church as a whole in the United States, have gone through a process of Americanization. This general process of adjustment to the American environment included certain features that were common to all the groups involved, such as the transition of generations and, for non-English-speaking immigrants, the language problem. But the working out of these common features of the process was conditioned by variable factors that differed from one group to another—such matters, for example, as the time of the group's arrival, its size, and distinctive elements in its specific cultural heritage. In tracing the development of the German-American Catholics in the twentieth century, I have tried to show how the assimilation of the group was shaped by its distinctive heritage and by various historical contingencies, and in particular to show how the interest of the group in social reform was related to the process of Americanization. The reader can judge for himself how well these aims have been achieved. My hope is that the results will have some value, not only for students of immigration and of American Catholicism, but also for sociologists who are interested in the way in which large social processes are influenced by contingent historical circumstances.

Whatever merit the book possesses is owing in large measure to assistance I have received from others. Most of those who have helped me are persons whom I have never met from whose writings I derived insights as well as information. It is a pleasure for me to acknowledge my obligation to Father Thomas T. McAvoy, Archivist of the University of Notre Dame, who first suggested this topic for investigation and who aided me as teacher, colleague, and friend. I am also grateful to Monsignor Victor T. Suren, former Director of the Central Bureau, and to Mr. Harvey Johnson, its present Director, for placing the materials of that institution at my disposal and for other assistance. Members of Frederick P. Kenkel's family also cooperated generously and I am especially obligated to Miss Eleanore Kenkel. The many others who gave me aid and encouragement cannot be named here, except my wife, Maureen.

I wish to express my appreciation to the United States Steel Foundation, the American Philosophical Society, and the University of Notre Dame for grants supporting my research. Parts of Chapter IV appeared in somewhat different form in the *American Historical Review* for December, 1967.

CONTENTS

ix

I

The Problem

Ten years ago an acute foreign observer wrote that American Catholicism could be summed up in a few words: " 'Immigration' to describe the past, 'Generosity and Courage' for the present, and 'Problems' for the future. . . ."[1] Perhaps he was overgenerous in describing the present, but the Chilean Jesuit quoted here could surely make a strong case for "immigration" as the single word that best epitomizes the history of the Catholic Church in the United States; and "problems" is still a good word for the future. In the past the two terms were practically interchangeable—the problems of the Church were overwhelmingly the problems of immigration. And to the degree that self-understanding is required to deal intelligently with the issues confronting the Church today, immigration is still a problem. For although we know in general that it has profoundly shaped the American Church, we do not know just how; nor do we know the extent to which the attitudes and social patterns of American Catholics are still conditioned by the immigrant past. To arrive at a more adequate

1

understanding of contemporary Catholicism—and specifically to grasp the real nature of the much discussed "emergence from the ghetto"— we need to know a great deal more about the complex processes of immigration, ethnic interaction, and the assimilation of the various elements composing the Catholic population.

The largest dark area in our knowledge of the immigrant past is the history of the non-English-speaking groups. For most American Catholics the life of these peoples has been rendered inaccessible by the language barrier; the histories written in their own tongues can be utilized only by specialists and by a declining percentage within each ethnic group. Moreover, the value of such histories is often reduced by reason of their annalistic approach and spirit of filiopietism. Yet because these groups are very important, research that would relate their development to the larger story of the Catholic Church in American society is greatly needed.

Among all the non-English-speaking Catholic groups, the Germans have been best served by historians. They have played too prominent a role to be overlooked, and a number of scholars have discussed their involvement in the story of American Catholicism. In *The Catholic Church and German Americans* by Colman J. Barry, O.S.B., we have an excellent detailed account of the group in the last quarter of the nineteenth century.[2] However, there remain many unanswered questions about the German-American Catholics. For one thing, most attention has been concentrated on the 1880's and 1890's, when the Germans became deeply involved in the controversies then dividing the American Church. The years after 1900 have been almost totally neglected, with the consequence that we know virtually nothing about the assimilation of the German Catholics in the present century. In one respect especially, the studies we have suggest a tantalizing puzzle but help not at all in solving it. The puzzle is this: How did a group that was deeply conservative before 1900 come to be regarded as progressive or liberal in the twentieth century?

Despite the ambiguities of terminology, there is no question that the Germans were on the conservative side in the disputes of the 1880's and 1890's and that they set their faces like stone against the tendencies described by Robert Cross as characterizing "the emergence of liberal Catholicism." But today the influence of German Catholicism is widely thought of as being associated with the more liberal and forward-looking developments in the American Church. Thus Edward Sheehan wrote in the *Saturday Evening Post* that the late Cardinal Ritter's open-mindedness and progressivism were partially explained by his having grown up "among liberal German Catholics [in Indiana] who felt no need to isolate themselves from Protestant society."[3] Thomas Beer seemed to think in the 1920's that German Catholics were more liberal than the Irish; and the more recent remarks of other non-Catholic writers like Reinhold Niebuhr and Richard Hofstadter indicate their belief that a stronger admixture of Germans as against Irish would have reduced the conservatism and anti-intellectualism of American Catholicism.[4]

The pioneering role of Midwestern German-American Catholics—especially the Benedictines of St. John's Abbey in Minnesota—in the liturgical movement has been a major factor linking them with the forward-looking tendencies and greater vitality which is generally thought to mark the Church in that region.[5] But another factor, perhaps less widely known, is the activity of the German-American Catholics with regard to social reform, or (to use the accepted term of the Progressive period) "the social question."

In 1909, as the Progressive movement was nearing its climax, the German Catholic Central-Verein began to publish a magazine called *Central-Blatt and Social Justice,* which was the first Catholic journal in the country to make the discussion of social problems its primary concern. Within a few years the Central-Verein had established its reputation as the most socially conscious of American Catholic organizations. Before the outbreak of World War I it had created a special office in St. Louis to coordinate its social reform work, had set up a day nursery in the same city, sponsored a number of lecture tours and social study courses, initiated a news service for religious and reform items for the Catholic press, and encouraged its membership to support a number of Progressive legislative measures. After the war the organization retained its interest in social issues during the doldrums of normalcy, and its leaders were closely associated with the beginnings of such groups as the National Catholic Rural Life Conference and the Catholic Conference on Industrial Problems. The *Central-Blatt and*

Social Justice also gave sympathetic attention to the liturgical movement long before liturgical reform became popular.

In view of this impressive record, we might be tempted to think either that the German-American Catholics radically changed their views in the twentieth century or else that they had not really been conservative earlier. We would be wrong on both counts. For not only were the Germans proudly conservative before 1900, they continued to think of themselves very definitely as conservatives after that date, even when they were at the same time pursuing a vigorous social reform campaign. Within the last two or three decades, the conservatism of their position has reappeared in more easily recognizable form: They have become severe critics of the welfare state and the sort of reform measures championed by American liberals since the New Deal. These puzzling transitions are dramatically illustrated in the career of *The Wanderer*. Now a spokesman for extreme conservatism in both the religious and political spheres, *The Wanderer* is the successor of a German-language Catholic paper founded in St. Paul in 1867.[6] It has been in the editorial hands of the Matt family since 1899; Joseph Matt, who took it over at that time, was one of the principal leaders of the Central-Verein when it took up the social question in earnest, and he consistently supported its social reform work. In the minds of the editors of *The Wanderer*, it is safe to assume, there is no inconsistency between the earlier reform interest and the position they now take.

Part of the seeming contradiction of these shifts from conservatism to liberalism and back again stems from the vagueness of the terms themselves and the simplistic way they are usually employed. But even if we make careful distinctions and guard against thinking that to be liberal on one point necessarily excludes being conservative on any point—or even if we discard the terms completely—the fact remains that the behavior of the German-American Catholics in respect to social reform is rather perplexing and invites closer scrutiny. It is the purpose of this book to provide that closer scrutiny.

But while the origin and development of social reform interest furnishes the principal thread of continuity running through this investigation, it is not really the main object of study. Our primary interest is in the historical evolution of the German-American Catholic group, and the reason for concentrating on the social reform program derives from its symptomatic value: what it tells us about the life of the group. The historical evolution of the German-American Catholics and their interest in the social question illuminate one another. On the one hand, the interest in social reform is simply unintelligible if not viewed in the context of the history of the group. But on the other hand, the social reform activities had the effect of making that history public and visible, embodying it in a clearly identifiable movement, and thus laying open its course for our analysis. And if we pay attention to the way in which the social reform program was shaped by both American and European influences, to the importance of linguistic and generational transition, to the imperatives of organizational self-preservation, to the difficulties of interaction with other religious and ethnic groups, and to other processes of immigrant assimilation—if we are attentive to all these matters, it soon becomes evident that the social reform program profoundly reflects the life of the group and its effort at adjustment to the ever-changing American scene. By analyzing these subtle developments in what has historically been the most important of the non-English-speaking elements in the Catholic population, we hope not only to learn more about the group but also to shed some light on the general theme of the Americanization of the Catholic Church in the United States.

The German-American Catholics and the Central-Verein

This study focuses on one German Catholic society, the Central-Verein, and the large themes just mentioned at times appear to be forgotten as we proceed into the intricacies of its organizational history. Therefore, it seems proper to explain what might otherwise seem to be an unduly narrow approach. The most obvious reason for concentrating on the Central-Verein is that it was the German Catholic organization that became most deeply involved with the social question. In 1901 it solemnly pledged itself to work for the reform of society according to the principles laid down in Pope Leo XIII's *Rerum Novarum,* and from that time forward it consistently made social study, social criticism, and social reform its leading concerns. Hence, if one wishes to understand the involvement of the German-American Catholics with the social question, the Central-Verein is indisputably the place to begin.

But how typical was the Central-Verein? That is the crucial question. Can we really consider this one society the authentic spokesman for the German-American Catholics? Are we justified in assuming that its activities are truly representative of the group as a whole? The answer to these questions is yes. In fact, the Central-Verein not only represents the group, but in a sense it *actually is the group* and to understand it is to understand the group as a whole. This may appear an extreme claim, but it is central to the entire study and so requires a rather extended theoretical justification.

The fundamental issue has to do with the identity of an immigrant group and the relationship of immigrant organizations to group identity. Obviously, we cannot arrive at any conclusions about the representative character of the Central-Verein until we know who constituted the group for which it claimed to speak. The first question to be taken up, therefore, is: Who were the German-American Catholics or, as they frequently called themselves, the German Catholics? The matter is not so simple as it might seem, as a German-American writer pointed out in 1909 in discussing the size of the "German Catholic" population in the United States. Not only were satisfactory statistics lacking, wrote Arthur Preuss, the American-born son of a Lutheran convert to Catholicism, but one also had to answer the question: "What is meant by German Catholics?"[7] Catholics living in the United States who had been born within the limits of the political state known as Germany were clearly German-American Catholics. But this criterion was too narrow because it excluded not only a large number of Catholic immigrants from Austria and elsewhere who considered themselves German but also the American-born children of German-speaking immigrants. On the other hand, difficulties also arose if one took the inclusive view that all German-speaking immigrants *and* their descendants constituted the German-American Catholic group. For in what sense was the son of an immigrant still a "German Catholic" if he worshipped in an "American" parish, married an Irish girl, and could speak only English?

As these considerations suggest, the German-American Catholic group could not be defined simply in terms of geographical origin or biological descent. At least equally important was how these people thought of themselves, how they identified themselves. Hence, the German-American Catholics may be described as those who thought of themselves, more or less self-consciously, as belonging to a group that was set off from other collectivities of human beings by the specific combination of American residence and civic loyalty, German origin and cultural descent, and Catholic faith. Because of the key role played by self-awareness, it is not merely tautological to say that the German-American Catholics were those who considered themselves to be such. For Germanness, Americanness, and Catholicity, while they were the essential ingredients or constituent elements of the group's social identity, were not sufficient of themselves to bring the group into existence and to maintain its life. Rather the group could not come into being until, and could exist only so long as, the individuals involved took thought of the fact that they shared these three characteristics and of the further fact that their sharing of the three characteristics consituted a principle of unity or distinguishing mark that set them apart from others in American society.

If the sense of self-awareness was so important, where did it come from? How did the Catholic immigrants from German-speaking lands become conscious of the fact that they formed a distinctive subgrouping in American society? Briefly, they became aware of who they were by becoming aware of who they were not. It was clear, first of all, that they were not just Americans, pure and simple, because they differed too much in language, religion, and cultural background from the native American majority to be able to consider themselves Americans without any further qualification. They did not wish to forget or to disassociate themselves completely from their German identity; and even if they had, they could not have done so because the native Americans made it impossible by regarding them as foreigners.[8]

But while these immigrants were very conscious of their German heritage and wished to preserve it as far as possible in the new world, they could not identify themselves unreservedly with the whole body of German-speaking immigrants in the United States, because of differences in religion and weltanschauung. Although they seemed a solid and cohesive bloc to the native Americans, the Germans were actually divided deeply among themselves, particularly along religious and ideological lines.[9] Catholics and Protestants were mutually antagonistic, and arrayed against both of these religiously oriented groups were the German liberals of the Forty-Eighter type. During the years of Know-Nothing nativism in the 1850's, Catholics of German origin probably suffered more from the hostility of anticlerical German liberals than they did from the anti-immigrant and anti-Catholic sentiments of the old-stock Americans.[10] These religious and ideological differences set the Catholic Germans off from the larger immigrant group of which they were linguistically a part. They were not simply Americans, because of their German heritage; nor were they simply German-Americans, because of their religious heritage.

Their Catholic faith was thus so fundamental to the identity of these immigrants that, to use a term that became popular in World War I, they were not only "hyphenated Americans" but also "hyphenated Germans." And they were also "hyphenated Catholics." For even the religion to which they clung so tenaciously through the upheaval of migration and adjustment to a new environment seemed different in the United States. Their steadfastness in the faith and loyalty to the Church was firm, but still things were not the same as they had been in Bavaria or Westphalia, where the Catholic Church was theirs alone and where Catholicism had been shaped as a social institution by centuries of association with Germanic culture. In the United States the German Catholic immigrants found themselves a cultural minority within a Church whose basic tradition had been set by an Anglo-American nucleus and which was dominated in the nineteenth century by immigrants from Ireland, whose faith, to be sure, was the same but whose linguistic, liturgical, and cultural traditions differed markedly from those of the Germans.[11]

Within the American Church, as in society at large and in the German linguistic group as a whole, the German Catholics were "different." Being alike and yet unlike other Americans, other German-Americans, and other Catholics involved a number of tensions and perplexities; it is understandable that those who found themselves in this situation sometimes felt that they were under fire from all sides. Thus the *Pastoral-Blatt*, a magazine published in St. Louis for German priests, complained in 1888: "On the one hand we are told: 'You Catholics are not Germans.' On the other hand we are told: 'You Ger-

mans are not Catholics.' What we are though, that no one tells us."[12]
The *Pastoral-Blatt's* implied question—"What are we?"—is answered
adequately by the term we have already used, German-American
Catholics. In fact, the threefold identity had been very clearly stated
just two months before the *Pastoral-Blatt's* comments were published.
A speaker at the Central-Verein's 1888 convention objected to what he
considered the "Germanomania" of some of his fellow delegates. He
rebuked them: "We are Catholics, we are Americans, and only then
are we Germans." The same tripartite identity was emphasized by
other speakers at the Central-Verein's conventions of 1908, 1916, and
1924.[13] The difficulties of social identity did not stem so much from the
elusiveness of the constitutent elements, which were in fact fairly easy
to pinpoint, as from the novelty of the three-way combination and the
lack of appropriate organs of corporate life. For there were no pre-
existing institutions—neither civic, nor nationality, nor religious—whose
social boundaries corresponded precisely with those of the group, no
institutions which were perfectly attuned to their inmost character and
in which the German Catholic immigrants could feel completely at
home, no institutions which could serve both as organizational vehicles
for their group life and institutional symbols of their common consciousness as a people. To meet these needs they had to create their
own institutions—and they did.

For the Germans, as for most other Catholic immigrant groups, the
national parish was the most important ethnic institution, not only
because it met their deepest religious needs but also because it furnished the social nucleus around which many voluntary associations
clustered. Some of the parish societies were devotional sodalities, but
the most important of the voluntary associations rooted in the parish
were various types of mutual benefit societies. These benevolent societies provided a congenial setting for sociability as well as material
assistance in sickness or misfortune. They were characteristically small
and local in scope, but they often grouped themselves into larger unions
covering a city or region; the Central-Verein, as we shall see, came
into existence as a national federation of such benevolent societies.
There were also more specialized organizations for particular groups,
such as a society for priests; other societies, like the St. Raphael Society

for the Protection of German Catholic Emigrants, were oriented around some particular activity.[14]

The whole complex of associational life—called the *Vereinswesen*—along with the national parishes and the German-language press, reflected the perception by the German Catholic immigrants of their distinctiveness in American society. More than that, this organizational complex was one of the most important means by which the unstructured collectivity of individual immigrants was transformed into a social group in the more formal sense. And since it furnished a tangible organizational reality with which the immigrant could identify himself and thus affirm his solidarity with the group, the *Vereinswesen* in a sense both objectified and symbolized the German-American Catholic group as a whole.

Although the *Vereinswesen* could not have come into being without at least an implicit recognition on the part of the German Catholic immigrants that they did not fully "belong" anywhere else, still the formation and support of their societies was more or less automatic when the group was predominantly composed of adults who had actually immigrated themselves. The "German Catholic" character of such persons was an obvious and given fact—they simply *were* German Catholics. They could converse comfortably only in the mother tongue; their memories went back to the homeland and the way of life they had known there; and, by a process which did not require a high degree of self-consciousness, they naturally formed associations with others like themselves, whom they were apt to find in considerable number in their immediate locality. A more fully conscious self-awareness was involved in the establishment of regional or national organizations, which were further removed from the concrete cultural milieu of the German Catholic neighborhood or parish where the local societies flourished. Existing as they did on a more abstract level than the local societies, these larger organizations required for their creation and maintenance a higher degree of self-consciousness in respect to their ethnic distinctiveness.[15] But with the passage of time, the need for ethnic self-consciousness increased all along the line.

It was the appearance of the second generation that created an urgent need for this self-consciousness. The American-born children of the immigrants could not be expected to think of themselves automatically as German. They had never known the German homeland; America was their birthplace and fatherland. Although German might be spoken in the home, English was their real mother tongue, and in a thousand ways they came into daily contact with strictly American influences, especially in the cities. Consequently, the second generation had to be *taught* what its identity was—had to be taught that although it was fully American, its heritage also included unique elements that set it apart from other groups in American society. And repeatedly the younger generation was exhorted to hold fast to this heritage—to know it, to cherish it, and to preserve it.[16]

The second-generation problem did not suddenly emerge from nowhere at the beginning of the present century; German immigration had been going on a long time and a number of second generations had already put in an appearance by that date. Nevertheless, the problem did become considerably more pressing around 1900, because the falling off of immigration from Germany largely eliminated the reinforcements which the first generation had been continuously receiving up to that time. The balance shifted decisively toward the second generation as the American-born children progressively outnumbered their foreign-born parents. In these circumstances, the group could survive in the twentieth century only to the degree that the loyalty of the second generation of German-American Catholics was won and retained. But if loyalty to their distinctive heritage was to be inculcated into these young people—if they were to be made conscious of the fact that they were German-American Catholics—then that heritage had to be defined and clarified, and appropriate ways of manifesting that loyalty had to be pointed out.

This brings us back to the Central-Verein and the question of its representative character. For in addition to using and cherishing the German language and supporting the German Catholic press, loyalty to the *Vereinswesen* was an indispensable means of manifesting one's identification with the German-American Catholic heritage. With the passage of time, however, and the eroding of the strongly German first-generation base, the *Vereinswesen* both contracted and subtly changed its character, becoming more "American" in orientation. And by a process to be described in detail in later chapters, the Central-Verein in the first decade of the present century not only adapted itself to the needs of the more Americanized second generation but also brought within its fold virtually the whole network of German-American Catholic organizations. Thus, for the years with which we are primarily concerned, the Central-Verein was for all practical purposes coterminous with the German-American Catholic *Vereinswesen.* It served as *the* organizational vehicle for those who thought of themselves as German-American Catholics, and to the extent that one thought of himself in these terms he had to identify himself with the Central-Verein, if not by actual membership in one of its branches, at least by thinking of it as the primary symbol—or what sociologists might call the most important reference group—of the German-American Catholics.

There were, of course, many persons of German Catholic ancestry who did not identify themselves with the Central-Verein, and their numbers grew as the century advanced. Some of them were active in the area of social reform, and we shall take note of their activities as we go along. The Central-Verein cannot be thought of as representing such persons. But were these people German-American Catholics or simply American Catholics of German derivation? Bearing in mind the subtle nature of the whole question of ethnic identity and the vital role played in it by self-identification on the part of the individuals involved, it seems legitimate to hold that they were *not* German-American Catholics. Certainly they should not be thought of as part of the same group as those *who did think of themselves* as German-American Catholics, who dedicated themselves to perpetuating their heritage, and who travailed much in spirit as they wrestled with the problem of relating their ethnic, civic, and religious loyalties in the most fruitful and harmonious way.

To return, then, to the point of our discussion, this book concentrates on the Central-Verein not simply because it was the German-American Catholic society that became most interested in the social question but far more because it was the only formal structure the group possessed on the national level. To the degree that the German-American Catholics constituted a self-conscious group, as opposed to an unorganized mass of individuals, that group was the Central-Verein. When we study the Central-Verein we are studying the German-American Catholics as such; and by tracing the origin and development of the social reform interest in this organization, we can gain a deeper understanding of the assimilation of an important element in the American Catholic population in the twentieth century.

But the German-American Catholics in this century were profoundly molded by their American past. We must begin our story with a review of their history in the nineteenth century.

II

THE NINETEENTH-CENTURY BACKGROUND

Beginnings and Growth

No one knew just how many German-American Catholics there were around the turn of the century, although there had been a good deal of speculation. Estimates ranged from two to seven million; but as the well-informed Arthur Preuss pointed out, all such calculations were "mere guesswork."[1] The writer of the article on German Catholics in the United States in *The Catholic Encyclopedia,* published in 1909, prudently refrained from making any numerical estimate of their strength.

In spite of the lack of reliable statistics, there was no doubt that the Germans constituted a large and important element within the American Catholic population. In 1906 there were upwards of two thousand Catholic congregations in which the German language was used either exclusively or in combination with English.[2] Fourteen years earlier, a biographical directory listed some 2,600 German-speaking priests in the United States; not all of them were German, but their distribution gives some indication of the location and relative concentration of the

German-American Catholic population. An examination of the directory confirms the popular impression that the German Catholics were most thickly concentrated in the Middle West: Fourteen of the twenty dioceses having fifty or more German-speaking priests fell within the region bounded on the east by Ohio, on the west and south by Missouri, and on the north by Minnesota.[3]

Cincinnati was the oldest important center of German Catholicism in the Middle West. It was the home of the earliest German-language Catholic newspaper, the *Wahrheits-Freund* (established in 1837), whose founder, the Swiss-born John M. Henni, became the first important German-speaking member of the American hierarchy when he was consecrated bishop of Milwaukee in 1844. By the 1880's and 1890's, the second generation of Cincinnati's German Catholics led all other dioceses in the number of vocations they contributed to the ranks of the German-speaking priests in the United States.[4] At the same time, however, and by a process not unrelated to the emergence of the second generation in Cincinnati, the Queen City was overshadowed by St. Louis and Milwaukee as leading centers of German-American Catholic activity.

The preeminence of the Midwest should not obscure the fact that such Eastern cities as Pittsburgh, Buffalo, Baltimore, Philadelphia, and New York were important focal points of German Catholic life. And of course the story of the German-American Catholics began around colonial Philadelphia. These very early beginnings deserve a brief review, because they remind us that the German Catholic group has roots going back to the first era of American Catholic history and, what is even more to the point, they reveal some characteristic features of German-American Catholic development.

Although there were relatively few Catholics among the German immigrants to colonial Pennsylvania, they nonetheless constituted a majority of the Catholic population of the province in the mid-eighteenth century. An enumeration made in 1757 showed that there were only 1,365 adult Catholics in all of Pennsylvania; two-thirds of this number were Germans.[5] Two German Jesuits arrived in 1741 to minister to their fellow countrymen, but it seems that there was no resident German priest in Philadelphia until almost two decades later, when Ferdinand Farmer began to share the labors of St. Mary's church with his Jesuit confrere, Robert Harding. German- and English-speaking Catholics had been worshipping together for a generation at St. Mary's, and during the lifetime of Father Farmer (who had anglicized his name from Steinmeyer) they continued to get along harmoniously. The purchase by the Germans of a separate burying ground in 1768 was the first important indication of a developing sense of group distinctiveness, and it foreshadowed the division of the congregation along ethnic lines.[6]

When Father Farmer died, in 1786, the Catholic population had increased to the point that a second church was needed; the Germans wished to have one of their own, in which a German-speaking pastor could be installed. They had already formed "The German Catholic Society" and had established a school; after Farmer's death they collected funds for the purchase of property and prepared to construct a church. The project was undertaken on lay initiative, and, in petitioning the Prefect-Apostolic for approval, the leaders explained their purposes by alluding to the need for a new church and to the fact that they were "warm wishers to keep up their respective nation and language." John Carroll, then Prefect-Apostolic and soon to be the first American bishop, was rather hesitant, but he did not stay the Germans from carrying out their plans. When the time came for cornerstone-laying, however, Carroll refused to participate because of troubles which had already begun with the German trustees.[7] Thus the German Catholics were not only the first to evolve the "national parish" as the characteristic ecclesiastical unit for dealing with non-English-speaking immigrants, but this first national parish also became embroiled at once in the "trusteeism" controversies over the control of church property and the right to appoint pastors that were to recur again and again throughout the period of heavy immigration.

The congregation of the new Holy Trinity church incorporated itself under the laws of Pennsylvania and claimed the right as owner of the church to appoint as pastor John Charles Heilbron, a Capuchin priest who had appeared in Philadelphia in 1787. John Carroll had already designated a different German priest as pastor of the Philadelphia Germans, but the first phase of the troubles ended amicably when Heilbron, who was functioning as pastor, was confirmed in his position by Bishop Carroll. More serious trustee difficulties arose in 1796, leading to an open schism which was not healed until 1802. The situation was too complicated to describe in detail, but again it involved the trustees' assertion of their complete control over the church, including the right to replace an unsatisfactory pastor. In this case, the congregation split, some adhering to Peter Heilbron (who had by that time succeeded his brother as regular pastor) and others supporting the trustees who deposed Heilbron and installed John Goetz, another German priest who had turned up in Philadelphia. For a time the rebellious faction controlling Holy Trinity entered into an alliance with a disaffected German congregation in Baltimore. Cesarius Reuter, the priest-leader of the Baltimore faction, wanted the support of Holy Trinity in appealing to Rome for the creation of an all-German diocese in the United States.

Although recounted here in barest outline, the story of the Germans in Philadelphia reveals several significant and characteristic features. Most notable is the fact that the consciousness of being a distinctive group developed hand in hand with the creation of distinctive German Catholic institutions designed to serve their special group needs—a cemetery in the 1760's; a society, a school, and a parish in the 1780's; and a request for separate ecclesiastical jurisdiction at the highest level in the 1790's. The evolutionary growth of German Catholic consciousness and institutions was accompanied by friction between German- and English-speaking Catholics. The details are not specified in the earlier phases,[8] but by the 1790's, when the Philadelphia and Baltimore Germans joined forces, the matter came into the open. The Germans in Baltimore saw themselves as resisting attempts "to change us all into Englishmen, rapidly and violently." Father Reuter especially "seems to have considered his long struggle with Bishop Carroll as a sort of crusade for 'the rights of my nation,' or 'the welfare of my nation'; he even declares that he is ready to die for his nation."[9]

But the trusteeism difficulties of the 1790's reflected much more than national or ethnic feeling, although that was often involved wherever trusteeism appeared.[10] In the most general terms, trusteeism can be understood as a by-product of the Church's adjustment to an unprecedented social environment. In the United States, the Church had to maintain itself as a religious organization dependent on the voluntary support of the faithful. Although it was placed on a basis of legal equality with other denominations, it existed in a society whose republican institutions were antipathetic to its hierarchical-authoritarian structure and principles of operation, and it existed among a people who regarded it with deep hostility. The libertarian spirit of the country, the state laws vesting property rights in legally incorporated bodies with trustees, the example of congregational polity among the Protestants, the lack of strong ecclesiastical organization or discipline in the early days, and the fact that the laity often constructed churches without any assistance from ecclesiastical authorities and before any pastor was available—all of these factors contributed to the feeling on the part of laymen that they should have the determining voice in the "temporalities" of the parish and even in the selection of a priest to minister to them. Add to this the difficulty of providing priests for the multitudes of immigrants, the seemingly inordinate number of itinerant clerics of doubtful quality, European precedents for lay control, and the social and psychic uprootedness of the immigrants themselves, and trusteeism becomes even more understandable. Indeed it is less remarkable that the difficulties arose than that they were overcome at all.[11]

Trusteeism was most threatening in the first few decades of the American Church because of the instability of the hierarchical structure in the early days. But while it was not so grave a peril in the later era, trusteeism continued throughout the period of massive immigration —that is, into the twentieth century—because each group went through much the same process of adjustment. In the case of the Germans, the Holy Trinity and Baltimore affairs were spectacular early episodes, but the heavy influx of immigrants after 1830 brought on a new rash of troubles. Some 40,000 German Catholic immigrants are estimated to have entered the United States in the 1830's; that number almost tripled in the following decade, and in the 1850's nearly a quarter of a million settled in the country.[12] By mid-century they were well distributed through the Mississippi valley, and throughout the whole area of their settlement recent immigrants from Germany were experiencing many of the same difficulties their brothers in Philadelphia had gone through years before.

The Troubled Scene at Mid-Century

The German Catholic immigrants entering the United States in the 1840's and 1850's did not receive a particularly hospitable welcome from native Americans. They were part of the heaviest immigration in American history in proportion to the total population, and the seeming danger that the country was being overrun by foreigners called forth a nativistic reaction. Nativism, or Know-Nothingism as it was called at the time, sprang from a number of roots. It has been interpreted as an inverted form of nationalism in which fears arising from domestic dislocations (such as slavery) were projected on the immigrants. Nativists also emphasized the dangers to cultural homogeneity and republican institutions posed by the hordes of ignorant and easily corrupted immigrants, and they feared the radical tendencies of the refugees who came to the United States after the unsuccessful revolutions of 1848. But the most prominent feature of mid-century nativism was anti-Catholicism.

Although the German Catholics suffered from American nativism—some of them died in the rioting in Louisville in 1855, and it was a Swiss-German priest whom the Know-Nothings in Maine had tarred and feathered a year earlier[13]—the aspect most distressing to them was the animosity displayed by liberal German immigrants of the Forty-Eighter type. For in spite of the fact that these liberal Germans too were objects of nativist suspicion, many of them endorsed the anti-Catholicism of the Know-Nothing movement. In fact, the German Catholics sometimes talked as though the German freethinkers were the main element in Know-Nothingism. Thus in 1857 the *Wahrheits-Freund* remarked, "Those fleeing from the various unsuccessful revolutions of Europe, . . . almost all without any religion and full of hatred toward Catholicism, came over to us and found a well-disposed audience for their declamations against the Papacy in the old bigotry of the masses." As a result, the paper went on, "Know-Nothingism began to spread itself throughout the land."[14]

No doubt the *Wahrheits-Freund* still retained vivid memories of the visit to Cincinnati in 1853 of the papal emissary, Archbishop Gaetano Bedini. The German society of Freimänner was chiefly responsible for the anti-Catholic disturbances that marked the occasion and caused

Bedini to cut short his American sojourn.[15] The famous German missionary preacher, Francis X. Weninger, S.J., claimed that German anticlericals twice made attempts on his life, and in Milwaukee feeling ran so high that Bishop Henni advised the superior of a community of nuns not to put any large windows in a chapel they were building, since the freethinkers could be expected to bomb it if it looked at all ecclesiastical. In the same city, anticlericals mocked the Catholic religion by leading a cow to the walls of the convent and baptizing it amid the grossest of vulgarities.[16]

The hostility of the liberals taught the German Catholic immigrants, if they needed the lesson, that they could not count on sympathetic support from their ethnic brethren at a time when their religion made them obnoxious to Americans. According to Father Joseph Salzmann, founder of a seminary designed primarily to train priests for work among the Germans, the attacks of the Forty-Eighters severely tried the faith of the immigrants. Salzmann wrote that thousands of immigrants testified: "Only here have I learned what it means to be a Catholic."[17] The hostility of the anticlericals thus made Catholic immigrants aware of their distinctiveness from other Germans; it also stimulated the development of their group life. Forty-Eighter enmity lent urgency to Salzmann's project for a German Catholic seminary and to the parish mission movement. Several German Catholic newspapers were founded to respond to the liberal polemic, and the danger that the immigrant might associate himself with groups like the Turners led German priests to encourage the formation of parish benevolent societies.[18]

The need to counteract the attractions of non-Catholic organizations was not the only factor in the formation of these mutual benefit societies. Mutual aid societies of this sort were the common response of almost all immigrant groups to the strangeness of their situation in a new environment. They have been called the basic type of immigrant organization, and it was natural that they should begin to develop among the German Catholics in the 1830's. The immigrants themselves were aware of the important social needs served by the benevolent societies. As an early leader of the Central-Verein emphasized, the uprootedness of the immigrant's life was the fundamental reason for the formation of the societies. "All of us," he said, "have been transplanted from our native soil into a strange land, as Israel was removed from Sion to the rivers of Babylon." The bonds of blood and social solidarity that supported them in the homeland were absent, and the German Catholic immigrants had banded together into societies to amend that loss as best they could.[19]

In the case of the German Catholics, the social instability which the mutual aid societies were designed to mitigate was not confined to the external threats of American nativism and Forty-Eighter hostility. On the contrary, it pervaded the life of their churches, manifesting itself in trusteeism and internal splits within the congregations. We must briefly sketch the extent of these dissensions, because they constitute the immediate background of the Central-Verein's formation.

Basically, the troubles reflected the uprootedness of the immigrant's condition. As a Wisconsin priest wrote in 1855, "All the resolutions made in Europe dissolve as soon as one feels the breezes of the American coastline; every tie, including the one with God, must be retied here and must undergo the American 'probatum est' before it can be said that it is secure."[20] The adaptation of old habits and institutions and the creation of stable new relationships which this astute observer had in mind were complicated in America by the heterogeneous coexistence of different ethnic groups. Tension between German and Irish Catholics was chronic, but the Germans also found it difficult to get along with each other. In rural northern Ohio, for example, Alsatians and Hessen-Darmstadters fell out over whose traditional hymns would be used in worship, and the quarrel became so bitter that the church was burned to the ground by disaffected elements. Difficulties also arose in Rochester, New York, over diverse local liturgical customs, and in southern Indiana an observer spoke of the "strife" that resulted from "the varying nationality of the multitudes thrown together from all regions of Germany."[21]

But regional jealousies certainly did not account for all the widespread turmoil in the German Catholic congregations at mid-century. It did not seem to be involved, for example, in the same southern Indiana community when the church had to be interdicted because an unruly element got control in 1849. And across the river in Louisville difficulties leading to a brawl in 1851 centered around the strictly American institution of the parish mutual aid society.[22] The same thing was true several years later in St. Boniface parish in Chicago—here a rebellious verein (society) and one loyal to the pastor fought a pitched battle in the middle of the church. St. Michael's German church in Chicago went through six different pastors between 1852 and 1860, and when the bishop wished to show the church to the superior of the Redemptorists and persuade him to take it over, the trustees locked the door against their bishop. The Redemptorists eventually brought peace to the parish, however. Further south in Teutopolis, Illinois, it was the Franciscans who restored order to a parish with an even worse record—six pastors in two years.[23] Internal dissensions were also recorded before the Civil War in German congregations in Wisconsin, Missouri, Maryland, and New York; and Holy Trinity church in Philadelphia, where it all began, was closed twice by trusteeism conflicts between 1849 and 1854.[24]

But it was in the state of New York that the most notorious problems arose in German parishes, and these quarrels are also most closely associated with the beginnings of the Central-Verein. Although all four of the German parishes in the diocese of New York were embroiled in trusteeism in the late 1830's, the case of St. Louis church in Buffalo was the most persistent and best known. After several years of trouble, Bishop John Hughes of New York interdicted the church in 1843. It was eventually reopened, but part of the German congregation split away and formed a new church. St. Louis was laid under interdict again in 1854 when the trustees refused to abide by the decision of Archbishop Bedini, who had gone there expressly to settle their dispute with John Timon, by then bishop of Buffalo. Aided and abetted by American nativists, the recalcitrant Germans remained under the ecclesiastical ban for a year.[25]

In Rochester a similar situation prevailed. St. Peter's church in that city was formed in 1843 when a disaffected group withdrew from the first German church, St. Joseph's. Hard feelings existed between the two parishes for a decade, and there were chronic trustee rumblings in St. Peter's. In 1854, however, Father Weninger gave a mission at St. Peter's which brought about a reconciliation between the two German churches. A few weeks later, what has been described as a "great love-feast" was staged to mark the new era of harmony among Rochester's German Catholics. The benevolent societies of the two parishes participated in this celebration, and representatives from several German Catholic societies in Buffalo were also present. A number of speakers dwelt on the desirability of "a reunion of minds and hearts under the sheltering arms of their common faith and race and language," and representatives of the eight vereins present rose together to pledge themselves to regard one another as brothers.[26] This "love-feast" was the immediate stimulus to the formation of the Central-Verein. As they returned to their homes and discussed the gathering in Rochester, the Buffalo men determined to work for a closer union of the German Catholic societies.[27] The fact that they sought and obtained the approval of Bishop Timon indicates that they were not associated with the "malcontents" in Buffalo; rather they were interested in an organization that would contribute to greater unity and order among the German Catholics under the aegis of regular ecclesiastical authority. In view of the troubled background of Know-Nothingism, liberal German anticlericalism, and widespread internal dissension, it seems reasonable to interpret the movement that led to the Central-Verein as part of the search for stability among an immigrant people who were undergoing serious difficulties of adjustment.

The Founding and Functions of the Central-Verein

After their return from Rochester, the Buffalo men worked first to unite the societies in their city; they hoped eventually, however, to effect a larger union, and in September, 1854, they addressed a proposal for a national federation to all the German Catholic benevolent societies in the country. In response to this letter, which specifically noted the "many trying situations" facing them and the need for "closer union . . . for the promotion of Catholic interests," representatives from societies in four states and the District of Columbia met in Baltimore in April, 1855, and established Der Deutsche Römisch-Katholische Central-Verein von Nord-Amerika.[28]

The new organization was a national federation of parish mutual aid societies, and although it gradually assumed the role of spokesman for the German-American Catholics on a broad range of issues, its original constitution defined its primary purpose as "the mutual support and assistance in cases of poverty or sickness of the individual members" of the affiliated benevolent societies. During its early years, the Central-Verein grew slowly and confined its attention rather narrowly to "organizational topics, constitutional amendments, and other routine matters" connected with its mutual benefit function.[29] This aspect of the Central-Verein's activities is best understood as furnishing the "manifest function" of the organization: that is, mutual aid activities were not only important in themselves, they constituted the raison d'être for the existence of an association which also fulfilled other needs —the "latent functions"—which might not by themselves have seemed sufficiently concrete and pressing to justify the creation and maintenance of a large national society.[30] In the most general terms, the latent function of the Central-Verein was to provide the organizational vehicle through which the German-American Catholics could participate as a group in the life of the American Church and American society on the national level.

The individual benevolent societies of which the Central-Verein was exclusively composed until the reorganization of 1900–1905 also fulfilled the same sort of functions on the local level, and a look at one of these societies may help to clarify the distinction between the manifest and latent functions. The St. Bonaventure Catholic Benevolent Society, formed in St. Francis parish in Milwaukee in 1872, will serve as our representative of the Central-Verein's local affiliates in the nineteenth century.[31]

Founded with twenty-one members, St. Bonaventure's enrolled 419 men on its silver jubilee; the members paid an entrance fee of three to five dollars, depending on their age, and regular monthly assessments of fifty cents. Benefits were paid out at the rate of eight dollars per week for loss of income resulting from sickness or disability. Life insurance protection was optionally available through affiliation with a larger association of the German Catholic societies of the city, and St. Bonaventure's also paid occasional benefits for special cases, such as the loss of a limb. In its first quarter century, the society had paid out a grand total of forty thousand dollars in benefits.

By providing a rudimentary form of protection against loss of earning power, the society was meeting a real economic need and fulfilling its manifest function of mutual aid. This, however, was by no means the only contribution the St. Bonaventure society made toward cushioning the adjustment of German Catholic immigrants to their new surroundings. In a variety of ways, the society fulfilled the latent function of mediating between the individual immigrant and the relatively strange social world in which he found himself. Most obviously, it provided for him (as the jubilee history specifically noted) a circle of friends to replace those he had left behind in the homeland. If he fell sick, his new brothers maintained a vigil at his bedside or at least called on him regularly. In health, his connection with St. Bonaventure's permitted him to contribute to significant projects, such as the erection of a normal school for German Catholic teachers. The society also brought him into contact with religious and social events of local importance. Hardly a year went by without the men of St. Bonaventure's assisting at the dedication of a church or the festival of some other Catholic society, and torchlight processions with musical accompaniment marked such occasions as Archbishop Henni's reception of the pallium in 1875. The following year St. Bonaventure's resolved to participate "*in corpore, mit Musik*" in the centennial observance of Independence Day. A flag was purchased for the event, and the society's chronicle painstakingly records the name of the symbolically important man—Jacob Bott, Jr.—who first had the honor of carrying St. Bonaventure's American flag on the Fourth of July.

Thus the local benevolent society enabled the German Catholic immigrant to participate in the life of his nationality group, his church, and the community at large. In time the Central-Verein performed the same function on the national level; and significantly enough, it was in the United States centennial year of 1876 that Father Weninger urged the national organization to undertake activities of the broadest scope for the good of Church and country. Weninger's remarks, which were given wide circulation in the English-language Catholic press and in pamphlet form as a "Centennial Address," took as their theme the destiny of the American nation and the role that Catholics and especially the Central-Verein should play in the realization of that destiny. He urged that, without abandoning its concern for mutual assistance, the Central-Verein should open its sessions to discussion of such topics as the care and education of Negroes and Indians, support of Catholic schools and the press, "and finally, union at the time of elections—not from mere political motives, but to protect the Church when her rights are endangered."[32]

The Central-Verein had already begun to move toward involvement in matters of general interest to the German-American Catholics more than a decade before Weninger addressed the society's twenty-first convention. As we have seen, the organization was brought into being by men concerned over the "many trying situations" facing the German immigrants, and the founders were also well aware of the role it could play by providing a forum "for mutual encouragement and the active advancement of our interests."[33] Hence, after a period of initial growth and consolidation, the Central-Verein began to expand its horizons beyond the limited function of coordinating the mutual benevolence work of its member societies. In 1863 it assumed the patronage of the German Catholic Normal School in Milwaukee, thus committing itself to the cause of the Catholic schools, an area in which the Germans had distinguished themselves from the earliest days. By appointing two agents to meet all incoming ships in New York and Baltimore, the Central-Verein, in 1868, involved itself in the field of immigrant care. As time passed, the organization continued to broaden the scope of its activities, and by 1892 a German priest could call the Central-Verein "the highest tribunal the German Catholics have in this country."[34] In the light of this gradual expansion of its interests, the assumption of social reform work after 1900 can be understood in part simply as the culmination of the Central-Verein's evolutionary development.

But before 1900 the Central-Verein went through its period of "storm and stress"—the controversies of the 1880's and 1890's. These quarrels deeply affected the attitudes of the German-American Catholics and hence exerted a profound influence on the development of the Central-Verein. Before considering the controversies more fully, we should take note here of two preliminary points: The first concerns the place of the Central-Verein within the spectrum of German-American Catholic organizations; the second has to do with the organization's manifest function of mutual insurance and how it helped the Central-Verein weather the stormy years of controversy.

Although the Central-Verein was the oldest and most inclusive element of the German Catholic *Vereinswesen* on the national level, it was not the only organization representing the group in the late nineteenth century. Many local mutual aid societies never affiliated with the Central-Verein, and there also grew up fraternal insurance societies and regional groupings of German Catholic vereins which were quite distinct from it. Moreover, several important associations were created to meet special needs; these were also independent of the Central-Verein and preempted certain fields of activity. Thus the American branch of the St. Raphael Society came into existence in 1883 as the first organizational daughter of the emigrant protective society founded in Germany by Peter Paul Cahensly. Just four years later, the German-American priests' society, the Priester-Verein, was founded in Chicago as a society taking within its purview all matters of concern to the German Catholic population. The Priester-Verein was the chief promoter of the German-American Catholic congresses (Katholikentage), which began in 1887 as annual mass meetings at which all issues of interest to the group were to be discussed. As a result of the first Katholikentag, a German Press Association and an organization for young men were also established, but neither of them prospered for very long.[35]

This extraordinary vitality of associational life reflected not only the numerical strength of the German Catholics during an era of heavy immigration, it was also a result of the high level of ethnic consciousness that accompanied the controversies of the period. The mere listing of these other organizations makes clear too that the Central-Verein did not monopolize the *Vereinswesen,* although it did enjoy a certain primacy. There was in fact a measure of ambiguity about the Central-Verein's position which protected it from some of the more adverse effects of the controversies even while causing it to become partially involved in them.

Because it was their oldest and largest organization, the Central-Verein could not avoid becoming involved to a considerable extent in the controversies in which the German-American Catholics played so conspicuous a part. Many of the leaders of the Priester-Verein, the most aggressive of the German societies, were also prominent in the Central-Verein. Indeed, it was one of these priests, Monsignor Max Wurst of Minnesota, who called the Central-Verein the German Catholics' "highest tribunal" and demanded that it take a stand in the so-called Cahenslyism conflict.[36] Another leader of the Priester-Verein, the Reverend Francis Goller of St. Louis, denounced the liberal Catholics from the platform of a Central-Verein convention and went to the extreme of describing the resolutions adopted at the Catholic Columbian Congress of 1893 as "Freemasonry resolutions."[37] But although the Central-Verein shared the position of the group, it had not been created primarily to champion the point of view of the German Catholics on the controverted issues; it did not play the leading role assumed by the Priester-Verein, and it was not considered by the opposing faction to be so nationalistic and divisive as the priests' society and the Katholikentage. On the contrary, both Archbishop William H. Elder of Cincinnati and Archbishop John Ireland of St. Paul, the outstanding liberal antagonist of the Germans, made a sharp distinction between the Central-Verein and these other organs of German Catholic activity. According to these prelates, the aggressive nationalism of Priester-Verein and the Katholikentage threatened to disrupt the unity of the American Church, but the Central-Verein was quite acceptable because it confined its activities to mutual benevolence and did not undertake to influence purely spiritual or ecclesiastical affairs. "The 'Central-Verein,'" said Ireland, after criticizing the priests' society and the German congresses, "has deserved in the past all praise. A close attention to its own legitimate business will deserve for it the same praise in the future."[38]

The expression of opinions such as these was doubtless related to a disagreement that arose within the Central-Verein at this time as to the proper scope of its activities. One faction thought the society should confine itself exclusively to matters relating to mutual insurance; the other contended that issues of more general interest should be taken up. Neither side to this dispute won a clear-cut victory. The consideration of "extraneous questions" transcending the narrow range of mutual aid was too intimately related to the function of an immigrant society to be dropped entirely, but the Central-Verein did move to dissociate itself from the more embattled organizations. Thus, after 1890 it no longer held its annual convention at the same time and place as the Katholikentage, even though the latter had begun more or less as adjuncts to the Central-Verein's meetings. This separation continued until 1896, by which time the general German Catholic congresses were well on their way to extinction.[39]

After the period of controversies ended, the Katholikentage and Priester-Verein passed quietly out of existence. The Central-Verein, however, continued into the twentieth century. A number of factors were involved in the Central-Verein's survival, but the point to be emphasized here is that its manifest function of mutual benevolence and the reputation it had won in the pursuit of this neutral and worthwhile activity not only justified the society's existence apart from any role in the controversies but also shielded it in some measure from the more destructive effects of the quarrels.

The Controversies

To list all of the disputed issues among American Catholics in the last quarter of the nineteenth century is to invite despair at the thought that some order has to be imposed upon them. There were controversies over the Knights of Labor, the theories of Henry George, the parochial schools, the founding of the Catholic University of America, the nationality question, the participation of Catholics in interfaith gatherings, secret societies, temperance, and—as a climax—over the alleged heresy of "Americanism." Obviously we cannot hope to give anything approaching a full review of all these issues.[40] Rather we shall try, first, to identify an important underlying theme in all of the controversies; and, secondly, we shall glance briefly at some of the leading issues from the viewpoint of the German-American Catholics.

The underlying theme is Americanization. All of the controversies reflected the general problem of how the Church was to adjust itself to the American environment, how it was to be related to American society and culture. On this basic problem, Catholics tended to divide into two camps—the liberals and the conservatives. The terms are not very satisfactory, and the two factions are best understood as rather vaguely defined orientations rather than as groups in any formal sense. Individuals sometimes shifted from one faction to the other on specific issues. Yet there was enough consistency in the positions taken that the terms "liberal" and "conservative" came into widespread usage, and the popular terms did correspond roughly to the two orientations. The most prominent of the liberals were Archbishop Ireland, Bishop John J. Keane, who was rector of the Catholic University of America at the height of the turmoil, and Monsignor Denis J. O'Connell, rector of the American College in Rome. On most issues the liberals also had the support of James Cardinal Gibbons of Baltimore, who was, however, temperamentally a most moderate man. The chief episcopal champions of the conservatives were Archbishop Michael A. Corrigan of New York and Bishop Bernard J. McQuaid of Rochester.[41] Most of the German clergy and prelates of the Middle West also aligned themselves firmly with the conservatives.

Although there were many differences on specific issues, in general the liberals took a more optimistic view of the relationship of the Catholic Church and American culture than did the conservatives. The liberals held that Catholicism and the institutions of the country were admirably suited to each other and that the prospects of the Church were brighter in the open society of the United States than in the tradition-bound states of Europe, where the dead hand of the past weighed heavily on all efforts to bring the Church into fruitful contact with the modern world. They also held, however, that in order to realize the fullest benefits from its American opportunity the Church must become Americanized. They did not, of course, advocate departures from orthodox Catholic doctrine. Rather they argued that since it appeared to Americans as a foreign institution, not only in respect to its structure and principles but also in terms of the population which adhered to it, the Catholic Church in the United States must do everything in its power to accommodate itself to the new circumstances and to adapt its practices and approach to the American scene. Hence, they called for flexibility and adjustment; they deprecated the tendency to view American civilization as wholly materialistic or basically incompatible with the beliefs or inherited values of Catholics, and they were opposed to the perpetuation of "foreign" languages or cultural traditions that did not accord with American expectations.

Insofar as it related to the Catholic immigrant population, the program of the liberals or "Americanizers," as they were often called, was strongly assimilationist in tendency. Archbishop Ireland denied, however, that he favored overhasty or forced assimilation. "What I do mean by Americanization," he told a group of German Catholics, "is the filling up of the heart with love for America and for her institutions. It is the harmonizing of ourselves with our surroundings, so that we will be as to the manner born, and not as strangers in a strange land, caring apparently but slightly for it, and entitled to receive from it but meagre favors."[42]

The more cautious conservatives, on the other hand, had reservations about the easy compatibility of Catholicism and the American spirit. They were less impressed by the glorious opportunity open to American Catholics in reconciling the Church and modern culture than they were by the indisputable Protestantism and periodic nativism of Americans; hence they emphasized the need to maintain the traditional integrity of Catholic life and thought as the surest means of maintaining the faith in the United States. To men of this persuasion, the flexibility commended by the liberals looked much like laxity, accommodation suggested compromise, and adjustment to the new environment resembled capitulation before the enemy. Since the program of the liberals seemed to require departures from the traditional stance in a number of areas, the conservatives were fearful of the possible consequences of Americanization; they urged that the preservation of the faith should not be endangered by the reckless adoption of novelties aimed at harmonizing the Church with American culture.

The conservative position recommended itself with special force to the German-American Catholics. For them Catholicism was bound up with a language and culture which seemed even more foreign to American society than that of the English-speaking Catholics, and they feared that Americanization might lead the German Catholic immigrant to jettison his religion along with his language and cultural outlook. Their conviction that the maintenance of his cultural heritage was the surest bulwark of the immigrant's religion was epitomized in the watchword "Language Saves Faith."[43] Although they recognized that assimilation was inevitable in time, they felt that men like Archbishop Ireland were trying to accelerate unduly what should be a slow and natural process. Hence, because of their dedication to the preservation of an inherited foreign culture, they opposed the Americanizers, and by a natural extension of this thinking they were predisposed to support the conservatives, even on ideological issues not directly related to the acculturation of immigrants.

A brief review of five of the areas of controversy may help to clarify the various ways in which the general theme of Americanization was involved in this phase of German-American Catholic development. The issues we shall consider are Cahenslyism, or the nationality question, and the controversies over Catholic schools, secret societies, temperance, and Americanism.

The nationality question (which became known as Cahenslyism after 1891) was the only controversy in which the place of the German Catholics in the American Church was the main issue and in which they played the leading role specifically as Germans.[44] The dispute raged fiercely from the mid-eighties, reaching a climax in 1891–92; for the next few years it smoldered on, adding a dimension of nationalistic bitterness to the other disputes with which it became hopelessly intertangled. The fundamental clash was between the determination of the German Catholics to preserve their language, culture, and ethnic identity and, on the other hand, the desire of the Americanizers to reduce the "foreign" coloration of the Church in the United States and to foster the assimilation of the immigrants.

For a number of reasons, however, the controversy had much of the character of a quarrel between the Germans and the Irish, of which there had been numerous earlier examples. For one thing, the leading Americanizers were of Irish birth or derivation. No doubt Archbishop Ireland and others like him were sincere in thinking they had completely shed their own "foreignism," but the German Catholics naturally thought otherwise, and they resented being lectured on Americanism by those who were as much immigrants as themselves. Hence there were really three nationalities intertwined in the nationality controversy—the American, the Irish, and the German[45]—and an almost infinite number of perplexing questions about the relationship of the three and about the essential nature of nationality itself. Was there, in fact, an American nationality? Some of the spokesmen for the German Catholics denied it;[46] but granting that there was, what was it ?And where did Americanism leave off and nativism begin? How was religion connected with nationality? How language? Were the Irish Catholics really closer to true Americanism, as they seemed to think, simply because they spoke English? Did the Germans have to drop their language to become real Americans? If they did, would their faith survive? Would their culture survive? Did Americanization require the disappearance of the German Catholics as a group?

All these were highly elusive questions, but they mattered deeply because they went to the very roots of personal and group identity. They were not—indeed, could not be—settled definitively by the controversy. The outcome was inconclusive in that sense, but it did set a limit to the institutional changes the Church would permit in accommodating to ethnic diversity in the United States. This becomes clear if we glance at two of the principal episodes in the controversy: the Abbelen Memorial of 1886 and the Lucerne Memorial of 1891.

The first of these was a petition carried to Rome by the Reverend Peter M. Abbelen of Milwaukee requesting a clarification of the status of German national parishes and discussing in general the relationship of "Irish Catholics" and "German Catholics" in the United States. The Abbelen mission aroused an angry reaction because it reflected unfavorably on the way American bishops had handled their pastoral problems, and it was interpreted as part of a "Germanizing" design to get special privileges for one national group within the Church. But in spite of the angry charges and the confusion resulting from the fact that the answer from the Congregation of the Propaganda was given in garbled form, it was unmistakable that the legitimacy and equal status of German national parishes was confirmed in the Abbelen episode. Rome was unwilling, however, to do anything to bind more firmly to the national parish the children of immigrants who could speak English; the second generation was free, on reaching maturity, to transfer to an English-language parish. Thus, to the degree that the national parish was at issue in the mid-1880's, it was confirmed but not extended.[47]

The national parish was the basic institutional device through which pastoral care could be provided for non-English-speaking immigrants. All American churchmen—including the Americanizers—agreed upon the necessity for national parishes and denied that they wished to relegate them to a lower status than that enjoyed by the English-language, territorially based parishes. But the Americanizers were not, of course, committed to the national parish in the same way that the German Catholic leaders were. The former could regard the national parish rather complacently as a transitional institution that would wither away as the immigrants became assimilated; for the latter, however, the withering away of the national parish was tantamount to the extinction of all that was dear and the disintegration of the group in whose destiny they were inextricably involved. The German-American Catholics therefore continued to be sensitive to the status of their parishes and to any other infringements of their "rights" or any evidence of neglect. In the Lucerne Memorial of 1891, it seemed that they were even calling for a new institutional modification to bolster their position—the creation of "national bishops" and reorganization of the hierarchy along ethnic instead of territorial lines.

Peter Paul Cahensly, the moving spirit behind the Lucerne Memorial and the man whose name became synonymous with the nationality question, was a zealous Catholic layman, a successful merchant, and a member of the Prussian House of Delegates.[48] His acquaintance with the physical hardships and spiritual hazards of emigration prompted him to establish the St. Raphael Society for the Protection of German Catholic Emigrants; and his concern for emigrant welfare eventually led him to take an interest in the religious situation in the United States, the country to which most of these emigrants were going. He set up a branch of his society in this country, was acquainted with the German-American Catholic leaders, and shared their views. Early in 1891, shortly after the European branches of the St. Raphael Society met in Lucerne and drew up a number of suggestions for improving the pastoral care of the immigrant Catholics in the United States, Cahensly presented this so-called Lucerne Memorial to the Pope. Although not a single American representative was present at the Lucerne meeting, it was popularly supposed that the "Germanizing" group in this country had a hand in the Memorial, not only because of Cahensly's ties with them but also because the Memorial paralleled the thinking of the German-American Catholic leaders. At the same time, Cahensly's membership in the Prussian Diet was made the basis of wholly unjustified allegations that the Memorial was politically inspired and was associated with Pan-Germanism. These circumstances, along with the distrust and hostility that years of controversy had generated, help explain why "Cahenslyism" seemed so offensive and even sinister and why the reaction was so explosive.

The Memorial covered familiar ground, both in charging that millions of immigrants were lost to the Church in the United States and in the suggestions it listed for remedial action.[49] In fact, most of the eight points it included were already accepted as policy in the American Church, although interpretations would naturally vary as to how they were to be applied. Even the controversial seventh point—dealing with the desirability of each immigrant group's having, as its representatives on the hierarchy, "several bishops of the same origin"—was not new. We have already seen that the Philadelphia and Baltimore Germans wanted "their own" bishop almost a century earlier, and the national background of episcopal appointees had been a tender issue on a number of occasions. But this recommendation was interpreted as calling for a fundamental restructuring of the hierarchy with ethnicity replacing territoriality as the organizing principle. Cahensly's defenders disavowed any such idea, but there were unprejudiced and reasonable men who believed that "national bishops" was what the Memorial, in fact, called for, and American Catholics almost universally opposed any such scheme.[50] The American hierarchy was virtually at one in rejecting the Memorial and in its indignation at such blatant meddling by officious Europeans.

The Lucerne Memorial was quietly pigeonholed at Rome, and no action on any of its recommendations was taken. Thereafter the nationality question itself simmered down, although national feeling remained inflamed among all the parties to the dispute. The results of this clash between the Americanizers and those devoted to preserving the German Catholic heritage were ambiguous. On the immediate practical level, the right of the Germans to be themselves, to use their language, and to maintain their parishes had been ratified but only provisionally and as transitional phenomena. And the reaction to the Lucerne Memorial made it clear that no effort to secure a firmer institutional anchorage for immigrant nationalities in the American Church could hope for success. From this perspective, the controversy ended with no better than a qualified and limited victory for the German Catholics. But viewed from another angle, the results were considerably less favorable. The uproar over the Lucerne Memorial threw the German Catholics on the defensive psychologically; their dedication to the cause of the *katholisches Deutschtum* was made to seem dangerous and divisive both to the Catholic Church and the American national community. This no doubt aggravated the inevitable strains of adjusting their multiple loyalties, and the feeling that they had been maligned and misrepresented added to the sensitivity of the German-American Catholics and made them even more ready to join issue with their fellow religionists in disputes over other matters.

The other controversies, which we must deal with in still more summary fashion, illustrate the manner in which ethnic interests were involved in quarrels in which German nationality itself was not the direct subject of dispute. The school controversy, which erupted violently in 1890, furnishes perhaps the clearest example of how ethnic and ideological elements became intertangled.[51]

This disagreement over the relationship of Catholic and public schools and over the respective rights of church and state in education had a very high ideological content—that is, questions of this sort tended then, as they do today, to divide Catholics into liberal and conservative factions, differing in their basic evaluations and policy approaches. But, at the same time, ethnic interests were vitally at stake for the German Catholics because the parochial school was a crucially important institution in the preservation of their language and cultural heritage.[52] They were unalterably convinced of the need for Catholic schools and regarded those who were less fully committed to them, or who were willing to grant any merit at all to the public schools, as dangerous compromisers whose liberalism was theologically suspect. Moreover, the liberals on the school question—those who conceded the state a legitimate competency in the sphere of education and who hoped for a more harmonious modus vivendi between Catholic and public schools—were also the most outspoken anti-Cahenslyites, and they sometimes interpreted the dedication of the Germans to parochial schools as springing principally from nationalistic rather than religious motives.[53] Here again, liberal Americanism took a direction that was both inimical to the ethnic interests of the German-American Catholics and, in their eyes, dangerous from a religious viewpoint. The German Catholics therefore aligned themselves wholeheartedly with the conservatives in the school question.

The secret society controversy was not nearly so important as the school question, but it, too, indirectly involved one of the institutions of German Catholic group life. The need to counteract the seductions of the Turners, the Sons of Hermann, and other non-Catholic and often anticlerical societies of German-Americans was one of the factors leading to the formation of societies among the German Catholic immigrants. The leaders of the group were steadfastly opposed to any weakening of the Church's prohibition of membership in secret societies, and they could not understand how anyone who was staunchly Catholic could view the matter differently. The liberals, however, argued that American fraternal and secret orders were merely social or economic organizations without offensive ideological trappings and that even the American brand of Freemasonry was an innocuous thing compared to the European variety. Excessive rigor in banning Catholics from harmless American societies was, in the opinion of the liberals, a misguided policy and one that could rebound to the detriment of the Church if Catholics came to believe that they were being forced to choose between their religion and membership in a society that was vital to their economic well-being or social advancement. As in the case of the school question the drift of liberal thinking was unacceptable to the German Catholics; they were determined to preserve their own institutions and felt that this was the surest way to preserve their faith.[54]

Nationality was somewhat differently involved in the temperance issue. No formal institution of German Catholic life, like the school or society, was threatened or called into question in this dispute, but a very deep-seated cultural tradition was. The Catholic temperance movement took the form of a crusade for total abstinence; it was led almost exclusively by Irish-Americans and was closely identified with the liberal, Americanizing wing of the hierarchy. The total abstinence advocates, whose dedication sometimes approached fanaticism, hoped to overcome a social problem that was especially pronounced among the hard-drinking Irish, but they also saw temperance as part of the great endeavor to bring Catholicism into line with the cultural norms of American society. From their point of view, the Germans' attachment to beer and the tradition of the "continental Sunday," while less socially destructive than the drunkenness of the Irish, was also inappropriate to the American scene. To some of them it seemed scandalous that the predominantly German-American monks of St. Vincent Abbey in Pennsylvania should actually manufacture and sell beer, and they asked if the initials O.S.B. (Order of St. Benedict) were to be interpreted as "Order of Sacred Brewers."[55]

The German-American Catholics were by no means abandoned to

demon rum. They were quite critical of certain American drinking practices[56] but were naturally offended by the polemics of the total abstinence men, whom they identified with American nativists and with the hypocritical tradition of "Puritanism." They believed in true temperance, or moderation, in the use of alcoholic beverages and could see "not the slightest objection to a workingman enjoying his glass of beer on Sunday in a saloon or in a beer garden."[57] The strident campaign of the Catholic temperance spokesmen affronted the self-respect of the German Catholics. They perceived very clearly that temperance and Sunday observance were part and parcel of the Americanizers' determination to eliminate from the Church in the United States those "foreign encrustations" that retarded its acculturation; but they responded that it was un-Catholic to emphasize the differences that existed among various groups of the faithful or to brand any one group, because of its language or characteristics, as "foreigners—barbarians!"[58]

In respect to temperance, as in the case of language, the German Catholics felt that they were being asked to change their ways very drastically for the sake of accommodating the Church to the American environment. Since their language and cultural traditions had always been closely linked with their Catholic religion, they naturally had some doubts about the orthodoxy of those who were pressing for so many accommodations. In the minds of some, total abstinence was simply heresy,[59] and the position of the Americanizers on education, secret societies, cooperation with Protestants, and many other questions seemed equally dangerous to the integrity of Catholic doctrine. In the controversy over "Americanism" the theological implications of the Americanizers' general tendency became the explicit issue: Americanism was identified with the condemned theological liberalism of Europe and was branded as plain heresy. The situation grew bewilderingly complicated after 1897, when Americanism became the focal point of the split between liberal and conservative factions within the Catholic Church in France, with each wing interpreting the American Catholic experience in the light of its own ideological and polemical interests. The dispute waxed so violent that Pope Leo XIII appointed a commission to study the whole question of Americanism and in 1899 issued the papal letter *Testem Benevolentiae*, in which—without saying that anyone actually held them—he condemned doctrinal errors imputed to the Americanists by their opponents, while excluding from his condemnation the qualities of society and government characteristic of the United States.[60]

The Americanism controversy divided Catholics along ideological lines rather than along ethnic lines, but the Germans were solidly in the conservative camp.[61] No doubt many of them would have been conservative as a result either of temperament or intellectual persuasion even if there had been no ethnic dimension at all to the question. It seems clear, however, that some element of ethnic feeling was inescapably present as a conditioning factor in their attitude toward Americanism as a theological issue. The Germans, after all, took a conservative position on all the specific practical issues of Americanization —language, schools, secret societies, temperance, and so on—and they did so not merely because of purely speculative convictions but because the preservation of their cultural tradition was involved. As a theological issue, Americanism represented a formulation, on the highest level of abstraction, of the same problem of Americanization of which the language question, the school question, and all the other specific questions were practical aspects. It is hardly surprising that after resisting Americanization in practice, the German Catholics should reject Americanism in theory.

Testem Benevolentiae ended the period of controversy, but it did not settle the question of Americanism. Rather the question was left in terrible ambiguity. Something called Americanism had been condemned, but it was not a doctrine expressly formulated by the champions of Americanization. Rather, the condemned doctrines were derived for the most part from the writings of conservatives who claimed that they were simply spelling out what was implicit in the Americanists' position. Yet the Americanists claimed that they never held the condemned beliefs, and they made no effort to defend them. At the same time, the Pope stated that he did not wish to repudiate Americanism if the term were understood as referring to the national characteristics of the American people or the "condition of your commonwealths, or the laws and customs which prevail in them. . . ."[62] The Americanizers could argue that all they had in mind was bringing the Church into harmony with Americanism understood in precisely that fashion.

Further analysis of the theoretical relationship between Americanism and Catholicism was postponed indefinitely after *Testem Benevolentiae.* Indeed, the American Church has still not confronted the task. The problem of adjusting the Church to American circumstances without sacrificing any of the essentials of Catholicity did not, of course, go away after 1899 simply because people stopped quarreling about it, but mutual exhaustion seemed to overspread both camps and new preoccupations arose. In the case of the German Catholics, interest in the social question became quite intense after 1900. While this concern for social reform might seem far removed from the issues of the 1880's and 1890's and considerably more progressive, the German-American Catholics retained vivid memories of the years of stress, and their attitudes were still in some measure conditioned by the passions then aroused.

The Legacy of Battle

The period of controversies came to a close with neither side having won a clear-cut victory and with both having absorbed damaging blows. The German-American Catholics regarded *Testem Benevolentiae* as sustaining their position, and from that point of view the controversial era ended triumphantly. But they did not emerge unscarred. In fact, the legacies of conflict which the German Catholics carried with them into the twentieth century were predominantly negative, although there was one important positive legacy: a heightened sensitivity to the weaknesses in American society. Negatively, the German Catholics had been embittered by the controversies; they had become mistrustful of their English-speaking coreligionists; they were also profoundly disheartened, and their self-confidence had been seriously undermined by the animosity displayed toward them and by the unfavorable outcome of some of the battles.

Even the pages of the Central-Verein's centennial history, written in 1955, give evidence of the bitterness aroused by the battles of the 1880's and 1890's. The recollections of the author, Joseph Matt, went back to the stormy era, and he confessed that "a perusal of the documents of those bygone days always stirs my innermost soul."[63] Cahenslyism was the issue that touched the most sensitive nerve. Whenever it came up after 1900 German Catholic spokesmen reacted with a promptness and vigor born of deep resentment. Whenever the allegation was revived that Cahensly's interest in American Catholic affairs was inspired by Pan-German ambitions there were immediate and indignant denials. In 1921 the Central-Verein characterized the circulation of such fables by Catholics as "playing into the hands of the Church's enemies" and was uncertain whether it sprang from ignorance or malice.[64]

No doubt the most distressing aspect of the Cahenslyism issue was that it put the German-American Catholics on the defensive. It required them repeatedly to clear Cahensly's name and their own, to establish the purity of his intentions and the genuineness of their own civic loyalty. In 1916, for example, the legacy of Cahenslyism weighed heavily on Central-Verein leaders as they considered what they might properly do to help Germany defend herself against Allied propaganda attacks. Although eager to assist their old homeland, they were determined to undertake no action that might lend substance to the fantasy that Cahenslyism was a movement to make the German-American Catholics the political tools of the Kaiser.[65]

The suspicion and mistrust for their fellow Catholics which the Germans brought with them out of the strife-filled nineties is best illustrated by an incident that occurred in 1913. The case concerns the relations of the Central-Verein with the American Federation of Catholic Societies, and it shows that even the social reform program of the Central-Verein was affected. There had been other difficulties between the two organizations, which we shall deal with in later chapters, but in 1913 the Federation offered to cooperate with the Central-Verein in establishing a school for social study. The Central-Verein had begun the project of the Ketteler Study House independently, and when spokesmen for the Federation expressed an interest in helping, provided their organization could also participate in its direction, the reaction was almost explosive. The German Catholics wished to do the job themselves, wrote Frederick P. Kenkel, the chief architect of the Central-Verein's social program; it would "cause consternation . . . and serious reaction" if the story leaked out that others were to participate in the erection and control of the Study House. "The mass of our people have no confidence in the English-speaking Catholics," Kenkel went on. "Nothing good has ever come to them from that quarter, they say. Honors and offices are for the Irish, they say; we are graciously permitted to work and to labor." These were the feelings Kenkel had heard expressed "a thousand times."[66] The Study House was never opened up, and it is doubtful that the assistance of the Federation of Catholic Societies would have assured its completion. But the Federation was not permitted to participate largely because of the sentiments of resentment and ethnic particularism described by Kenkel.

The feeling of somewhat embittered estrangement on the part of the German Catholics and the suspicion with which they regarded their coreligionists were related to the extreme discouragement which gripped them at the end of the period of controversies. While this near-demoralization was partially caused by changes in the social basis of the group, it was also associated with the quarrels, most specifically with the unhappy struggle over Americanism at the Catholic University of America and with an episode involving Monsignor Joseph Schroeder.[67]

The Catholic University of America, which began to function in 1889, had as its first rector John J. Keane, one of the best known leaders of the Americanizers, and although there were some conservatives on its faculty, the University was regarded as a hotbed of liberalism. Monsignor Schroeder, who was brought from Cologne as professor of dogmatic theology, was the most noteworthy spokesman for conservatism at the University; he also became perhaps the most active critic of Americanism in the country and was looked upon by the German-American Catholics as their special champion. Schroeder played so important a role in the Americanism controversy that he was characterized by one intemperate observer as a "Professional Jonah" who had caused "this storm in the American Church."[68] In 1897 his numerous enemies succeeded in having him ousted from the University; after much rather discreditable bickering—including charges that Schroeder frequented saloons—he was forced to resign and returned to Europe.

The shabby treatment accorded Schroeder was bitterly resented by the German-American Catholics. The Central-Verein, which had already petitioned Rome to keep him on at Catholic University,[69] had a special reason to lament his unceremonious departure. At Schroeder's urging, the Central-Verein had already pledged itself, in 1896, to strengthen the representation of German Catholic opinion at the University by subscribing twenty-five thousand dollars for the creation of a Chair of German Language and Literature. Schroeder, who was called "the soul of the undertaking," proposed naming the Chair in honor of the Central-Verein, and he promised to make sure that its holder would be both thoroughly German and thoroughly Catholic— that is, not a "liberal."[70] Although the campaign to raise the money was initiated in a businesslike way, the results were disappointing. Central-Verein president Adolph Weber reported after a year of agitation that less than half of the amount had even been pledged, and he added that many local vereins were following a sort of wait-and-see policy. While the hard times of the middle nineties were partially responsible, Weber was sure that the principal reason the campaign was so phlegmatically supported by the press and clergy was quite different. The reason, he said, was "the uncertainty about what is going to become of us German Catholics here in America," and he suggested that the Central-Verein seek to determine whether the German Catholics were on a level of equality with other nationalities or "whether we shall merely be tolerated."[71]

The outlook was much more depressing when the Central-Verein met a year later. By 1898 Schroeder had already been dismissed, and his departure made the continuation of the campaign for a German Chair "completely pointless."[72] According to a well-qualified observer, the discouragement caused by the Schroeder case was noticeable in German Catholic ranks for several years thereafter. In 1903 they received another disheartening blow when Monsignor Denis O'Connell, a notorious Americanist, was appointed rector of the University.[73] Curiously, it was at just this time that Father Anton H. Walburg of Cincinnati, a prominent German apologist in the nationality controversy, undertook personally to establish a German Chair at the University, using his own funds and whatever he could collect from other sources. Walburg, whose views were not notably clear or consistent, was able to persuade the Ohio state league of German Catholic societies to support his movement, but when the matter was brought up at the Central-Verein's convention in 1903 it was rejected as "inopportune at the moment." Feeling ran so high that when Archbishop Sebastian G. Messmer of Milwaukee rose to speak in behalf of Walburg's proposal, he was at first shouted down and only regained the platform when the delegates realized what an affront they had offered the prelate who was the leading German-speaking representative in the American hierarchy.[74]

Eventually the Central-Verein took a more positive interest in the German Chair which Walburg succeeded in establishing, and they regarded its occupant as a bridge between the University and the German-American Catholics. By 1912, another prominent German-American prelate, Bishop Joseph Schrembs of Toledo, could congratulate the organization on its improving relations with the University. He asserted that although there might have been a time "when icy winds blew upon us Germans, . . . now the weather has changed" and the atmosphere at Washington was much more congenial.[75] But the very date of Schrembs's remarks indicates how long the alienation of the German Catholics from the University persisted, and the background of the case shows clearly that their estrangement was intimately associated with the resentments and disappointments arising out of the Americanism controversy.

Yet the results of the experience of controversy were not all negative. There was also a positive legacy, although it was, in a sense, merely the obverse side of the negative legacy. For the same conflicts that left the German Catholics resentful and disheartened also sharpened their critical powers and made them keenly sensitive to the weaknesses in American life. At least in part, it was precisely because they were estranged and mistrustful that the German Catholics were predisposed to take an interest in the social question. They needed no muckrakers to tell them that all was not well in American society. They had known that all along. After more than a decade of resisting the misguided enthusiasms of the Americanizers, the German Catholics were well practiced in the criticism of American weaknesses, for in the course of defending their own language and culture they naturally had occasion to examine the imperfections of the culture they were being called upon to embrace. Flaws, of course, there were, and the German Catholics pointed them out: limitations in such key institutions as the public school and failings in the national character, such as the prevailing materialism and worship of mammon.

After 1900, the German Catholics became more aware of the labor question and other social and economic problems which they had been too busy to take much note of during the storms of battle. But this shift was more a matter of changing the focus of their criticism of American life and modifying its spirit than of developing a wholly new sensitivity to defects in the national culture and institutions. Thus their resistance to the Americanizers served as a sort of apprenticeship in social criticism; and although this was by no means the only factor in the Central-Verein's embarking on a program of Christian social reform, one can hardly doubt that it made the work of criticism and reform seem more congenial and more necessary.

The year 1900 thus found the German-American Catholics in an ambivalent and uncertain condition. They constituted a large and influential element in the American Church and had figured prominently in the Catholic life of the country in the last two decades of the century. They had benefitted from the active leadership of a fairly sizeable elite, composed mainly of priests but also including a few laymen; they had become a highly self-conscious group supported by numerous institutions, such as press and societies; and their organizational life had been unusually vigorous through the latter half of the century. The controversies of the 1880's and 1890's had been a severe trial, but they ended with a statement from the highest authority which, in the minds of the German Catholics, vindicated their position.

However, there was a darker side to the picture. The years of controversy had engendered in the German Catholics a beleaguered and defensive mentality and had undermined their self-confidence. Moreover, as the controversies ended and a new epoch began, there were ominous signs of dissolution in the seemingly solid fabric of the group itself, and several new external perils arose. The Americanizers had been fought to a standstill on the level of polemics and ecclesiastical politics, but Americanization as a social process could not be overcome by arguments or Roman pronouncements. By 1900 it had reached the point where prompt action was required to adjust to changes that had been going on unnoticed beneath the storms of battle.

III

CRISIS AND REORGANIZATION

The Crumbling Deutschtum

The first decade of the twentieth century was a time of critical transition for the German-American Catholics. Spokesmen for the group were keenly aware of this fact and often warned that the most thoroughgoing adaptations were needed or their cause would be lost. In the 1890's they had been beset by external enemies who demanded an Americanization equivalent to "national apostasy" from their language and culture;[1] after 1900, they could no longer close their eyes to the effects de facto Americanization was having on the internal composition of the group. The same phenomenon could also be observed among non-Catholic German-Americans—*das Deutschtum* was beginning to crumble all along the line.[2] The fundamental cause was the same in both cases: a drastic falling off of immigration from Germany which coincided with the emergence of the second generation as the preponderant element among the German-Americans.

Between 1820 and 1920 about six million Germans came to the United States. But the tide of German immigration did not flow evenly throughout the hundred-year span; rather, mass migration from Germany was "a phenomenon practically confined to the nineteenth century, and . . . essentially a mid-nineteenth century movement."[3] As the industrialization of Germany provided more employment, immigration dropped precipitously in the 1890's and especially after 1900. There are no records of the religious affiliation of entering immigrants, but the most elaborate study made to date indicates that the number of Catholic arrivals reflected the same downward trend at the end of the century. According to the best estimate,[4] the figures for German Catholic immigration between 1820 and 1920 are as follows:

1820–1830	2,197
1831–1840	38,876
1841–1850	110,831
1851–1860	244,887
1861–1870	210,000
1871–1880	175,000
1881–1890	400,000
1891–1900	105,000
1901–1910	36,500
1911–1920	10,000

These figures are only probabilities, but they doubtless represent the general tendency; they show that less than five percent of the German Catholic immigrants during the century of mass migration entered the United States after 1900. Since half the total number immigrated between 1840 and 1880, many of the original immigrants were dying off by 1900 and their places were being taken by the more Americanized second generation. At the same time, the first generation was only weakly reinforced by the diminished stream of immigration.

The census of 1900 confirms that the displacement of the first generation was already far advanced: Some 2.6 million German-born were enumerated, as opposed to 5.1 million native whites of German parentage. The fact that the second generation was seventeen percent more numerous than the first among those the Census Bureau called "male breadwinners" reveals that a large proportion of the American-born Germans were sufficiently mature to take their places in the labor force. Analysis of the occupational distribution of the second-generation

Germans also shows that many more of them were working in white-collar jobs than was the case with the immigrant generation.[5] Since these occupations demanded greater proficiency in English and thorough familiarity with American ways, it is clear that the second generation was acquiring the skills and outlook needed to move upward on the ladder of social and economic status. Ascent of the status ladder was not infrequently accompanied by a move out of the original neighborhood, which in the case of Catholics often meant away from the national parish.[6]

But these evidences of the inroads of Americanization were not nearly so disturbing as the decline in the use of the German language, which many observers deplored. The Catholic German-language press was still numerically impressive in 1900, but, like the German press in general, it had already passed its peak. In the century after the founding of the *Wahrheits-Freund* in 1837, some sixty-four daily or weekly German Catholic publications appeared in the United States. Twenty-six had already succumbed before 1900; fourteen more expired between 1900 and 1918; and only three new ones were begun between 1900 and 1937.[7] The pioneer *Wahrheits-Freund,* which complained in 1900 that the young people would have nothing to do with the "Dutch language,"[8] struggled manfully against the current but was forced out of business in 1907.

There were widespread efforts to check the "decay of German" and stringent rebukes for those who adopted a defeatist attitude. In Cincinnati, for example, there had been a widely publicized controversy the year before the *Wahrheits-Freund*'s demise, when Archbishop Henry Moeller recommended that Catholics of all nationalities should make the transition to English as quickly as possible. One of Moeller's objections to the overlong retention of German was simply that Catholic schoolchildren who learned their catechism in that language did not understand it well enough to have an adequate grasp of their faith. A columnist in the *Herold des Glaubens* of St. Louis, a priest who had long defended the German Catholic cause, confirmed Moeller's point about the catechism. "English is in the air," he added; "children born in this country drink it in with their mother's milk." His question, therefore, was not whether it was desirable to preserve German but whether it was possible and how it might be done.[9] A writer in the

Pastoral-Blatt had some suggestions in 1912—among others, the dropping of all dialects since it was too much to expect children to learn three languages.[10] Occasionally a society was formed specifically to foster the mother tongue—as in a famous stronghold of staunch German Catholicism, the Mother of God parish in Covington, Kentucky. But the conventional response to the linguistic challenge was exhortations to use German in family, school, and society, and to preserve such traditional customs as the greeting: *"Gelobt sei Jesus Christus."*[11] Interspersed with these were recriminations against parish dramatic clubs that performed plays in English and against those who voted for strong resolutions on the language question and then went home to cancel their subscriptions to the German Catholic newspaper because *"Meine Boys and Girls sprechen nicht mehr deutsch."*[12]

So rapidly was English gaining ground that in 1900 a German-born bishop, Frederick Eis of Marquette, issued an instruction that English was to be preached at least once in the Sunday Masses in his diocese. "The Bishop bases this order," reported the Milwaukee *Excelsior,* "on the claim that the immigrants are rapidly and in great numbers becoming Americanized and that particularly the young people are more familiar with the English language. . . ." In Green Bay, Bishop Sebastian G. Messmer, soon to move to the important see of Milwaukee, followed suit almost immediately with a similar order.[13] There was some sniping at these edicts from those whom Arthur Preuss characterized as "ultra-Germans," but the vast majority, according to Preuss, held the "sane and sober view" that such measures were necessary because of the linguistic transition. Since "the salvation of souls is the supreme law," as the *Katholisches Sonntagsblatt* of Chicago explained, "it would be a grave neglect to ignore the actual condition of affairs for reasons of nationality."[14]

To Preuss, who read the signs correctly in 1893 when he founded his *Review* as an English-language vehicle for German Catholic commentary, there was a world of difference between the "wise regulation" of Bishops Eis and Messmer and the abhorred Americanizing program of Archbishop Ireland. The Franco-American and Polish-American Catholics, however, failed to appreciate the distinction. The French press regarded the Eis order as "an Americanizing ukase," and Polish newspapers "fiercely denounced" the Messmer directive.[15] Since Preuss always respected the ethnic rights of other groups, he tried to clarify the difference between forced Americanization and adjustment to changing realities; he also warned the French-Canadians of New England to take heed of making Americanization such a scare word that they blinded themselves to the real needs of the time. The German Catholics had learned "almost too late," he said, that the only way to "save" many of their city parishes was to make room for English.[16]

Time was bringing changes in other German Catholic institutions besides the parishes. The parochial schools were of course affected by the language shift. A less obvious but related facet of Americanization in the schools was the replacement of male lay teachers—often combination schoolteachers and church organists—by nuns. The use of women religious conformed to the prevailing American Catholic pattern and could perhaps be likened to the earlier displacement of the old-fashioned schoolmaster by the schoolmarm. There was still a national organization of German Catholic lay teachers during the Progressive period, but their numbers decreased markedly after 1900. In Stearns County, Minnesota, a bastion of German Catholicism, a local society of lay teachers disbanded in 1905 after an existence of eighteen years.[17]

Other sectors of the German Catholic *Vereinswesen* were in very bad shape. After 1898 there were no more Katholikentage of the sort that had flourished during the years of controversy; the once doughty Priester-Verein passed out of existence so quietly that no one seemed to mark its dissolution. The St. Raphael Society had also entered a decline; its hospice in New York, the Leo-Haus, was having trouble making ends meet. An organization for young men set up in 1887 had fallen apart completely by 1900. In the Central-Verein, discouragement and apathy were widespread. Some delegates to the 1902 convention predicted despairingly that its days were numbered, and so few priests were present on the opening day of the proceedings that the usual Solemn High Mass had to be foregone.[18] To make matters worse, Bishop Messmer, the leading German-speaking member of the hierarchy, seemed a good deal more interested in the American Federation of Catholic Societies than he was in the Central-Verein.

These developments, along with the demoralizing effect of the Schroeder dismissal, made the situation of the Central-Verein little short of desperate. The older generation, who had once needed the society to cushion their adjustment to American life, were dying off, and the society would die with them unless some way were found to attract the more Americanized younger generation. But in courting the "young men," the Central-Verein could not alienate its old-line members, without whom it would collapse altogether. Moreover, its extremely loose organization added to the difficulties of reshaping the society's purposes and program. It was a national federation of local benevolent societies with no permanent headquarters or staff; the few days of annual convention was really the only time the national organization had much more than nominal existence. And there was also the fundamental problem of knowing just what sort of program ought to be formulated to attract the more assimilated second-generation German-American Catholics.

As it turned out, the solution to the latter problem had to be postponed until three immediate organizational challenges were met. First, the Central-Verein's life insurance subsidiary, the Widows and Orphans Fund, was tottering and threatened to drag the parent organization down to destruction. Second, state leagues (*Staatsverbände*) of German Catholic societies had grown up which did not belong to the Central-Verein, although they rivaled it in size and strength. Third, the creation of the American Federation of Catholic Societies in 1901 made it imperative for the Central-Verein to set its own house in order so that it could properly represent all the German Catholics within the Federation. Americanization and the emergence of a more assimilated younger generation figured in each of these problems, but we will begin with the crisis over the Widows and Orphans Fund.

The Crisis of the Widows and Orphans Fund

As an insurance organization, the Central-Verein's functions were confined to coordinating the work of its affiliated societies, transferring the benefits due to men who moved from one to another, and so on. There were suggestions in the 1870's, however, that the national federation provide mutual life insurance to supplement the sickness and disability protection which was usually all that the local societies offered. In 1881 the Widows and Orphans Fund was established for this purpose; it was a subsidiary of the Central-Verein, and membership in it was personal and voluntary. Those who took out insurance with the Fund had to be members of a society affiliated with the Central-Verein. Although the two societies were distinct, they held their annual conventions together, and the Fund was explicitly recognized as an adjunct of the Central-Verein.

The Fund, which never had many more than five thousand members, was organized as a mutual life insurance company of the "assessment" type. Such companies abounded in the late nineteenth century but were actuarially unsound; by 1900 "the countryside [was] strewn with the wreckage of assessment companies," as one of the Fund's unhappy members put it.[19] The defect was in the assessment principle itself. Under this scheme, the insured did not pay fixed premiums but periodic assessments to meet claims made against the company. So long as the members were young there were relatively few claims; assessments were infrequent, and the cost of insurance seemed modest indeed. But claims multiplied as the members grew older. Since no adequate reserve had been built up, the assessments multiplied with the claims, becoming a greater and greater burden upon the aging membership. No new members would join a society that had reached such a pass; hence an ever-decreasing membership was called upon to meet a constantly accelerating incidence of claims.

The Widows and Orphans Fund was entering this critical stage of its career in 1900. It was losing members, and those who remained averaged about forty-eight years of age. The leadership was well aware of the need to attract "new blood"; their discussions of the matter suggest the changes assimilation was bringing in the attitudes of the younger generation. Fund president C. A. Mueller remarked in 1899 that "Our German Catholic Vereinsmen are beginning to grow indifferent." Tried and true organizations like the Fund were "too Catholic" for the newer taste, he complained; everywhere they were being abandoned for "new, modern, non-Catholic, non-Church-affiliated societies."[20] Those dissatisfied with the condition of the Fund argued, however, that young people avoided it because of the unreliability of its insurance.

Just as the Fund members were beginning to face up to their great financial problem, a new blow fell. An accountant's review of the books turned up a shortage of over thirteen thousand dollars. The responsible officer was none other than the founder of the Fund and long-term president of the Central-Verein, Henry J. Spaunhorst. It appeared that Spaunhorst's son had been keeping the books, and doing it, as the accountant noted, "in a very loose and careless manner."[21] Negligence and inefficiency rather than dishonest intent seem to have been Spaunhorst's offenses. But those were grievous enough from the viewpoint of the membership, and even Spaunhorst's character and reputation as the leading German Catholic layman of his generation did not shield him from worse suspicions. A more damaging incident could hardly be imagined for a society seeking to win new members.

The Spaunhorst case also brought to light a fact most disquieting to the Central-Verein. When the officers of the Fund initiated court proceedings against Spaunhorst to recoup the loss, they discovered that their society had no legal existence, since it was unincorporated. The suit against Spaunhorst had to be brought by the Central-Verein as the incorporated body of which the Fund was a subsidiary. This was merely an inconvenience in cases where the Fund was the plaintiff, but in suits brought against it the possibilities were alarming: Perhaps the Central-Verein would be held accountable for all the liabilities of the Fund. Such a case came up in 1898–99, and it prompted Central-Verein president Nicholas Gonner to ask: "What are the obligations which the 50,000 members of the Central-Verein have legally undertaken in regard to the 5,000 members of the Widows and Orphans Fund?"[22]

At the same Peoria convention where Gonner asked this ominous question, the Fund delegates formulated a new plan, one clause of which released the Central-Verein from any financial obligation. But no one could say whether this disclaimer would stand up in court, and since the remainder of the new Peoria plan drastically reduced the benefits payable to Fund certificate holders, it gave rise to several more law suits. The Central-Verein's financial obligations vis-à-vis its life insurance subsidiary were still in doubt as late as 1904.

The Peoria plan was frankly adopted as a stopgap measure. Since it lowered the benefits precipitously, it caused an exodus of members from the Fund and made the task of attracting "new blood" impossible. By 1903 only about one member in a hundred was under thirty years of age.[23] The younger men who remained wanted to abandon the assessment principle entirely and adopt the "level premium" plan of the "old line" commercial companies. The crucial discussion took place at the 1903 convention; it found the "young men" and the "old guard" arrayed against each other as two quite self-conscious groups. The personal insurance needs of the two groups diverged, of course, but the debate also revealed more general differences in the thinking of the two generations. The old guard persisted in the view that they should stick to the methods of the past, although it should have been clear that this was the road to bankruptcy. Some of the younger men showed a distinct lack of reverence for the achievements of their fathers. One spokesman for the level premium plan said scornfully that the basic trouble was that the Fund had been "patched together by cobblers and not by persons who understood anything about the [insurance] business." But the younger men who were still in the Fund in 1903 were fundamentally loyal to the institutions of their fathers or they would not have been there; their aim was to lend new life and vigor to the organization, and their arguments carried the day. The new plan was approved by a three-to-one vote against the bitter-enders among the old guard.[24]

One of the most prominent of the young men who took part in this debate was Nicholas Gonner, a Missouri-born newspaper editor of Luxemburger background, inordinately pompous at the age of twenty-nine when he became president of the Central-Verein.[25] Gonner, who held office from 1899 to 1903, was naturally pleased that the new plan would put the Widows and Orphans Fund on sounder footing, but he really wanted it separated completely from the Central-Verein. The fact was that the Fund had become an albatross around the neck of the larger organization. The task of the Central-Verein's reorganization consisted essentially in bringing the state leagues of German Catholic societies within its own structure. But these *Staatsverbände* were understandably reluctant to associate themselves with the apparently doomed Widows and Orphans Fund. Gonner overcame this difficulty straightforwardly—he simply promised that the Central-Verein would cut itself free from the Fund.[26]

Such cavalier treatment aroused displeasure in the Fund, but the parent organization was determined to cast it off. Although the first motion for separation was introduced in 1904, the complicated process was not completed for two years. After 1906, however, the Fund drops out of the history of the Central-Verein. The separation facilitated the Americanization of both organizations: It left the Central-Verein free to adapt itself to the exigencies of the moment, and the reorganized Fund conformed itself to the insurance laws of Illinois and was incorporated as the Marquette Life.

The Problem of the Vereinswesen

The reorganization of the Central-Verein which had so decisive an influence on the destiny of the Widows and Orphans Fund was first agitated at the same convention in Peoria that saw the beginning of the Fund's struggle for survival. The American Federation of Catholic Societies was also mentioned for the first time at this gathering in 1900. Reorganization and the question of the Federation were intimately related, with the latter acting as a stimulus to the former.

The complicated and unhealthy condition of the *Vereinswesen* resulted from the growth of the *Staatsverbände;* their development in turn reflected the shifting organizational patterns that accompanied the assimilation of the German-American Catholics. The state leagues originated in the 1890's largely in response to the passage in various states of educational legislation inimical to the Catholic schools, particularly those in which a foreign language was used. In Wisconsin the bitter battle over the so-called Bennett Law led to the formation of the *Staatsverband* in 1890; the Edwards Law in Illinois prompted the German Catholics there to form a federation of their societies three years later. Within a few years similar *Staatsverbände* came into existence in most of the states in which the Central-Verein had member societies.[27]

Although these organizations had been formed with the Central-Verein's blessing and its affiliates usually belonged to them, the state leagues as such were not part of the national federation. Many of the societies belonging to the state leagues were local branches of insurance fraternals that were ineligible to join the Central-Verein. The fraternals were newer and reflected the influence of the environment in the heyday of American fraternalism. The American stamp was best illustrated in the "lodge" character of societies like the Catholic Order of Foresters. Even the Western Catholic Union, a society established without lodge features by German Catholics in Illinois (1877), had to adopt a "ritualistic form of work" to satisfy the state insurance requirements for a "Fraternal Beneficiary Society." The Knights of St. George, founded in Pittsburgh in 1880, was a fraternal "order" from the outset.[28] The branches of such fraternals were participating units in a larger insurance scheme, and they did not necessarily practice strict mutual benevolence on the local level. Among the societies making up the Central-Verein, however, local mutual aid was required: Each society had to take care of its sick or injured members out of its own resources. Another difference between the two types of societies was that the fraternals were often less strictly German than the Central-Verein. The Western Catholic Union dropped the German language in the minutes within two years of its establishment, and very soon names like McInerney and McGinnis began to appear in its records.[29]

As early as 1893, Spaunhorst noted that the older type of benevolent society was losing ground.[30] Within a few years it was evident that the Central-Verein would be in serious straits unless it adapted itself to the newer taste. But in 1897 it flatly rejected the proposal that a ritual be introduced to woo the younger men away from the Foresters and other lodges.[31] While the Central-Verein stood fast, the more accommodating state leagues continued to expand; indeed, it seemed that they were on the- point of setting up a national organization that would bypass the older federation entirely. Michael Girten, a thirty-year-old Chicago lawyer, reported in 1902 on a plan to link together the "vigilance committees" of all the state leagues into a network designed to defend German Catholic interests in matters of national scope. When this idea was first suggested at a meeting of the Illinois *Staatsverband,* a speaker objected that the Central-Verein had performed this very function for almost fifty years. The Illinois men felt, however, that the Central-Verein did not represent the entire *katholisches Deutschtum* and that it was too exclusive about accepting new members.[32]

Assimilation seemed to be proceeding faster in the more urbanized Eastern centers, and Central-Verein leaders from that area were particularly concerned over the need for reorganization. John B. Oelkers of Newark and Joseph Frey of New York, two middle-aged German businessmen, were among the most forthright in calling for changes. Oelkers, who made the first definite proposal looking to the incorporation of the *Staatsverbände* into the Central-Verein, served as president from 1902 to 1910; he was succeeded by Frey, who held office until his death in 1919. Oelkers' 1900 proposal was rejected, but reorganization was the principal issue at every convention until 1905, when the plan finally decided upon was conclusively approved.

The details of the struggle for reorganization need not detain us; one effort at revivifying the Central-Verein—Gonner's pet Volksverein scheme—will be considered in the following chapter. The plan ultimately adopted was largely the work of Joseph Matt, the editor of *Der Wanderer* in St. Paul.[33] Then a young man in his mid-twenties who had emigrated from the Palatinate in 1895, Matt remained one of the giants in the German-American Catholic community until his death in 1966. The essential transformation wrought by the plan he proposed was that the Central-Verein was changed from a loose confederation of autonomous local benevolent societies into a more tightly knit national federation of state federations. To make possible this *Anschluss* of the state leagues, the Central-Verein dropped the requirement that its local affiliates must practice mutual benevolence, discarded some of its stricter religious specifications for membership, and permitted the proceedings of its member units to be conducted in English in exceptional circumstances, although German was retained as the official language.[34] The overall result was that the *Vereinswesen* was clarified, made more rational, and enormously strengthened. Virtually all the societies of German-American Catholics—both the older type and the more Americanized variety—were brought under one roof; within two years of the plan's adoption the membership of the Central-Verein almost doubled from the 1900 figure of about fifty thousand.[35]

Although it proved to be strikingly successful, the reorganization aroused great opposition, especially in the early stages. Four aspects of the debate deserve mention here: discouragement on the part of some members, insistence on the need to change with the times by others, the split between the older and younger generations, and the influence of the American Federation of Catholic Societies on the whole movement.

Discouragement was sounded especially by the older members, like Theodore Fehlig of St. Louis, who said at one point:

It is only natural that when a man gets old, he dies; and so goes it with the Central-Verein. But I really cannot see why it should be given a sudden death blow. Let it die a natural death. The entire proceedings as they have been conducted here today must convince every thinking man that the days of the Central-Verein are numbered.[36]

The younger men agreed that the prospects were bleak unless changes were made, but they were unwilling to give up without a fight. In 1903 Nicholas Gonner, whose insight was sound enough although he was not much of an executive, spoke for the American-born generation who wished to preserve their heritage with the necessary modifications:

We find ourselves in a period of transition both in regard to the state leagues and in regard to the whole system of Catholic societies in America. . . . [I believe] that the circumstances of the time require that we adjust ourselves to the *Zeitgeist*, without sacrificing principles. The Central-Verein has become in a certain sense—in respect to organization, not principles—an outmoded institution.[37]

Even some of the older members were driven to reluctant agreement with these sentiments. "Nowadays," said G. L. Goetz, of St. Louis, "anyone who wants to use old machinery that was in use thirty or forty years ago is regarded as a fool. We are forced to go along with the times."[38]

Goetz prefaced his remarks with a confession that makes explicit the feelings of the older generation: "I belong to the class described by Herr Frey as rather old. It is certain that sooner or later the younger generation will push us to the wall—*nolentes volentes*. We, of course, will hold on as long as we can. But I have come to the conclusion that whoever swims against the current is lost."[39] Another veteran member went considerably further in recognizing the justice of the younger men's claims. For too long, he said, a young man who tried to speak up in the organization was invited to resume his seat and was told, "You don't know what you're talking about." If such an attitude persisted, he warned, "we will alienate these young people and they will be slowly but steadily driven out of our camp."[40]

Many of the young people had already drifted away, but youthful leaders like Matt, Girten, and Gonner, along with seasoned men like Frey—who was nearing fifty although he spoke as a champion of the younger generation—felt that the cause could be redeemed; they aimed to "bring about a combination so that we will represent a solid *Deutschtum*" with the Central-Verein as its backbone.[41] For in addition to giving the Central-Verein a new lease on life, the reformers hoped to forge it into a sort of counterpart of the Catholic Centrum in the fatherland; it was to furnish the nucleus of an organization "in which all Catholic Germans can consider themselves represented." The German-American Catholics wished "to march in a closed phalanx," said Gonner, and the Central-Verein was to be the unifying agency.[42]

German Catholic unity became a matter of crucial importance with the development of the American Federation of Catholic Societies, and the latter organization was never far from the minds of the Germans when they contemplated the distressing fragmentation of the *Vereinswesen*. The problem in a nutshell was that if the Central-Verein did not manage to incorporate the state leagues within itself, there was every likelihood that they would be absorbed piecemeal into the Catholic Federation. This meant that they would be lost forever to the Central-Verein; even worse, it raised the possibility that the German-American Catholics would be divided in the Federation and, as a result, unable to take their own part against the English-speaking Catholics should the need arise. It was clearly more desirable that all their forces should be united under what one delegate called "the German standard" before they ventured into association with others who had so recently maligned and wronged them. For this reason, Oelkers reported to a friend in 1905 that he had prayed earnestly that the Pennsylvania *Staatsverband* would not join the Federation directly. When his prayer was answered, Oelkers took it as a sign that God willed the preservation of a united "*katholisches Deutschtum*."[43]

But while it loomed as a threat to their organizations, the German Catholics were at the same time heartily in favor of the idea of the Federation and were among its earliest supporters. The story is a complicated one, but we must explore it in some detail because it reveals so clearly the ambivalent situation of a group caught in the crosscurrents of assimilation.

The Challenge of the Catholic Federation

Regardless of what others might think, American Catholics had known for a long time that they were anything but a monolithic group; in the late nineteenth century they made a number of attempts to unite their scattered forces. As early as November, 1868, the *Catholic World* discussed the feasibility of Catholic congresses similar to those held regularly by European Catholics. Two such congresses actually took place—in Baltimore in 1889 and in Chicago in 1893—and were important milestones in the history of the American Church, but they left a good deal to be desired from the viewpoint of unity among Catholics. Not until the turn of the century did the movement to consolidate by linking together the myriad of Catholic societies gain any real momentum.[44]

Hopes for Catholic unity flickered low in the embattled days following the Columbian Catholic Congress of 1893, but they did not expire completely. Vehement Catholic reaction to the Spanish-American War and the ensuing church-state problems in the new possessions seems to have supplied the psychological spark needed to rekindle interest in unification. A Catholic Truth Society was formed in 1899 to correct misrepresentations of the Church's position in the Friars' Land question and other issues, and the Catholic press was filled with stories of "mistreatment of the Church in the new possessions, apparently at the hands of American officials and soldiers."[45] Some perennially troublesome issues, like the treatment of Catholic Indian schools, were heating up at the same time.[46] It was against this background that in the summer of 1899 the Knights of St. John, a Catholic fraternal with headquarters in Indiana, initiated a movement looking to the federation of Catholic societies. The response was very favorable and the movement elicited enthusiastic episcopal support from Bishop James A. McFaul of Trenton and Bishop Messmer. A series of preliminary conferences in 1900 and 1901 paved the way for the first general convention of the American Federation of Catholic Societies (AFCS) in Cincinnati in the second week of December, 1901.[47]

The Central-Verein took note of the agitation for a federation from the very outset, and German representatives were present at all the preliminary meetings. The *Wahrheits-Freund* commented after the

Cincinnati convention on the prominent role played by Germans and the recognition it won for them. Bishop Messmer was later said to have claimed the AFCS owed its origin primarily to the Central-Verein.[48] But despite its contribution to the Federation, the relations between the two organizations were always troubled, and many German-American Catholics entertained deep misgivings about the AFCS.

There were three major reasons for German Catholic support of the Federation. First, important German leaders heartily endorsed the idea; second, the Federation appeared in the beginning to be a movement in the opposite ideological direction from that represented by the Americanizing liberals; and third, the group had reached the point of de facto social Americanization where it was prepared to cooperate with other Catholics across ethnic boundaries.

Undoubtedly Bishop Messmer's was the most influential German voice raised in support of the idea of federation in its early stages; as his episcopal collaborator noted, Messmer's support "counted a great deal among the Germans."[49] His first important statement was made before a German Catholic gathering at Fond du Lac in the summer of 1900.[50] Here Messmer listed the problems requiring the united efforts of Catholics, among which he gave much greater prominence to the social question than most other promoters of the Federation. He also called attention to the splendid example of unity afforded by the Catholics of Germany and asserted that an American "Centrum" was needed to mobilize Catholics "socially, religiously, and, if necessary, also politically." Like McFaul, Messmer disclaimed any intention of forming a Catholic political party, but it was clear that he visualized the Federation's acting, among other things, as a massive pressure group—"a closed and well-ordered phalanx, ready to fight in the battle of the age, under the leadership of their ecclesiastical superiors, for justice and truth, for home and family, for God, Church, and country."

Messmer was willing to cooperate with non-Catholic groups; he also felt that well-intentioned Protestants would not fear this Catholic body, but would welcome it as a means of achieving a better social order. He did, however, expect opposition from the "pusillanimity and false wisdom" of those timorous Catholics who trembled at the prospect of a manly assertion of Catholic rights and who preferred to leave such matters to the diplomatic handling of "our political prelates." But

Messmer's aim was not to rake over old quarrels, and he did not dwell on the failings of the "pusillanimous." Indeed, in his emphasis on unity, he used language startling for a convention of German Catholics. "Away with all un-Catholic and pernicious national self-conceit!" he exclaimed. "In this battle we are neither Germans nor Yankees, nor Irish, neither French, nor Polish, nor Bohemian, only Catholic, keeping our eye on one thing only, religion and church."

Messmer followed up his Fond du Lac speech with a similar appeal before the Central-Verein's Peoria convention a few weeks later; then he drew up an organizational plan which Gonner and the president of the New York *Staatsverband* took with them to one of the preliminary AFCS meetings held in New York.[51] But while Messmer played the key role, he was not alone among German Catholic leaders in promoting the idea of federation. Another influential voice was that of Arthur Preuss, the frail and scholarly but slashing editor of *The Review*. His discussion of the federation movement made explicit the overtones of reaction to liberalism apparent in Messmer's discourse.

Preuss was undismayed by the prospect that the Federation might become engaged in politics. Despite "numerous and vehement anathemas," he held to his belief "in the expediency of a Catholic Centre Party for the United States." Nor did the possibility of an American Kulturkampf frighten him, for that would bring in its train "a consequent regeneration of Catholic life."[52] Other conservative Catholic spokesmen, both German and non-German, shared Preuss's conviction on the need for political action and his reaction against the Americanizers' preference for working quietly to make the Church more acceptable to their fellow citizens. Preuss's longest discussion of the connection between "'Americanism' and the Movement for Catholic Unity" used as a springboard an article appearing in the *Sacred Heart Review* of Boston. Seconding the view expressed there that the Federation would have the healthy effect of "toning up" the "weak-kneed" and "servile" among American Catholics, Preuss added:

> The reason why the Catholics of this country have, in the langauge of Msgr. McFaul, been "wasting energy and accomplishing little," lies precisely in the fact that many, if not most of them, . . . have been "forever explaining away and whittling down the meaning of Catholic doctrine." Therefore we of *The Review* have hailed the Apostolic Brief "Testem benevolentiae,"

which was directed against this pernicious tendency, not only as an important doctrinal pronouncement, but as a providential basis of energetic practical Catholic action in this country.

.   .   .   .

"Americanism," more than anything else, has been our bane hitherto. Until it is thoroughly eradicated we may not hope for better things.[53]

While many German-American Catholics welcomed the Federation because it promised a departure from the liberalistic approach of the Americanizers, their very willingness to participate in it betokened a new plateau of Americanization on the sociological level. Although Spaunhorst, a moderate in the nationality quarrel, had taken part in the earlier congresses of 1889 and 1893, other German spokesmen had been highly critical of these affairs. By 1900, German Catholic cooperation in the federation movement contrasted not only with their earlier aloofness but with the refusal of the Franco-American and Polish-American Catholics to have any part of the AFCS. These two groups were still at such an embattled stage in defending their linguistic and national "rights" that participation in the Federation was out of the question. Preuss, who could never be suspected of being an Americanizer, warned the French that they could gain nothing "from a policy of rancorous isolation."[54]

But if the Germans were prepared to work with Catholics of other nationalities, they were by no means willing to countenance assaults on their language or to have their organizations absorbed by the overwhelmingly English-speaking Federation. These interrelated ethnic interests accounted for most of the difficulties between the AFCS and the Central-Verein, but there were several other relatively minor points of difference.

Many of the Germans were displeased, for example, that the Federation voted at its first convention to admit women's societies to membership. Some were also disappointed that it proved considerably less aggressive than they had hoped (and than liberals like Ireland had feared) and that its leaders had renounced any intention of influencing American politics. Irritation with the leadership reached a climax after AFCS president Thomas B. Minahan of Ohio, annoyed by the strictures of the German Catholic press, addressed an open letter to Arthur Preuss. In this grotesquely injudicious epistle, Minahan replied to what he called the "black vomit" of Preuss's "carping criticism." Preuss's rejoinder matched the "billingsgate" discharged upon him: He spoke of the Federation president's "expectorations" and his "cold, clammy, dead-fish-like hand of fellowship."[55]

The really substantive difficulties of the Central-Verein with the Federation were less colorful than the Minahan-Preuss episode but more enduring. Even before the first AFCS convention in Cincinnati, Gonner had served notice that no infringements of linguistic or nationality rights could be tolerated and that no organizational plan encroaching on the interests of the Central-Verein or the state leagues would be acceptable.[56] But the Central-Verein was poorly situated to speak for the whole *katholisches Deutschtum* in 1901, because all the state leagues were free to determine their relationship to the Federation strictly on their own account. Still more regrettable, from the Central-Verein's viewpoint, was the confusion that attended efforts to set policy for its own participation in the Cincinnati convention. Gonner and Central-Verein secretary Peter J. Bourscheidt, a Peoria druggist who had long been active in the mutual insurance business, first instructed the local vereins not to send anyone to the AFCS gathering because the Central-Verein as a whole would be represented by two delegates. Their reasoning was that direct participation by the locals would set a bad precedent and might lead to disunity among the representatives of the German-American Catholics. But other spokesmen, including Oelkers and Louis J. Kaufmann (president of the New York *Staatsverband*), who were on the AFCS preparatory commission, countermanded the Gonner-Bourscheidt instruction, since they deemed it absurd that the fifty thousand members of the Central-Verein should speak with only two voices at the Federation's formative convention.[57] Local vereins were directly represented at Cincinnati as a result of this contretemps, along with German organizations unaffiliated with the Central-Verein.

Although several German Catholics were elected to high office in the Federation, the outcome of the meeting was not altogether satisfactory. The crux of the matter, as the Central-Verein men saw it, was the distinction between true federation and what they called amalgamation or centralization. They opposed plans which called for meshing all societies together in local and state subunits of the Federation, fear-ing that such fusion would undercut existing national organizations like the Central-Verein. The German Catholics were especially conscious of these problems because the question of nationality was involved. What they proposed in Cincinnati was that separate state federations of nationalities be formed; these subfederations would then cooperate in the national AFCS, which would serve as a sort of parliament of ethnic organizations. When this scheme was rejected, the Central-Verein bent its efforts toward obtaining for itself a special position within the Federation as the national representative of all German-American Catholics. According to this arrangement, local societies and the *Staatsverbände* need not affiliate directly with the AFCS or any of its subordinate divisions, since they were already considered part of the Federation by virtue of belonging to the Central-Verein.[58]

At the Federation's second convention, held in Chicago in the summer of 1902, substantial concessions were made to the Central-Verein's demands: It was made the "national representative" of the German-American Catholics and its per-member dues to the AFCS were drastically reduced. These favorable changes in the Federation's structure induced the Central-Verein to affiliate itself formally with the AFCS later in 1902.[59] But the problems of cooperation were not to be solved by constitutional formalisms, and the issue remained a chronic one. In the very next year after the Chicago changes were approved, a representative of the Pennsylvania *Staatsverband* warned the officers of subordinate divisions of the Federation to "keep hands off of our German societies"; tampering with them would "undo that for which we have labored many years and the fruition of which we see here now in the fraternal clasping of hands of the different nationalities." Three years later, German delegates were so uneasy that they pushed through a resolution by which the AFCS guaranteed the linguistic rights of non-English-speaking groups.[60]

The Central-Verein's willingness to participate in the Federation in spite of these tensions was indicative of the waning sense of ethnic exclusiveness among the German-American Catholics. Some, like Bishop Messmer, went much further than others, and there was even an occasional suggestion that if the Central-Verein was doomed to extinction it could perform its last great service to the Church by contributing as decisively as possible to the emerging organization of all

American Catholics.[61] But the characteristic reaction was to insist that the Central-Verein must strengthen itself so as to avoid being absorbed by the Federation even while cooperating with it. The German-American Catholics wished to belong to the AFCS "as a compact whole, not dismembered and cut to pieces, without helm or rudder," in secretary Bourscheidt's words. Consequently, the emergence of the Federation made reorganization a "pressing necessity."[62] The Federation had the paradoxical effect of both leading the German Catholics into closer contact and cooperation with others and at the same time spurring their efforts to forge stronger organizational bonds and to solidify their ethnic cohesiveness.

The Vereinswesen Reconstituted

Just two or three years before its 1905 golden jubilee convention there were probably not many people who expected the Central-Verein to endure very long after that milestone. Two generations was certainly a decent lifetime for such a society; the Irish Catholic Benevolent Union, much like the Central-Verein in purpose and structure, was on its last legs at the same time and it had been formed fourteen years later than the Central-Verein.

But the golden jubilee convention marked the beginning of a new life for the Central-Verein. The reorganization plan approved there was clearly taking effect two years later; a membership of almost one hundred thousand was reported at the Dubuque convention in 1907, an enthusiastic gathering honored by the presence of the Apostolic Delegate and marked by the most impressive public sessions (a modified Katholikentag) the German Catholics had mounted for a decade. Confidence, at an all-time low just five years earlier, was fully restored. Monsignor Francis Goller, a veteran of the Priester-Verein, captured the spirit of the convention in the words of a student song, "Noch ist Polen nicht verloren"—roughly equivalent to "I have not yet begun to fight!"[63]

The leaders had every reason to be proud of their achievement, for it was very great. They had adapted their organization to new conditions, and in doing so they had unified virtually the whole complex of German-American Catholic associational life. A new level of Americanization had been reached which might easily have dissolved the organizational structure of the group; but the process had been contained, the challenge of the AFCS had been met, and the *Vereinswesen* emerged from the period of crisis in incomparably better shape than it was earlier.

The restructuring of the *Vereinswesen* was part of a much larger movement of organizational realignment that took place in the American Catholic subculture at the opening of the twentieth century. This realignment has never been studied, but it seems to have been a response by the maturing Catholic minority to the increasing complexity and bureaucratization of American society. The wave of business consolidations in the late nineteenth century was the most obvious aspect of the tremendous movement toward complex, specialized organization that characterized American society as it assumed its contemporary urban-industrial form. These massive changes made it imperative for all groups within society rationally to organize or reorganize themselves to cope with the challenges created by the ongoing process. The quickened organizational life among farmers, laborers, and sectors of the middle class were all part of this movement which the historian, Samuel P. Hays, has called "the response to industrialism."[64]

Within the Catholic minority, the movement to federate Catholic societies can be interpreted as part of the effort to cope with the changing situation. But the establishment of various Catholic professional associations early in the present century was a more significant landmark. One of the earliest and most important of these groups established to systematize Catholic activity in specific functional areas was the Catholic Educational Association, which came into being in 1904. The National Conference of Catholic Charities (1910), the Catholic Press Association (1911), and the Catholic Hospital Association (1915) were part of the same overall movement to coordinate specialized activities and keep abreast of professional developments. Accompanying the new emphasis in Catholic organizational life and in keeping with Pope Pius X's motto "to renew all things in Christ," there was a flurry of interest in the layman and the important role he could play.[65]

Considerable discussion took place in the German Catholic press and within the societies on the need for educated lay leadership. Several speakers at the Central-Verein's Dubuque convention in 1907, including a visiting dignitary from the Center Party in Germany, sounded the same theme. As a result of this heightened consciousness of the demands being made upon the laity, a committee was appointed at Dubuque to investigate the means whereby more young German-American Catholics might receive higher education and be prepared for constructive participation in public life and the professions.[66]

The appointment of this committee was a vital step in the Central-Verein's process of Americanization for two reasons. First, it showed that the German-American Catholics were responding to the newer trends and endeavoring to make their activities relevant to the emerging needs of the day. Secondly, the work of this committee was essential to the modernization of the Central-Verein's purpose; that is, it was through the committee that the organization found a mission, a raison d'être, in keeping with the times and attuned to the interests of its more assimilated clientele.

Up until 1907, the Central-Verein's reorganization was primarily a "structural" Americanization: It had accommodated itself to the more Americanized forms of organizational life which the *Vereinswesen* had assumed among second-generation German-American Catholics, and it was prepared to cooperate with other Catholic societies in areas of common concern. But the Central-Verein still lacked a distinctive work to do, some task which would justify its existence as a separate organization for German-American Catholics. Ethnic self-consciousness was, of course, still its fundamental reason-for-being. But at a time when the transition to a new generation had significantly changed what it meant to be a German-American Catholic and when the newest trend was for Catholics to organize themselves professionally to pursue specific functions in society, the Central-Verein needed a clear-cut mission to which it could point and say: "This is the task providence has assigned to us German Catholics. Let us be up and doing!"

When the Committee for *Heranbildung* (continuing education) was appointed in 1907, it was not yet clear what the Central-Verein's new mission was to be. But by the time the committee reported in 1908, its designation had changed to "Committee for the Further Education of our People for the Catholic Movement for the Renewal of Society," and after that date it was simply "Committee for Social Propaganda."[67] Christian social reform was the new mission of the Central-Verein.

IV

Early Stirrings

When the Central-Verein launched into the work of social reform in 1908–1909 it was not embarking on a wholly new undertaking. The mutual assistance provided by its constituent societies from the earliest days was a type of social welfare work, although it could not properly be called social reform as some of the organization's spokesmen have since maintained. German-American Catholics also showed an awareness of the larger aspects of the social problem in their attention to immigrant aid. Shortly after the Haymarket Riot in 1886, the *Pastoral-Blatt* emphasized that immigrants should be given all possible assistance to forestall their joining the ranks of the unemployed and aggravating the social unrest.[1] And while the social question was a quite secondary interest for the Central-Verein before 1900, it did manifest some concern over the problems of labor and the threat of socialism.

The creation of employment bureaus was the most practical early step taken by the organization in the area of social and economic issues. In 1886 the convention passed a resolution calling upon each affiliated society to appoint a committee to watch the local labor market and seek to bring employers and job-seekers together. In large cities having at least five affiliated vereins, the chairmen of these committees were to form themselves into a "labor bureau" or employment agency. Several such agencies were established. In St. Louis, Central-Verein president Spaunhorst served on the labor bureau, which worked with Polish as well as German Catholics. The 1898 report of the Milwaukee bureau furnishes an example of the scope of its services. The secretary complained that too much was expected of him and conceded that' he had been unable to place the many applicants for office work; he had, however, found work for 228 applicants, most of whom were laborers or craftsmen.[2]

The Central-Verein's stand on the broader aspects of the labor problem was closely related to its fear of socialism and anarchism. The same was true of most other American Catholics of the period. Trade unionism "won little, if any, recognition in Catholic circles until the mid-1880's"; only then did prominent Catholic spokesmen begin to distinguish between the labor question and socialism.[3] Previously Catholics had tended to lump labor unions together with socialist organizations; the secrecy and lodge-like features of the Knights of Labor also aroused suspicions which were not settled until the issue was taken to Rome in 1887. But because German immigrants played so prominent a role in socialist and anarchist agitation, the Central-Verein members were perhaps even more sensitive than other Catholics to the dangers of these radical movements.

"Scientific" socialism was brought to the United States by German Forty-Eighter immigrants. The first two organizations in this country to join Marx's International Workingmen's Association were German: Ferdinand Sorge's Communist Club and the General German Workingmen's Union of New York. The First International dissolved in 1876, but the Socialistic (later Socialist) Labor Party that succeeded it in the following year was also dominated by Germans. Throughout the next decade the German language was used in its meetings and the convention proceedings were printed in German. Friedrich Engels realized that the strong Teutonic flavor did little to speed the acceptance of socialism among Americans, and he thought it would be a good thing for the movement if these doctrinaire and belligerent "*alte*

Genossen" could be eliminated.[4] German radicals, the most notable of whom was Johann Most, were also conspicuous among the anarchists. And although Andrew Carnegie was an immigrant himself, he probably spoke for most Americans when he called these movements the work of "a parcel of foreign cranks."[5]

Many American Catholics bracketed socialism with Germans. In 1878, for example, the *Catholic World* discussed the dangers of "German Socialism," and a few days after the Haymarket Riot, Cardinal Gibbons preached to the German Catholics of Baltimore on the menace of immigrant-led radical movements. Archbishop William Elder of Cincinnati was also thinking of the Haymarket affair when he observed that the German language in America was "a vehicle of socialism." (This remark "brought some odium on me," Elder reported later, because through a mistake in copying he was represented as contending that German was "a language of sensualism.")[6] In the midst of the nationality conflict, the Americanizers Ireland and Keane did not fail to draw attention to the prominent role played by Germans in the socialist movement.[7] Under these circumstances the German-American Catholics were particularly anxious to dissassociate themselves from the radical activities of their ethnic brethren.

In the same year that the *New Yorker Volkszeitung* was established as a socialist daily (1878), the Central-Verein passed a series of resolutions on the social question and revolutionary agitation. Asserting that only the Christian religion could furnish an adequate solution to the ills of the time and admonishing employers to treat their workers justly, the Central-Verein also warned that Catholic workingmen could take no part "in agitation which has for its purpose revolution in any form, or from which revolution would follow as a consequence." The English-language Catholic press noted these resolutions with approbation.[8]

The Catholic press also reported the discussion of the Knights of Labor issue at the Central-Verein's convention in 1887. This convention was held in conjunction with the first German-American Katholikentag, an important episode in the nationality conflict, and the reporting of the incident relating to the Knights had heavy overtones of that controversy. George Mitsch, a leading German Catholic layman of St. Paul, introduced a resolution condemning the Knights of Labor and linking it with anarchists, socialists, and prohibitionists. He supported his resolution in a brief speech which the convention proceedings do not reproduce and which was variously reported in the press. According to the most sensational version, Mitsch said that German Catholic workingmen should consider it a disgrace to be ruled by the "Irish ignoramuses" who dominated the Knights. But another version quoted Mitsch as saying, "It is a disgrace that the German-speaking residents of America should be held responsible for a few fanatics and frauds who pose as Anarchists and exponents of diverse types." The resolution was rejected, and after Terence V. Powderly wired the convention defending the Knights of Labor, Mitsch clarified his position by saying he was not opposed to unions but only to anarchism and revolutionary socialism.[9]

The labor question was discussed at the 1887 Katholikentag by Father William Robbers of Covington, one of the leaders of the Priester-Verein. Robbers' treatment was rather conservative, as was typical of Catholic thinking at the time. He granted that the labor problem was a real one but did not believe it was as serious as some commentators would have it. Labor unions, he argued, were useful if properly directed but could also do much damage if they fell into the hands of the wrong leaders. In any event, they alone could not solve the problem; a return to Christian principles was indispensable. Robbers commented, "German character and Catholic life and faith are the first prerequisites to the solution of the social and labor questions." His most positive contribution was the suggestion that special Catholic societies, with subdivisions for workingmen, be set up to study the social problem. Robbers listed child labor, immoral language, the "dangerous working together" of men and women, and Sunday work as examples of the sort of abuses these societies might take up.[10]

Aside from the proposal for a more systematic approach to the problem, there was nothing in Robbers' speech that was in advance of contemporary Catholic social commentary. The same was true of the Katholikentag's resolution on the labor question, which tended to minimize its seriousness.[11] Not until the turn of the century were the German-American Catholics to assume a position of leadership on the social question. No doubt they were too deeply engaged in the controversies over Cahenslyism, education, and Americanism to devote themselves consistently to other matters. But they were aware throughout the troubled nineties of the continuing presence of the social question. In 1891 both the Central-Verein and the Katholikentag passed resolutions hailing Pope Leo XIII's encyclical *Rerum Novarum*.[12] The following year a Newark lawyer, Charles Herr, examined "The Social Question" in the light of the papal encyclical. Herr's speech was undistinguished but it reflected the uneasiness occasioned by the bloody Homestead strike of 1892. As the *Freeman's Journal* observed, Herr "criticized very freely the labor leaders who live lives of luxury, travelling in palace cars and stopping at expensive hotels, fomenting strife between capital and labor for their own interests."[13] During these years the Central-Verein repudiated "so-called Christian Socialism" and touched on related problems several times. When it declared in 1895 that employers were obligated "to treat workmen as human beings, rather than as machines," Archbishop Ireland's paper, the *Northwestern Chronicle,* commended "the German Catholics . . . [for] thus placing themselves in line for the advancement of the cause of labor on the only true basis."[14]

But as this comment indicates, the Central-Verein was merely "placing itself in line"; it had not yet forged to the front in American Catholic social thought. Indeed, the name of Bishop Wilhelm E. von Ketteler of Mainz, the great champion of social reform in Germany, was not even mentioned in the Central-Verein's sessions until 1900; the man who did so then was Bishop John Lancaster Spalding of Peoria.[15] The Central-Verein's remarkable burst of interest in the social question after that date was, therefore, a real novelty in the development of the organization.

The Sources of Social Reform Interest

The factors involved in the Central-Verein's concern with the social question reflect its situation as an organization of German Catholic immigrants midway along in the process of Americanization. While becoming more responsive to the influences of the society in which it dwelt, the Central-Verein was still quite conscious of its German heritage and drew its inspiration in part from the fatherland. Its course of action was also molded by recollections of the controversial era of

American Catholicism. In addition, organizational needs and the socia concern of individual leaders played a part.

The influence of the American social environment is the most obvious of the forces which acted upon the Central-Verein. The first decade and a half of twentieth-century American life was dominated by "the quest for social justice." Theodore Roosevelt dramatized the commitment to reform at the highest level of government, and Presidents Taft and Wilson were also reformers although they differed widely in temperament and approach both from Roosevelt and from each other. Progressivism was a powerful force on the state and local levels, and the muckraking exposure of social ills was the newest fashion in popular journalism. Moreover, the cause of Progressivism enlisted the support of middle-class groups who stood aloof or opposed the agitation of Populists and workingmen in the 1890's. American Catholics, Germans and others as well, were carried along in the powerful groundswell of reform that moved through nearly all sectors of society. In these years Father John A. Ryan emerged as the first Catholic leader of national stature whose reputation rested exclusively on his identification with social reform.[16]

The great upsurge of socialist activity in the Progressive period was by far the most important single element among the currents of reform that influenced the Central-Verein. It was only in 1901 that the creation of the Socialist Party of America (SPA) brought some measure of unity to the socialist movement and mobilized diverse native American groups behind the banner of socialism. Optimism soon reached an all-time high among party members; the feeling was general that the realization of a socialist America was inevitable and near at hand. From Kansas the radical newspaper *Appeal to Reason* proclaimed that nothing could stop the march of socialism, and in Milwaukee Victor Berger noted with delight that there was greater enthusiasm among Social-Democrats than he had ever seen before. The SPA picked up an average of almost ten thousand new members a year between 1901 and 1912; and the socialist presidential vote increased nearly tenfold between the elections of 1900 and 1912. These facts justify David Shannon's conclusion that socialism seemed "destined to become a major force in American life."[17]

Few Catholics regarded "the rising tide of socialism" with detachment, and in their fear of the movement they probably exaggerated its real strength.[18] They were fearful that Catholic workingmen would fall victim to its snares, especially since socialists could point to two priests—Thomas McGrady and Thomas J. Hagerty—who were avowed socialists and whose writings and speeches were exploited to woo Catholics to the movement. To neutralize these perils, a veritable crusade against socialism was mounted by Catholics in the decade preceding the outbreak of World War I. The Catholic press resounded with denunciations, meetings of the American Federation of Catholic Societies and other groups featured critiques of socialism, and Catholics affiliated with the labor movement fought fiercely to prevent the American Federation of Labor from falling into the hands of the comrades.[19]

Since there was still a strong German tincture to socialism in several strongholds, the Central-Verein was particularly sensitive to the need for social enlightenment so that all could "refute with clearness the sophisms of socialism," whose "syren [sic] voice" was tempting "even Catholic laborers . . . from the path of safety."[20] In Milwaukee, where Germans formed the backbone of socialism, Archbishop Messmer set a vigorous example: He forbade Catholics to belong to the local Social-Democratic party or to vote for its candidates.[21] Socialists were numerous and aggressively anti-Catholic elsewhere in Wisconsin. Peter Mannebach, a Sheboygan furniture factory worker, reported in 1902 that for years he had listened to socialist attacks upon the Church and witnessed mockeries of Catholic ceremonies. He called for countermeasures from the Central-Verein and said he would quit the organization unless it met the situation with something more energetic than resolutions. Conditions in Evansville, Indiana, were described in the same terms and Hoosier members were also prepared to support the Central-Verein in the struggle against socialism.[22]

German Catholics in Arkansas were similarly troubled by the growth of socialism and were ready to lend a hand in combating it.[23] St. Louis was still another trouble spot. The trade unions there were heavily infiltrated by socialists, especially in the German-dominated brewing industry, and Catholics complained that all workers were forced to subscribe to the German-language socialist paper. To offset this propaganda among Catholic workers, parish workingmen's societies of the type suggested earlier by Father Robbers were organized. These societies were eventually federated in a city-wide Arbeiterwohl (working-men's welfare society), and after the Central-Verein established its Central Bureau to direct the reform program, it pressed for the adoption of the Arbeiterwohl system in all industrial cities.[24]

In 1901 a similar workingmen's society was established independently in Buffalo, and there was another in Dubuque.[25] A more broadly based Christian Reform Society made up of German Catholics from all walks of life was also active in Buffalo. This society entered the lists against the socialists, reporting in 1903 that it helped reduce the socialist showing in the most recent local election to a mere four hundred votes. It did not, however, restrict itself to the narrowly negative purpose of fighting socialism, since its ultimate aim was to lead the existing German Catholic societies into positive action to reconstruct the social order according to the principles of *Rerum Novarum*. Hence the Christian Reform Society was on the lookout for such abuses as the exploitation of labor by municipal contractors, and it advocated the dissemination of Christian social teaching, closer cooperation between Catholic workers and employers, the creation of workingmen's reading rooms, and other positive reform measures. The leaders of the Buffalo society were in demand as speakers as far away as Chicago, and in 1901 one of them urged the Central-Verein to adopt the methods it was pursuing in reform work.[26]

But while the German Catholics were sufficiently Americanized to be profoundly affected by the prevailing social ferment and swept along in the currents of reform, there were also strong emotional links to the fatherland which made the example of German social Catholicism relevant to their awakening interest in the social question. Since the pioneering days of Bishop von Ketteler in the mid-nineteenth century, the Catholics of Germany had become increasingly attentive to the social question; after the Kulturkampf abated they developed an extensive program of reform on both the practical and theoretical levels. The proverbial German talent for organization was turned to good account by these Catholics, who mobilized all classes of society into specialized organizations for rural folk, workers, employers, professional people, and intellectuals. The annual Catholic congresses were great mass meetings at which representatives from all these groups gathered for mutual encouragement and to examine the pressing problems of the day. The Center Party provided political leadership; the Christian trade unions were created to offer the worker an alternative to the socialist-dominated Free unions, and the Volksverein für das katholische Deutschland, organized in 1890 with a very active Central Bureau in München-Gladbach, carried on intensive work in the fields of popular social education and antisocialist agitation.[27]

The social reform activity of Germany's Catholics was so impressive that the papal representative at the Cologne Katholikentag of 1903 exclaimed "Germania docet," and Leo XIII himself referred to Bishop von Ketteler as his "great precursor." The German example was also widely hailed by English and American Catholics as a model for emulation.[28] German-American Catholics were of course interested in developments in their old homeland. They had watched the Kulturkampf with the greatest admiration for Ludwig Windthorst and the other Catholic leaders, and the association of Windthorst's name with the activities of the Volksverein was in itself sufficient warrant for the sort of work it was doing. As Arthur Preuss's comments on the movement to federate Catholic societies indicate, some felt that the example of the Center Party was worthy of imitation by American Catholics in the political sphere. The leaders of the Christian Reform Society in Buffalo were consciously patterning their approach after the system followed in Germany. And when Ernst Lieber, Windthorst's successor as leader of the Center Party, visited the Milwaukee Katholikentag in 1898, Nicholas Gonner asked him to describe the methods of social action used in Germany.[29] Four years later, when Gonner established his Volksverein für Amerika, he borrowed not only the name but also the organizational structure from the German original.

The example of social Catholicism in the fatherland thus provided a stimulus and warrant for interest in the social question; but the Central-Verein's more immediate heritage as a German-American Catholic society just emerging from an era of ethnic-religious controversy also played a powerful role. For although social reform interest was in keeping with the Progressive impulse of the times it would be mistaken to assume that the Central-Verein was becoming "liberal." On the contrary, its tradition was one of opposition to all forms of liberalism, ranging from the doctrinaire anticlerical variety of the German Forty-Eighters to the social and procedural liberalism of the

Catholic Americanizers. The German Catholics interpreted Leo XIII's *Testem Benevolentiae,* which appeared shortly before the Central-Verein turned its attention to the social question, as vindicating their conservative religious and ideological position. While their new interest in social reform might appear to be virtually a repudiation of the German Catholics' traditional position, in fact there is a clear continuity between their earlier conservative stance and the more progressive reform interest.

As we have noted, Catholic liberals like Ireland and Keane held that the Church and American institutions were admirably suited to one another, and they felt that the future of Catholicism was more promising here than in the tradition-bound states of Europe. Most of the German-American Catholics disagreed; they held less sanguine views on the excellence of American society and the easy compatibility of Catholicism and American civilization. Even after the disputes over Cahenslyism, the schools, and Americanism subsided, the German Catholics retained the conviction that the liberals were mistaken in their enthusiasm for American institutions. The liberals were too complacent, too satisfied with the status quo; they glossed over the defects and shortcomings of American life and were insufficiently critical of the blemishes on the American scene. The liberal Catholics, according to this interpretation, were so bedazzled by the supposed excellencies of the American way that they believed "We have no Social Question."

If anything were needed to persuade the German-American Catholics that we most assuredly did have a social question, nothing could have served the purpose more admirably than the conviction that the Americanizers denied its existence. Thus, the Germans later took great pride in their entry into the field of social reform at a time when other Catholics were indifferent to the need for such activity. Central-Verein spokesmen never precisely identified who it was who said "We have no Social Question," but the evidence points unmistakably to an article by Bishop John J. Keane as the statement they had in mind.[30]

Keane's article, entitled "America as Seen from Abroad," appeared in the *Catholic World* in March, 1898. It was not, however, a treatment of the social question as such—Keane had earlier dealt with that in two notable commentaries on *Rerum Novarum.*[31] Rather it was a document in the Americanism controversy. Writing from Europe,

Keane attempted to show that Catholics in the Old World misunderstood American Catholicism and its relation to American civilization because they were misled by false parallels between conditions existing in the United States and those prevailing in Europe. Thus European Catholics could not appreciate the true significance of the American separation of church and state, and they wrongly believed that the nation was dominated by a spirit "hopelessly Voltairean, infidel, anti-Christian." By clearing away these misunderstandings and interpreting the American situation more favorably (and as he saw it, more accurately), Keane hoped to acquit American Catholics of charges of theological liberalism and show how a faithful Catholic could also be an enthusiastic "Americanist."[32]

Keane's efforts were lost on the German-American Catholics, who saw in his article further evidence of the wrongheadedness of the liberals. The topic was most fully treated by the Reverend Dr. Anton Heiter at the Central-Verein's convention in 1901.[33] A very active man who combined pastoral work with his editing of a Catholic newspaper, Heiter was a prominent antisocialist and a leader of the Buffalo Christian Reform Society. At the convention in Bridgeport, Connecticut, he urged the Central-Verein to take action on the social question, referring to the summons of Leo XIII and citing the example of Catholic reform activities in Italy, France, Belgium, Switzerland, and "above all" Germany. Then, interrupting himself dramatically, Heiter exclaimed: "But there I hear a noisy voice shout triumphantly, 'We have no social question.'"

Without identifying the souce of the objection, Heiter gave a caustic summation of the argument advanced in Keane's article. America's free institutions were invincible against the machinations of the socialists. The relations between church and state were "so wonderfully wise and perfectly ordered that it would be an unpardonable crime to disturb them. . . ." The incomparable American school system was the best in the world. Our industries ruled the world market, and workingmen enjoyed unparalleled benefits. Prosperity was coming "with all sails set," and the horn of plenty was overflowing upon a people "reveling in abundance."

These views Heiter could not accept. Fatuous optimism of this sort, he maintained, betrayed total ignorance of the causes, extent, and consequences of the social question. One who denied we had a social question simply was confounding sickness with health. In listing the symptoms of social sickness in America, Heiter included not only the menace of socialism, the "gigantic strikes" of the recent past, and the existence of trusts and monopolies, but also several other points not usually considered part of the social question by Progressive reformers. The separation of church and state, the reduction of religion to the sphere of private conscience and its exclusion from the realm of public affairs—these Heiter considered the most telling indications that we did indeed have a social question in the United States. Additional evidence was furnished by the irreligious public school system and the injustice of Catholics' being forced to support schools they could not in conscience allow their children to attend.

Heiter laid greater emphasis on these symptoms of social sickness in America than on economic or political evils. In so doing he highlighted the continuity between the Central-Verein's conservative position in the earlier controversies and its social reform interest in the Progressive era. For in a very general way the Central-Verein's stand was the same in both periods. There were certain features of American life that the German Catholics found unacceptable or at least unsatisfactory. In the 1880's and 1890's they had been compelled to fight a defensive battle to keep the Americanizers from carrying the day completely; but after 1900 they took the offensive with a social reform program that would refashion American society along more suitable lines. Time had brought changes and was bringing more; hence it would be absurd to say the Central-Verein intended through social reform to reinstate the same conditions the older generation had labored to preserve. Yet there was an underlying continuity of spirit. The same partial nonacceptance of American ways that had animated German Catholics in the battles over Cahenslyism and Americanism found a more constructive outlet in the Central-Verein's efforts to reconstruct American society according to the principles of Christian social reform.

Another factor that made social reform an inviting subject was that it promised to serve an important organizational need at a time when the Central-Verein found itself caught in a profound crisis of generational transition. As we have already seen, it was in a very shaky position at the opening of the twentieth century. Faced with several

organizational challenges and confronted by the growing preponder-
ance of a new generation of German-American Catholics whose outlook
and interests differed from their fathers', the Central-Verein managed
to stave off dissolution only through the heroic struggle for reorganization. A fundamental problem which was never very explicitly discussed
was the need for a new mission, a new purpose that would accord with
the interests and bind the allegiance of the younger generation, who
no longer required the same sort of organizational support to ease their
transition to American life and who were not attracted by the Central-
Verein's insurance features. To employ the distinction introduced earlier,[34] we might say that while the Central-Verein's latent function
remained the same (i.e., to provide an organizational vehicle for those
who identified themselves as German-American Catholics), its older
manifest function (mutual insurance) was outmoded. The problem,
therefore, was to find a manifest function in keeping with the exigencies
of the moment and at the same time appropriate for an organization
of German-American Catholics.

In this connection, the Catholic societies of Germany offered an
example that was not lost on Nicholas Gonner. For while the American vereins were, as Gonner put it, "vegetating," the Catholic *Vereinswesen* in Germany presented a spectacle of purposeful activity and
vigorous life. Hence Gonner seized the opportunity of Ernst Lieber's
visit in 1898 to question him publicly on German methods. The following year, when he submitted a resolution calling for the Central-Verein
to take up the study of the social question in earnest, Gonner remarked
pointedly that such a move was not only timely but that it would also
"be of the greatest usefulness in invigorating" the *Vereinswesen*. "You
may call me a dreamer (*traumhaften Politiker*)," Gonner conceded,
". . . but I tell you that in the future the Central-Verein must place
itself upon such a footing that all Catholics can follow it. And if the
Central-Verein succeeds in demonstrating that we are of a mind to
represent the economic interests of the people," he concluded strongly,
"then the future is secure for us."[35]

Gonner's prediction that social reform work would galvanize the
Vereinswesen into action was vindicated by events. The Central-Verein
experienced a great surge of new life, especially after 1908 when Frederick P. Kenkel assumed leadership of the social program. Kenkel

himself was well aware of the relationship between social reform work and organizational vigor; he wrote in 1914 that the Central-Verein would "probably resemble a dying tree" had it not entered into that field.[36] The closeness with which the organization's German Catholic identity was wedded to its reform function was illustrated by the remarks of a speaker before the youth section in 1913. The Central-Verein had found the true solution to the social question, this speaker asserted, but it was necessary that its doctrines be diffused among the younger generation. "The young German-American of today," he continued, "is to be the bearer of the standard for which his father . . . stood and fought, and to prepare him for this mission it becomes imperative that steps be taken to conserve that German tradition, sentiment and feeling and to win the young German-American for the cause for the which the Central-Verein stands."[37]

But it was one thing to suggest that social reform work might be an appropriate function for the Central-Verein and quite another to shape a successful program. The role of leadership was of tremendous practical importance. More than any other single individual, Nicholas Gonner led the Central-Verein into the work of social reform. Gonner was more effective as a prophet and pioneer than as an administrator, however, and his first organizational approach to the task of reform was a failure. Nonetheless it was during his presidency that the Central-Verein committed itself to the work.

The year 1901 marks the official beginning. The delegates to the convention at Bridgeport, after listening to Father Heiter's rousing address, added a clause to the constitution ampifying the Central-Verein's purpose to include "decisive championing of the cause of religion in public life according to the principles laid down by Leo XIII in his encyclical on labor."[38] A separate twelve-point program of "Social Political Action" spelled out the organization's stand on contemporary problems. The points followed very closely the outline of Heiter's speech, repeating his position on the school question and the exclusion of religion from public life. It emphasized the need for "the influence of religion" in the economic realm and especially in the relations between labor and capital; it likewise called attention to the menace of socialism and declared "we need societies for workingmen and Christian trade unions, such as our Christian brethren of Germany have organized. . . ." The program concluded by reiterating the necessity of "enter[ing] into the Christian social movement which Leo XIII has so happily inaugurated and to which our Catholic brethren of Germany owe their great successes."[39]

The delegates also investigated the possibility of creating a Central Bureau, or permanent headquarters, which would take over the work of distributing popular treatments of the social question both to the press and the local vereins. In addition, the printed proceedings of the convention provided in an appendix an eleven-page bibliography of "Reliable Sources for the Study of the Social Question."[40]

It was Gonner who suggested compiling this book list. As the editor of three weekly newspapers, two in German and one in English, he had great faith in the power of the printed word. His newspaper work also familiarized him with the stirrings of reform on the American scene, and since he had been educated in Luxemburg, the ancestral homeland, he had some firsthand acquaintance with European Catholic life.[41] As we have seen, he was mindful of the functional value that social reform could have for the Central-Verein. He also had the notion that if the German Catholics could no longer maintain a national organization of their own, they might still erect a lasting monument— one that would endure the "changing of nationalities"—by leading the American Federation of Catholic Societies, in which he was deeply involved, into the work of Christian social reform.[42] It was an amalgam of these ideas that moved Gonner to propose in 1902 that the Central-Verein organize a Volksverein für Amerika."

Gonner's Volksverein: An Abortive Beginning

Aside from alluding very briefly to the Volksverein für das katholische Deutschland, Gonner did not explain how his Volksverein was to function, and there were doubtless many delegates to the 1902 convention who wondered exactly what it was they were being asked to support. However, discussion of the proposal revealed widespread concern over the advances of socialism, and, largely because of the belief that something had to be done to check it, the convention voted five hundred dollars for the new experiment.[43]

The structure of the Volksverein was patterned closely after that of the German original and was quite simple. At its apex was a Central Bureau in Chicago, presided over by the secretary. The primary function of the Central Bureau was to disseminate Christian social teaching through popularly written pamphlets which were to be spread abroad by the Volksverein's parish "business managers." These officials, appointed on the local level, would be assisted by an "agent" for each of the districts into which the parishes were subdivided. The agents were to enroll the individual members of the Volksverein by collecting from them the yearly dues of twenty-five cents. For this trifling sum, the members were to receive all the publications through the business manager and agent.[44]

Since there were no regular meetings to attend, the Volksverein was more a reading circle than a society, and Gonner claimed that it thereby avoided adding another competing association to the already overcrowded *Vereinswesen*. The hope was that the Volksverein would act as a leaven among all the German Catholic societies by directing their attention to the social question. To this end it was to institute special gatherings where the social question would be aired and to set up courses of social study for those who wished to deepen their knowledge. One did not have to be a member of the Central-Verein to belong to the Völksverein. The Central-Verein had not yet reorganized itself, and Gonner hoped through this new experiment to reach out to the societies affiliated with the state leagues and bring them into the orbit of the Central-Verein's activities. His ultimate dream was that the Central-Verein, impregnated by the spirit and method of the Volksverein, would lead the AFCS (already "practically taken in hand" by the Central-Verein, according to Gonner) into a grand movement to mobilize all American Catholics behind the social reform effort, for he recognized that the German-American Catholics alone could not bring about a reconstruction of society according to Christian principles.[45]

The purpose of the Volksverein, Gonner said, was "the furtherance of the Christian social order and the combating of all principles which are in opposition to it." He was vague about what the Christian social order was but stated categorically that it had never existed in America. The few Christian principles that still made themselves felt in American society were merely imported "fragments" of the earlier Christian social order of Europe. Hence the task of the Volksverein would be more difficult in the United States than in Europe, where the Christian order had once been a reality. Nonetheless, the restoration of the Christian social order was the "grand ideal" of the Volksverein für Amerika.[46] Gonner was more specific in identifying the forces antipathetic to the Christian order of society. There were three: liberalism (in both its economic and religious aspects), socialism, and anarchism. The struggle would require men of dedication and principle, Gonner asserted, and he paused to commend not only the zeal of the socialists but also their commitment to principles. In this respect, they contrasted favorably to the Democrats and the Republicans, who had nothing but "platforms"; the socialists "at least" *had* principles, even though they were mistaken ones. Socialism constituted the gravest immediate threat. The two traditional political parties were doomed to go under with the sinking liberal economic system, Gonner believed, and everything would fall to the socialists unless Catholics were in a position "to oppose to the liberal and socialist parties, a *Christian* party *with a Christian social program.*"[47] This somewhat doctrinaire analysis of the political situation indicates that Gonner had in mind a comprehensive and well-articulated system, but he himself never spelled out his "Christian social program."

Was wollen wir (Our Aims), a leaflet published by the Volksverein in 1905, reiterated Gonner's argument on the need for a Christian social party but was more specific in describing the Volksverein's reform program.[48] "Next to religion," the anonymous writer proclaimed in boldface type, "the chief task of Christian social politics is the proper restoration of the corporative order of society [*Ständeorganisation*]." Since the Christian social order depended upon the structuring of society on the basis of "its natural classes and estates [*Stände*]," it was desirable for workers to be organized in unions, farmers in alliances, and industrialists in business combinations. This sort of organization needed to be carried much further in the United States, the writer maintained, alluding to the example given by Germany where even priests and theology students had their own associations. The Germans organized so industriously "simply because they wish to achieve in this fashion the *natural* social order according to vocations and estates, which has been willed by God." The corporative order could be fully realized only on the basis of religious unity and a general return to Christian principles. But the impossibility of attaining the ideal did not absolve one of the duty of striving to implant the Christian order in the United States, even in the face of religious divisions and anti-Christian prejudice.

Citing several authorities among the Catholic social theorists of Europe,[49] *Was wollen wir* intimated that the organization of the people into vocational estates or "corporations" would eventually have to be made legally obligatory. It also insisted that the vocational corporations be recognized in law as competent to deal with all matters touching upon their "class interests." Each vocational corporation should have the power to bind its members to follow its rules and regulations; each should also be free to enter into agreements, national and international, with other organized social estates. In this manner, "these organizations will replace with *design* and *order* the chaos of the present liberal system, which is built upon naked selfishness and serves private interests solely and exclusively."

As the capstone of the Christian corporative order, *Was wollen wir* demanded that the vocational corporations be represented in the legislature—"in the United States at least in the *state* legislatures." The Volksverein spokesman was quite dissatisfied with the prevailing system of political representation which he called a "delusion." His treatment of the point deserves quotation at some length:

Especially here in America, the country is governed by professional party politicians and not by the people. It is not a political party but simply the organized classes, these natural strata of society, that in reality can give the people representation in the legislatures. The government of a country must base itself upon the people of that country, and the people . . . are not merely citizens, they are rural folk, farmers, workers, businessmen, and the like, grouped according to their natural occupations. [A government based upon these groupings] would indeed be closer to the *natural, divinely ordained order of a country than the modern popular representation through professional politicians,* which treats, classifies, and exploits the people . . . only according to their character as voters.

.   .   .   .

We demand a public representation in which every citizen is represented not only as a voter but also according to the interests of his social estate [*Standes-Interessen*]. We demand a hierarchically articulated popular representation that will form a chain by which the people, with their interests and occupations, will be reflected in the parliament. All Christian sociologists must pursue this plan if we wish to work in a definitive way for the removal of our present social evils in the state. The overlordship of capital must be replaced by the dominion of the natural corporative order [*Ständeordnung*] and the reign of justice.

As Gonner observed, the Volksverein's task in America would not be easy. The creation of a Christian social political party would be difficult enough; the ultimate introduction of a corporative order among a people to whom the concept of a "social estate" was utterly exotic was almost by definition hopeless. Yet the desirability of a corporative order remained a basic premise of the Central-Verein's social program. It was never again presented, however, in so extreme or rigid a formulation.

Judging from the response it met, the Volksverein and its program aroused little enthusiasm among the German-American Catholics to whom its first appeals were directed. After a full year of agitation it enrolled only "about 1,000" members. In 1903–1904 it added eight hundred more members and took in $665.84; in 1904–1905 its income dropped to $464.67.[50] Considering its slim resources, the Volksverein did a commendable job of distributing timely literature on the social question. Two years after its foundation, the secretary reported proudly that almost thirty thousand copies of seven different brochures and leaflets had been circulated and two new ones were in preparation. It had also sponsored a social study course at Dubuque, given by the Jesuit Father John J. Ming, an antisocialist writer. Gonner, who lived in Dubuque, attended the course and pronounced it a "brilliant success" and "the first fruit" of the Volksverein für Amerika.[51]

But either because he was disappointed at the slow progress the Volksverein was making under the aegis of the Central-Verein or because he felt the moment was propitious to carry the movement directly to the English-speaking Catholics of the land, Gonner initiated steps to transfer the Volksverein to the American Federation of Catholic Societies. The matter was officially broached at the meeting of the Volksverein's executive committee in January, 1905, and Archbishop Messmer, who was present as a guest, was commissioned to present the idea to the AFCS executive board. The Federation's officers approved the plan in March and appointed a committee that included both Gonner and Messmer to look after the details. A few months later the Central-Verein's golden jubilee convention voted unanimously to allow the AFCS to take over the Volksverein and the Federation's 1906 convention completed the transfer.[52] Thus ended the Central-Verein's first major undertaking in the field of Christian social reform. Not even its founder tried to claim that it had been a success. In fact Gonner acknowledged in 1910 that the Volksverein "went kaput,"[53] and the poor support it received shows that the rank and file of the German-American Catholics took little interest in it. Nor can it be supposed that the Central-Verein would tamely hand over to the Federation an organization it really prized, for there was still mistrust of the AFCS among many of the Germans. In the same convention in which it adopted the Volksverein, delegates from the Central-Verein and the New York *Staatsverband* felt constrained to push through a resolution safeguarding the rights of nationality and language. And one of the leaders of the Central-Verein later said that the "sellout" of the Volksverein to the AFCS caused discontent among the German-American Catholics.[54]

There were several obvious reasons for the Volksverein's failure. Its program, for one thing, was bombastically unrealistic. It was simply fatuous for the leader of an organization that seemed on the point of expiration to talk of creating a new political party that would reconstruct the whole of American society along corporative lines. Although the Central-Verein later carried on an educational campaign in favor of corporative reconstruction, the notion of organizing a political party was never again entertained. Thereafter the Central-Verein consistently ignored purely political questions even though it vigorously supported specific social and economic reform measures.

Secondly, the Volksverein proved abortive because it was launched at the wrong time. The Central-Verein had its hands full between 1900 and 1906 with the problems arising from the near collapse of the Widows and Orphans Fund, the reorganization, and the threat posed by the AFCS. It is true that Gonner was keenly aware of all these difficulties and hoped to overcome at least some of them through the Volksverein. Part of its function was to stimulate the German Catholic societies and to tie them more closely to the Central-Verein. Gonner also seemed to regard the new organization as a sort of bridge which would enable the German Catholics to move from their older nationality organization (the Central-Verein) into a leading position in the newly emerging multi-nationality group (the AFCS). But these two aims were not wholly compatible; Gonner seemed to waver between the conviction that the Central-Verein could be resuscitated as an independent organization and the feeling that the best it could do was bow gracefully out of the picture, bequeathing to the Federation the legacy of a socially awakened Catholic citizenry.

As is often the case with projects that aim at inconsistent ends, Gonner's Volksverein was not very effective in either direction. In spite of his claims to the contrary, it did add a new and ambiguous element to the already overcrowded and complicated German Catholic *Vereinswesen*, and it made new demands for voluntary contributions. What was needed (and what the reorganization eventually provided) was not a new society but a realignment of the existing ones that would simplify and rationalize their mutual relationships. On the other hand, the influence of the Volksverein upon the Federation of Catholic Societies seems to have been slight. It was incorporated within the AFCS not as a separate entity devoted to social reform but as an organizational device that permitted individuals unaffiliated with a society to become "associate members" of the Federation. As in the original Volksverein plan, the associate member's dues entitled him to receive the publications of the Federation. It was probably as a result of this innovation that the AFCS began to publish its *Bulletin*.

However, the Volksverein was by no means a total loss. It doubtless created greater interest in social reform among the German-American Catholics, and for the Central-Verein it furnished the precedent of a major organizational commitment to the social reform function. It also pioneered the technique of social study courses which the Central-Verein was to employ effectively in later years. Gonner was correct in thinking that social reform offered a promising line of action for the Central-Verein. His mistake was in trying to achieve too many different aims by taking on the social reform function. His Volksverein was ill-designed to bring about the structural reorganization that the Central-Verein badly needed. But once the *Vereinswesen* had been restructured and solidified, the Central-Verein as a whole was ready to assume the mission of social reform which he had earlier assigned to a specialized unit. The Central-Verein itself became a new sort of Volksverein für Amerika.

V

The Volksverein experiment had not been very encouraging, but the Central-Verein's need for a new mission still existed. After the reorganization overcame the threat of dissolution, the energies of the organization were freed for new work; indeed, it became even more pressing to find some activity to which the membership could devote itself. The impetus to the Central-Verein's second foray into the field of social reform came from the highly successful convention in 1907, which was a sort of climax and celebration of the reorganization and a prelude to the next era of organizational development. As we have noted, the prevailing contemporary concern over the need for educated lay leadership led to the appointment of a committee to investigate ways in which "needy young German-American Catholics" might be assisted in preparing themselves for "the higher lay callings."[1] After a year of deliberations, this committee was transformed into the Committee for Social Propaganda.

The details of the committee's evolution from concern with the general problem of lay leadership to its specific focus on social reform are not clear. The factors which made social reform an attractive field were still operative, and Nicholas Gonner, who suggested the creation of the committee and was its chairman, was no doubt predisposed to see in social action the most appropriate area for concentration. As the committee led the organization into social reform work in the winter of 1908–1909, he hailed the process which was transforming the Central-Verein into a new Volksverein. Joseph Matt, one of the principal architects of the reorganization and a member of the committee, was also convinced of the need for social reform. He was responsible for bringing into the committee the man who was to become the great leader of the social reform program and the dominant figure in the Central-Verein from 1908 to 1952—Frederick P. Kenkel.[2]

Kenkel was not a member of the Central-Verein in 1907, but his work as the editor of a German Catholic paper impressed Matt so favorably that he suggested Kenkel's inclusion on the Committee for *Heranbildung* (as it was called at first). Kenkel's preeminence on the committee was signalized by his being chosen to present its first report at the 1908 convention; he also became the director of the Central Bureau, or headquarters for the social reform program, when it was established in the following year, and he continued in that capacity until his death in 1952. As social reform work assumed ever-greater importance in the organization, Kenkel's authority grew correspondingly. Since he shaped the Central-Verein's course for almost half a century, an understanding of Kenkel's background and character are indispensable.

Frederick P. Kenkel—The New Leader

Although no longer a young man when he came into the Central-Verein, Kenkel was a member of the American-born *Deutschtum*.[3] His parents, Henry and Albertine Voll Kenkel, had emigrated from Oldenburg as newlyweds in 1848. Both were active in the German theater in this country; eventually they settled in Chicago, where Henry Kenkel entered the business world and where Frederick Albert Philip Kenkel was born on October 16, 1863. The family seems always to have been comfortably situated financially. The parents were persons of cultivated tastes and high ideals; the influence of his mother, who gained some

distinction as an actress, is credited by the family tradition as having
forcefully impressed itself upon young "Fritz" Kenkel.
The Kenkels were of Catholic background, and Frederick was bap-
tized in St. Michael's church when he was ten months old. He grew
up without religious instruction, however, since his parents had fallen
away from the practice of their faith, and Kenkel later spoke of himself
as having been "New Pagan."[4] When the fire of 1871 destroyed their
home, Albertine Kenkel took her son and an older sister to visit relatives in Germany. After returning to Chicago, Fritz Kenkel was educated at private schools in the city and later at a Lutheran college at
Watertown, Wisconsin. As a boy, Frederick loved history, archeology,
and geology; but when he grew into young manhood without definite
ambitions, Henry Kenkel became impatient with his son's failure to
"find himself." Apparently under some pressure from his family, Frederick therefore returned to Germany at the age of eighteen and
enrolled at the Royal Academy of Mining in Freiberg, Saxony. Here,
however, he "knew the fencing school and other such places better
than the lecture rooms of the professors." One year of minerological
studies convinced him that his interests lay elsewhere, and he left the
mining academy in the spring of 1882.
It is possible that Kenkel's social consciousness was partially awakened by observation of conditions in the mining areas of Saxony,[5] but
he makes no mention of such matters in a review of his life written in
1891. Judging from this "Curriculum Vitae" (which seems to have
been written as an exercise in Latin), Kenkel's interests while on the
Continent were artistic and historical.[6] He reports that upon leaving
the mining academy he traveled through Austria and Italy, admiring
the many ancient cities and works of art he saw along the way. After
this tour he settled in Dresden, where he joined a classical society and
spent the next two years in private studies of a broadly humanistic sort.
His passion for history was nourished by travels through regions
steeped in legend and the romance of past ages. He records visits to
the tombs of Goethe and Schiller; his recollections of the Rhine are
couched in deeply romantic language. Just as the tide ebbs and flows,
he wrote, "so also in my mind comes the yearning for the Rhine."[7]
Kenkel describes himself as having been a vain and arrogant young
blade and reports that in the lusty celebration of a holiday he tried to

provoke a duel with a traveling Spaniard. He "despised the man who
. . [declined and] cheated me out of a rare fight."[8] But gallantry and
romance soon affected him in a more conventional form—he fell in love.
The girl was young and beautiful, but marriage also meant responsi-
bilities. In the summer of 1885 Kenkel made a hurried trip to Chicago
to find a suitable means of livelihood, and the family helped him buy
a partnership in a combination bookselling and publishing business.
The following spring Frederick P. Kenkel, "businessman," (as his pass-
port described him), returned to Germany. In May, 1886, he and Elisa-
beth Puttkamer were married in Wiesbaden by a Lutheran minister.

Although he was always a bibliophile, Kenkel did not get along too
well with his partners in the bookselling business. His domestic life
was happier but only for a short time. Two years after their marriage,
his wife, Else, fell sick. For a year her life ebbed away so gradually
that her husband could not credit her presentiment of death; but, as
Kenkel put it, "when a certain autumn day was already far advanced,
her heart stopped and her soul took flight."[9] She was buried on October 16, 1889—Frederick Kenkel's twenty-sixth birthday.

Else's death was, in Kenkel's words, "that death which gave me
life." Bereaved and shocked, "this man who before was unwilling to
believe" felt himself a stranger in his home, whose reminders of past
happiness aggravated his remorse over fancied shortcomings as a husband. During a winter of loneliness and sorrow, Kenkel came to the
realization "that we are all strangers in the world," and he began "with
the greatest zeal" to search for something that could give meaning to
his life. His family watched this search with compassion and earnest
prayers, for, led by Kenkel's sister, Marie, they were one by one returning to the practice of the Catholic religion.[10]

Frederick Kenkel had earlier resisted attempts to direct him to the
Catholic Church, but now grief and the example of his family led him
to the priests of old St. Peter's church in Chicago. His conversion
brought Kenkel abundant religious consolation. In his early fervency,
Kenkel felt that he might have a vocation to the religious life, and
after his Confirmation in May, 1891, he departed for the Franciscan
monastery and college at Quincy, Illinois.

Kenkel's eight month stay with the Franciscans seems to have had
more the character of a lengthy retreat than of a postulancy in the

order. He lived in the college rather than the monastery, dined at the head table, and had his quarters cared for by a lay brother who won an enduring place in his affections. He was not a regular student, but his room was next to the college library and he was free to pursue his studies as he wished. He read industriously; Dante and Janssen's history of the German people he mentions specifically, and he alludes generally to other works in philosophy and biography. Perhaps it was during these months that he became acquainted with the writings of Bishop von Ketteler and other German Catholic social theorists whom he cited so frequently in later years.[11]

Twice a day Kenkel walked from the college to the adjoining monastery to be tutored in Latin and Greek by Father Solanus Hilchenbach, O.S.F. These sessions were usually prolonged by a half-hour of friendly "disputation" between the earnest candidate and the young Franciscan, Kenkel's senior by only four years. Father Solanus was ordained in this country in 1883, after having been expelled from Germany with the Friars during the Kulturkampf. He was a teacher of theology and philosophy and was also an accomplished classicist. He shared Kenkel's interest in history and like him was "a great devotee of the Germanic Middle Ages, of Gothic art and German poetry."[12] A close friendship developed between them while Kenkel was at Quincy, and after he returned to the world it was to Father Solanus that Kenkel opened his heart and from whom he received advice and solace.

Kenkel's life of prayer and study at Quincy was deeply satisfying, but he was torn all the while by his attraction to Ella von Kamptz, a young woman whom his sister had engaged as a tutor. The two had met shortly before he went to Quincy, and through the summer and fall of 1891 Kenkel wrote her lengthy letters of a highly spiritual nature. They met again in January, and the meeting determined Kenkel's interior struggles over his vocation: He left the college in February, and in May he and Ella became engaged.

Ella's mother had died a short time before, and at Kenkel's suggestion she made a trip to Germany in the summer of 1892, while he set himself up in an insurance and real-estate business and furnished an apartment. Kenkel's letters during Ella's absence reveal that he was deeply in love. But perhaps even more than most lovers he demanded repeated assurances of her reciprocating love, and he reproached her for her coldness and reserve. As he had told her earlier, he required much of the woman who would be his wife: She must find her complete fulfillment in him and so bind herself to him "that it practically amounts to the renunciation [*Aufgeben*] of her own individuality." This demand—which he conceded might seem self-centered—corresponded to his "deepest character," Kenkel wrote, for he had always been a person of "sharply stamped individuality" and needed a wife who would feel as one with him "in all the situations and questions" of their life together. He felt that this sort of perfect unity was possible, especially if it were grounded "in that absolute, highest principle of all love and beauty, in God."[13]

Their separation, which Kenkel found increasingly irksome, ended in the autumn, and they were married on November 15, 1892. According to the Chicago *Saturday Evening Herald,* the wedding was an event "of unaccustomed beauty and elegance." "Richly mounted equipages" drew up to St. Peter's church and deposited "an ultra fashionable assemblage" of relatives and friends. The outstanding social luminary at the ceremony was Marshall Field, Jr., and afterward Field and his wife—Kenkel's niece—entertained the wedding party and opened their home for a "brilliant reception."[14]

As the account of Kenkel's wedding indicates, he had connections in the upper circles of Chicago society, and from his earlier life it would seem apparent that he was accustomed to almost aristocratic leisure and was undisturbed by economic pressure. The future architect of the Central-Verein's social reform program was clearly not made conscious of the social question by any personal experience of want or close identification with the working classes. Yet Kenkel suffered grievously under the prevailing social order; the nature of his discontent is revealed in a series of letters to Father Solanus Hilchenbach.

Kenkel first wrote to Father Solanus about a month after his wedding. His real-estate and insurance business seemed to leave him much free time, for he reported that he was studying industriously and inquired whether the Franciscan did not share his opinion that monastic life in the eighteenth century had "suffered severely from the influence of the zeitgeist."[15] Kenkel never referred to the quarrels that were raging then among American Catholics, nor did he allude to the depression or social unrest of the day. He read little of recent works but found himself returning to older books time and again.[16] He was, in fact, immersing himself deeply in the past, and it is through his historical interest that we must trace his approach to the social question. The study that was most significant in this respect was undertaken within six months or so of his marriage. Kenkel became interested in the way in which the churches of the Middle Ages served as historical museums as well as places of worship, "since, as a result of numerous vows [made by the faithful], weapons, banners, bits of costume, etc., were deposited and exhibited there." He worked on this project for at least a year and a half, and although it is not clear whether the results were ever published, the study had an important influence on his thinking. "The deeper I work my way into the topic," Kenkel told Father Solanus, " . . . the greater becomes my admiration for the church of the Middle Ages, which achieved something then which it does not achieve today—the complete permeation of all the relationships [*Verhältniss*] of the state and of individuals. And the church buildings, the churches, were an image of this."[17]

In developing this theme, Kenkel revealed his tremendous admiration for the medieval social order. No greater contrast was imaginable, he wrote, than that between a medieval church and "a modern Protestant prayer-barracks, which is closed up at 12:30 on Sunday, to stand there empty, cold, and desolate during the coming week." In the medieval church, the guilds met, held elections, and distributed food and alms. "Everything was sanctified through the life with the Church, which took an interest in all the affairs of her members." Hence Kenkel regarded as foolish the charge that the Catholic Church preaches estrangement from the world. Rather it was Catholicism alone that could dispose all of men's powers in the service of a great idea, could teach men to dedicate themselves to the good of the whole. Protestantism, on the other hand, had generated in the modern world "only a diseased and exaggerated esteem of the individual ego," which had reached such proportions that it was difficult to preserve any bonds of unity in human society. "The flight of individuals from the world," Kenkel concluded, ". . . was never the hindrance to humanity, to culture, that the raging pestilence of individualism is."[18]

The fragmentation of modern life disturbed Kenkel profoundly, and he repeatedly expressed to Father Solanus his anguish with the times that were so radically out of joint. He spoke of "the dissonance of life," "the shattered, distracted character of our modern weltanschauung," and "the evil influence of humanitarianism." He described one of the articles he was writing as "a mild protest of the past against the Machine Age," and declared that there were many similarities between the present age and the days of Roman decadence in the fourth and fifth centuries.[19]

Quite naturally a man so out of sympathy with modern civilization had difficulty adjusting himself to it and was misunderstood by his contemporaries. Kenkel's discontent reached the stage of black depression in the mid-nineties. He felt damned that fate had cast his lot in a "great city of shopkeepers" where life resembled a monkey-show. One who lacked the talent for pushing his way ahead with "solid fists and strong elbows" was better off drowned at birth. Kenkel would have preferred birth in a slave's cabin, he wrote, for no corporal yoke could be so galling as life amid such spiritual desolation.[20]

Such thoughts often plagued him, Kenkel confessed to Father Solanus, and he identified the crux of his problem as an inability to reconcile himself to the "contemptible, ordinary baseness [*Niedertracht*] that besoils the world." Mediocrity, hypocrisy, "stupid pride," and "petty avarice" were more distasteful than the large-scale roguery of a robber or murderer. And because he had never been content with mediocrity for himself, because he despised flattery and conventional lies, because he loved truth and followed it in his own way—because of all these things, Kenkel was regarded with "a certain mistrust." "Everywhere," he complained, "I am thought of as an eccentric [*Sonderling*], and am accordingly avoided."[21]

Completely out of tune with his times and misunderstood by those around him, Kenkel was in a state of near-despair. He felt his life was wasted and found his "*only joy*" in his family. He recognized that his mental state was unhealthy and deeply appreciated the steadfast friendship of Father Solanus, who responded to his most despairing letter with twenty-four pages of solace and encouragement. Slowly, his spirits recovered, but the effects of his depression were noticeable for more than a year. Even after he was more fully restored, Kenkel remained extremely sensitive to the meanness and mediocrity of others. In 1896 he became the business manager of the Chicago Catholic paper, the *New*

World, but was unenthusiastic about those associated with him in that work. With one or two exceptions, Kenkel found his co-workers "petty, egotistical, susceptible to flatterers," and not receptive to an honest expression of one's opinion.[22] He also confessed to difficulty in controlling his indignation and rebellious spirit. Associates in the Central-Verein later remarked on his explosions of impatient anger and the pride and self-assurance that gave others the impression of an autocratic personality.[23]

Kenkel realized that excessive self-centeredness was involved in his depression, for he said it was partially owing to "a Narcissus cult." He also felt some frustration that he lacked the sort of university training that would enable him "to accomplish something in history, etc."[24] But like Henry Adams—whom he also resembled in his appreciation of the unity of the Middle Ages as contrasted to the multiplicity of modernity —Kenkel associated his personal malaise with the degenerating course of Western civilization.

He was particularly sensitive to the "shattered" and "distracted" condition of the modern world because, he explained to Father Solanus, "I was a New Pagan—and a powerful lot of that still sticks in my bones." It was only when he became aware of the far-reaching effects of the fissure that had opened three centuries earlier (presumably with the Reformation and Renaissance) that Kenkel perceived the resultant disunity to be the cause of his own "sickness." When he gained the insight that it was the intellectual confusion, spiritual uprootedness, and religious unbelief of the age which lay at the bottom of his own melancholy, Kenkel attempted to "get the thing out of his system" by writing a story in which he would illumine the errors of the modern mind.[25] This was the genesis of his novella, *Der Schädel des Secundus Arbiter.*

This tale of "The Skull of Secundus Arbiter" concerned an eccentric nineteenth-century German named Strobil, a believer in phrenology who conceived the idea of using phrenological techniques to learn more about the past. Since he held that the configuration of the skull revealed human character, Strobil reasoned that skulls taken from archeological diggings could reveal hitherto inaccessible facets of human history. Pursuing these researches, he came upon a skull exactly like his own in every measurement. At first stunned by the coincidence,

Strobil gradually became obsessed by the notion that he was a rein-carnation of the person whose skull he had discovered. Since the skull had been taken from the excavation of a Roman settlement, Strobil, now a confirmed believer in the transmigration of souls, immersed himself in the history of the late Roman Empire. He identified as his alter ego one Secundus Arbiter, a Roman trader who had been active in the Rhineland in that era. Striving to learn more by translating himself back into his earlier existence, Strobil began to live like a latter-day Roman. As a result of his effort to establish contact with the world of Secundus Arbiter and to reexperience his previous life, Strobil strayed further and further from reality, ending in complete madness.

The tale reflected Kenkel's interest in archeology and also his admiration for highly imaginative, as opposed to realistic, literature. But the basic motive for his writing lay much deeper than distaste for the prevailing literary fashion. He intended the story to illustrate the maxim: "Whoever does not allow himself to be overcome by truth will be conquered by error." In Strobil he meant to portray a man who was the victim of contemporary intellectual confusion and spiritual poverty. Kenkel said that very few would grasp the real meaning of the story, for he realized it was a paradoxical way of establishing the need for religious and intellectual unity. Nonetheless, his purpose was:

> to show, in this Herr Strobil, whither the lack of a unified weltanschauung leads, and that the belief in immortality is so deeply impressed in the soul and is such a necessity that, no matter how one tries to annihilate it, the totality [of mankind] and each individual is always striving—often unconsciously and against his own volition—to replace . . . [through inadequate substitutes] the bridges, now destroyed by materialism, which once spanned that abyss in which Horror [*das Grauen*] dwells.[26]

The *Schädel* was privately published in 1898; the edition consisted of only 250 small and distinctively turned out copies which Kenkel distributed among his friends. It was his only published book; the remainder of his prodigious literary output was devoted almost exclusively to Catholic journalism. Kenkel's interest in history also led him to become a charter member of the German-American Historical Society of Illinois and to contribute a couple of articles to its journal.[27]

His signed contributions to the *New World* were mostly sketches of the lives of the saints.

In 1901, Kenkel became the editor of a German-language weekly in Chicago, the *Katholisches Wochenblatt*. This was the beginning of a distinguished career in the field of German Catholic journalism. It was work for which Kenkel was temperamentally and intellectually well suited, and by providing a vocation to which he could devote himself wholeheartedly it probably assisted him in overcoming the personal problems that had disturbed him so profoundly a few years earlier. Kenkel's work on the *Wochenblatt* also brought him to the attention of the national leaders of the German-American Catholics, with whom he had no earlier connection. In St. Paul, Joseph Matt was greatly impressed by "this newcomer to the German-American Catholic press." He became Kenkel's champion in Central-Verein circles, ultimately initiating the move that brought him into the Committee for Social Propaganda.[28]

Arthur Preuss had so high an opinion of Kenkel's abilities that he approached him to take over the editorship of the German Catholic daily, *Die Amerika*, in St. Louis. Kenkel accepted the position in May, 1905, thus becoming the editor-in-chief of the most influential Catholic German-language newspaper in the United States. Under his leadership, *Die Amerika* maintained its high standing. One admiring reader, a priest in southern Illinois, feared only that Kenkel's acute and scholarly editorials were "caviar to the American reader."[29]

As a journalist, Kenkel had to concern himself with contemporary affairs rather than history. He seems to have become more involved in the social question while still in Chicago. He organized among his friends there an informal discussion group called the "Ketteler Club" after the famous reforming bishop of Mainz, and as editor of the *Katholisches Wochenblatt*, he featured articles on the threat of socialism. In editing *Die Amerika*, Kenkel was very conscious of the influence this widely read journal could have among workingmen.[30] By 1908, when he was asked to join the Central-Verein's committee on *Heranbildung*, he was quite concerned over the social question. The evils of individualism and spiritual disunity which had caused him so much personal suffering had not lessened, and the newer menace of socialism loomed even larger. Although he was by temperament anything but a "joiner," Kenkel could hardly refuse to associate himself with the Central-Verein's efforts to meet the problems of the day, and it seems likely that he was instrumental in giving the *Heranbildung* committee the special focus that transformed it into the Committee on Social Propaganda.

Although it is rather risky to attempt a summary description of so complex a figure, it will be helpful to bring together some tentative conclusions about Kenkel's experience and character before tracing the first year of the Central-Verein's social program under his leadership.

Forty-five years of age in 1908, Kenkel was a seasoned journalist of high standing who had also had considerable experience in private business and in managing enterprises of some scope. He was also a person of tremendous energy and devotion to his work, with a keen appreciation of the importance of *Kleinarbeit* (attention to detail). A strong personality of rather autocratic tendency, he found it difficult to accommodate himself to direction by others or to work smoothly with those who differed with him on matters of principle or policy. Yet his gifts of mind and character inspired confidence in his leadership, and he soon became the key figure in the Central-Verein.

Kenkel had deep religious faith and devotion, and after his conversion he never wavered in his dedication to Catholicism in spite of personal problems such as he experienced in the 1890's or family tragedies such as the death of one of his children in 1913. Although he was not involved in the controversies that absorbed the German-American Catholics in the 1890's and seems to have had no connection with the group until he became editor of the *Katholisches Wochenblatt*, Kenkel identified himself with them in the twentieth century. His association with the *Vereinswesen* did not begin until he was invited to join the Committee on *Heranbildung*, but from 1908 onward his personal career was intimately tied to the organizational life of the German-American Catholics. In that respect Kenkel personally symbolized the Central-Verein's success in attracting the interest of the second generation through its mission of social reform.

It seems clear that Kenkel's own interest in the social question sprang from what today would be called his "alienation," rather than from any close personal acquaintance with economic exploitation or political corruption. The disordered condition of modern society impressed itself upon him through the spiritual estrangement and psychological malaise he experienced in the 1890's. He reacted against the whole of the life around him and the prevailing ideas of the age; it was the general *quality of life* in the modern world, not the specific dislocations and inequities of industrial capitalism, that Kenkel detested. To Kenkel's way of thinking, the solution of the social question required much more than the reform of a few obvious abuses. It required instead a fundamental restructuring of society and a concommitant reordering of attitudes and values so that human life could again be lived in something like the organic, integrated community that had obtained in the Middle Ages.

Kenkel's interest in the social question, therefore, had a deeply conservative cast, although it envisioned as an ultimate goal a very radical reconstruction of society. It was the same sort of conservative orientation that characterized the thinking of many early nineteenth-century German romantics who reacted as Kenkel did against the rationalism and liberalism of the Enlightenment and who found in the medieval past a social and intellectual climate more congenial to their spiritual needs. It would hardly be too much to say that Kenkel approached the social question in the spirit of a latter-day German romantic, and he certainly could have applied to his own studies of the Middle Ages a remark made by one of the great German romantics, August Wilhelm Schlegel: "The subject I am working on transports me completely into times of old, while I loathe the times we live in."[31]

However, we must guard against thinking of Kenkel as a dreamer who heedlessly led the Central-Verein into unrealistic undertakings. His vision was surpassingly ambitious, but he combined with it an awareness of practical possibilities and attention to organizational needs. The conservatism of his leadership in this sense becomes apparent in the first year of his association with the Central-Verein's social program.

The Creation of the Central Bureau

The program presented by Kenkel to the convention in 1908 on behalf of the Social Propaganda Committee was educational and agitational in character. The emphasis it placed upon the participation of young men in the *Vereinswesen*, its suggestion that they attend social study courses at München-Gladbach, and the proposal that the Central-Verein provide financial help for deserving young German Catholics studying sociology all reflected the committee's original mandate to concern itself with the formation of an educated German-American Catholic elite. The committee also called for the arrangement of short courses of social study of the type earlier sponsored by Gonner's Volksverein, and it had in mind the eventual establishment of a center affiliated with some Catholic university where students could receive thorough grounding in the principles and methods of Catholic social reform. Finally, the committee urged that a site be chosen for a Central Bureau, a permanent headquarters whose director would oversee the entire reform program.[32]

To get this program under way, the committee asked authorization to send out three appeals for funds to the German-American Catholic laity and clergy. The delegates to the Cleveland convention responded handsomely: They approved the report of the committee, pledged over $1,600 in personal contributions for the work, and adopted a resolution on the social question that recognized labor's right to organize and called for the application of Christian principles to correct the evils arising from the liberalistic economic system. Kenkel's presentation of the committee report impressed even the doubtful older members. The next day one of the "old guard" approached him and said: "Herr Kenkel I was very fearful that this business would not turn out well, but according to the way you explained it yesterday, I must say that the thing pleases me and I believe it will turn out all right."[33]

The committee's original plan was to devote the year 1908–1909 exclusively to preparatory work—collecting money and awakening the "dead masses" of the German Catholic population through special press releases. Through the fall and winter a lengthy series of articles appeared promoting the Central-Verein's social program. These discussions called attention to the example of Germany's Catholics and presented the social reform work as a continuation of the earlier dedication of the Central-Verein to high ideals, but they were very generalized in content. The ninth installment in February, 1909, expressed the hope that the program would not fail through lack of enthusiasm or remain mired down "in the swamp of German oratory."[34] Some of the membership had already become concerned that the ratio of talk to action was disproportionately high. As a result of this uneasiness, a meeting was called in Chicago on February 11 and 12, 1909, which led to a notable quickening of the tempo of the social reform program. The Chicago meeting was prompted by a group from Cleveland led by Father Peter E. Dietz; representatives of the *"Clevelander Herren"* took part in the meeting along with members of the Social Propaganda Committee. The enlarged committee determined to establish the projected Central Bureau immediately in St. Louis, with Kenkel as resident representative of the Social Propaganda Committee and pro-tem director of the Bureau. It was also decided that the *Central-Blatt,* a monthly begun the previous year by Rudolph Krueger, financial secretary of the Central-Verein, should be expanded and transformed into the *Central-Blatt and Social Justice,* a bilingual magazine devoted specifically to examination of the social question in the light of Christian principles. Father Dietz was to be the editor of the English-language section, while the Reverend Dr. August Breig of Cleveland would edit the German section. In addition, the Chicago meeting authorized Father Dietz to arrange a social study course the following September in Oberlin, Ohio, where he was stationed.[35]

Central-Blatt and Social Justice made its first appearance two months later. The opening German-language section contained two articles explaining the social reform mission of the Central-Verein and outlining the role of the magazine and the new Central Bureau. The third article quoted from a German-language organ of the Socialist Labor Party to prove that socialism was inimical to religion. The concluding German piece, *"Socialreform und Charitas,"* was written in outline form to facilitate its use as discussion material in meetings of the local societies. Father Dietz opened his section with an essay on "Social Justice," and followed with some observations on the "Central-Verein and the English Language." He also presented several short items on socialism. Father Dietz intended to make "The Open Court of Social Justice," a question box, a regular feature of his section. A half-dozen additional pages of German-language organizational notes on the Central-Verein made up the last section of the magazine.

Central-Blatt and Social Justice was well-received by the Central-Verein's leadership and members, and within five months it had over 6,000 subscribers. By September the Central Bureau had also distributed some 4,500 copies of pamphlets on social topics; most of them were leftovers from Gonner's Volksverein, but the Committee for Social Propaganda had prepared two new ones as well. The Central Bureau was much more successful than the earlier Volksverein in winning financial support: The Social Propaganda Committee collected just over $7,000 in its first year of active work and had a balance on hand of $4,676.53 when the 1909 convention met in Indianapolis. Moreover, the committee could boast that Dietz's Oberlin study course, held shortly before the convention, was a successful adaptation to American circumstances of the sort of popular social education that Catholics carried on so fruitfully in Germany. The Central Bureau had also provided subventions to enable two American students to attend courses at the München-Gladbach headquarters of the German Volksverein.[36]

The Central-Verein's program won praise from John A. Ryan, who had already become the most prominent Catholic figure in social reform matters; it also generated a good deal of interest among the branches, to judge from the number of communications received by the Central Bureau and the emphasis upon the social question in the state leagues.[37] The reform-mindedness of the organization is suggested by the detailed resolution on the social question adopted by the 1909 convention. Among its thirteen points were recommendations for social study circles in the local vereins; close cooperation with the American Federation of Labor, the National Civic Federation, and similar organizations; stricter regulation of women's and children's labor and industrial safety in general; and the creation of Catholic workingmen's societies.[38]

But in spite of the first year's impressive activities, serious stresses had developed in the Central-Verein as a result of its new departure. Some were matters of personality. Father August Breig, for example, lost interest in the *Central-Blatt and Social Justice* within six months, leaving Kenkel to edit the German-language section. Trouble was brewing too between Kenkel and Father Dietz, which was to lead to Dietz's ouster in 1910. But the establishment of the Central Bureau also created problems in the areas of finances and organizational authority, which would have existed no matter who were the personalities involved.

Finances were naturally a crucial matter. Kenkel would accept no compensation for his indispensable labors as director of the Central Bureau, but, even so, the outlays required for the publication of the

magazine and pamphlets and for Kenkel's assistants were very considerable. After only five months of full-scale activity, the Central Bureau's
expenses totaled more than $2,300. Because of the anemic condition
of the Central-Verein's treasury, funds to cover these expenses had to
come from subscriptions and voluntary contributions.

Central-Verein secretary Krueger, who was unenthusiastic about the
ambitious plans of some in the organization, outlined the "sad situation" of the exchequer shortly before the Central Bureau went into
operation. In 1900, when its membership stood at just under 50,000, the
Central-Verein had taken in almost $3,500 and had a treasury balance
approaching $5,000. By 1908 its membership had more than doubled,
but income had dwindled to some $1,900 and there was a balance on
hand of only $1,068.22. This anomalous situation grew out of the need
to persuade the state leagues to associate themselves with the Central-
Verein. The reorganization was so imperative to the Central-Verein's
survival that the reluctance of the *Staatsverbände* was overcome by
"opening a Bargain Counter" for affiliation with the national organization. The dues for some affiliated societies were lowered from five cents
to one or two cents per member. As a consequence, the treasury was
exhausted, current income did not cover immediate costs, and the
Central-Verein had to borrow money to meet its operating expenses.[39]

The financial problem was never satisfactorily solved if by that we
mean that a completely adequate flow of money was assured. The
membership did care enough about their organization to assure its
continued existence, however; and there was sufficient response to
Kenkel's repeated pleas for special contributions to the Central Bureau
to permit that institution to maintain and expand its operations. Kenkel's livelihood depended on his editorship of *Die Amerika*, which he
carried on in addition to the work at the Central Bureau until 1920.
When he resigned from the newspaper, he accepted a modest salary
as director of the Bureau, and in the 1920's a special endowment fund
drive gave the St. Louis headquarters a more secure financial basis.
However, its work was always hampered by its limited financial means.

The problems of organizational structure that arose from the need to
fit the Central Bureau into the framework of the Central-Verein were
not so persistent as lack of funds, but they caused considerable tension
for the first year or so. In setting up the Central Bureau, the parent

organization had created, without consciously intending it, a permanent headquarters whose director performed the functions of an executive secretary. As the Central-Verein identified itself more and more intimately with the social reform mission, which was the special province of the Bureau, the center of gravity in the organization shifted inevitably toward this institution and its resident director. This development of course reduced the influence and prestige of the Central-Verein's national officers, who were scattered about the country, out of touch with the increasingly important nerve-center in St. Louis. Some apprehension on their part naturally resulted.

Some of the older leaders of the Central-Verein feared that the Committee for Social Propaganda, under whose authority the Central Bureau functioned, was dominated by fuzzy idealists; they felt that these "scholarly gentlemen" needed the guidance of the more seasoned older heads. One product of such thinking was a complicated proposal which appeared shortly before the 1909 convention and called for the division of the Social Propaganda Committee into two parts: One would concern itself with social education; the other—the practical men—would manage the finances.[40] This scheme was rejected at the convention in Indianapolis, but the committee was bedeviled by such attempted "palace revolutions against the academicians" for at least another year.[41]

These maneuvers were annoying to the men directing the social reform program, but their opponents were not simply benighted obstructionists. The Central-Verein was not an association of learned sociologists or apostles of reform. The membership was composed of tradesmen, farmers, and workers who belonged to German Catholic fraternals or mutual aid societies, and the task of leading this group into participation in social reform posed some very delicate problems. It was therefore quite natural that there should be disagreements over the proper course of action, especially since geographic factors were involved and because some of the older leaders felt they were being shunted aside in favor of an untried newcomer. The complaints of John B. Oelkers reveal the sort of misgivings that troubled the critics.

Oelkers, a veteran of the struggle for reorganization, was president of the Central-Verein when the Bureau was established. After his bid for reelection was defeated in 1911, he explained to Father Dietz that his downfall had been engineered by the forces dominated by "the Triumvirate of Kenkel, Gonner, and Matt." "Kenkel is the real President of the Central-Verein now," he went on; "Gonner and Matt almost go into a fit, if Kenkel threatens to withdraw and do anything he wants them to do." Oelkers feared that "this arrogant Kenkel" would destroy the organization by undertaking ambitious projects that would impose a crushing financial burden. Oelkers continued:

The Central-Verein is an Idealistic society. No material Benefit. Each member pays 3–5 cents. Members mostly workmen, poor, have to contribute to numerous wants for school and church. When asked to pay more—trouble. . . . I am glad I have not the duty to combat the Utopian Plans of Kenkel. . . . My retirement is hailed by our Eastern societies. We can now organize for special work as we see fit in the states: Pa., Del., Maryl., N.J., N.Y., and the N.E. states. What consideration can we expect from the men living on both sides of the Mississippi for our need now! They have the Central-Verein mostly in the west.[42]

In another letter to Dietz a year and a half later Oelkers returned to the charge. Concerning the Social Propaganda Committee's influence in the Central-Verein, he wrote:

Even some priests told me in Toledo [site of the 1912 convention]—if this Special committee goes on this way, we don't need no Central Verein Convention. . . . Must give Kenkel credit for his hard work, but it is dangerous for an organization to depend on *one man*. . . . Kenkel, Gonner, and Matt neither one understands the every day people. They have no affiliation. Kenkel goes to the places to make a speech but he does not mix with the rank and file. The same is true of Gonner and Matt.[43]

Oelkers' analysis of personalities and the organizational situation was fairly shrewd, and his emphasis on the divergent needs of the *Vereinswesen* in the East and the Midwest is particularly interesting. But it is astonishing that a man so well acquainted with the situation should have complained to Dietz that Kenkel was a visionary likely to overextend the Central-Verein! Compared to Dietz, Kenkel was the soul of prudence and moderation. In fact, one of the chief sources of tension between them was the divergence in their views on the scope of the social reform program and the speed with which it should be effected.

Kenkel and Dietz

It is true that Kenkel was a "utopian" in the sense that the solution he proposed to the social question envisioned a fundamental restructuring of society. But he combined with this ultimate aim a keen awareness of what was immediately feasible with the means at hand, and he was deeply convinced that the social reform work must proceed in slow stages with constant consolidation of small gains. Kenkel realized that the Central Bureau was a very fragile institution in its first years, and he knew that a misstep could easily spell disaster. No doubt it was precisely because his ultimate vision was so sweeping that he insisted on the need to concentrate at first on awakening the "social sense" of the people and on creating a cadre of trained leaders. For Kenkel held that the social question could only be solved through the introduction of an "organic," or corporative, social order, but this could only take place after the people were made to understand how fundamentally defective the prevailing social arrangement really was. Hence Kenkel was adamant that the Central-Verein should not commit itself to immediate action programs requiring mass participation and support.[44]

Father Dietz, on the other hand, had no such long-range object in view, and he was impatient to plunge into the work of correcting the most glaring of existing social and economic abuses. He had no particular commitment to the *Vereinswesen* or to the preservation of the cultural identity of the German-American Catholic group. It seems that he regarded the Central-Verein strictly as an instrument through which he could bring some leverage to bear in the area of social reform. He was heedless of the special problems created by the fact that the organization existed first of all as an expression of the ethnic consciousness of a people rather than as an agency to reform society. Moreover, Dietz was temperamentally impetuous and hard to get along with. He was something of a stormy petrel in the Catholic reform movement of the Progressive era, but after the first World War he dropped out of the social action picture completely and passed his days as an obscure pastor until his death in 1947.[45]

In 1908 Dietz stood at the beginning of his career in social reform. He was a priest of the diocese of Cleveland and attended his first convention of the Central-Verein in that city in September, 1908. Here he listened to the report of the Social Propaganda Committee, delivered by Kenkel, who was also making his first appearance in the Central-Verein's sessions. Obviously impressed, Dietz wrote to Kenkel three weeks later suggesting that the city of Oberlin (a mission attached to the pastorate at Elyria, where he served as curate) would be the ideal site for the projected Central Bureau. "I want Oberlin to be the centre of a Catholic social service campaign, similar to that at München-Gladbach in Germany," he wrote. The ten thousand dollars that he estimated would be required to begin operations did not loom as a major obstacle in Dietz's mind. Kenkel apparently chided him for his hastiness, but Dietz was not discouraged. In a second letter he proposed that the Central-Verein buy a twenty-room colonial mansion in Oberlin and establish there a permanent school for social study with a three-year curriculum in economics, sociology, journalism, and related subjects.[46]

There seemed to be no response to this suggestion, and since he got no encouragement from Kenkel, the ambitious priest changed his tactics. In January of 1909 a ringing demand that the tempo of the social reform campaign be immediately stepped up issued from a group of Central-Verein men around Cleveland. Dietz was one of those calling for more energetic action, and he was no doubt chiefly responsible for the manifesto.[47] Kenkel was reluctant, but he had to acquiesce in the demand that a special meeting be held in Chicago to discuss the ideas of the dissidents from Ohio. The meeting was held in February, and although there were some unpleasant moments, the outcome was less upsetting than Kenkel had feared.[48] As we have already noted, the decisions taken at Chicago resulted in the immediate establishment of the Central Bureau and the publication of the *Central-Blatt and Social Justice*, with none other than Peter E. Dietz as one of its editors.

These steps did not satisfy Dietz, however, and in September, 1909, he outlined a "Scheme of Larger Organization" for the guidance of the delegates to the Indianapolis convention. This grandiose plan for social action bristled with administrative councils, central administrative councils, president-generals, general executive secretaries, and other bodies and offices. The kernel of the plan was that the Central Bureau be expanded into a large national headquarters under the direction of a general executive secretary, who would be provided with a staff large enough to operate five major departments—Organization; Press and Lyceum; Records; Agriculture, Industry, and Sanitation; and Legislation. Dietz said nothing about where the money for this magnificent operation was to come from, but it is clear from other sources that he envisioned for himself the strategic position of general executive secretary.[49]

Dietz's impractical proposal got nowhere, but a man who dealt in such overambitious projects was bound to collide with the prudent Kenkel. Dietz also acted somewhat precipitously in the extremely tender matter of language. He originally wanted the Central-Verein's social reform journal to be written entirely in English; the manifesto of the Cleveland group, which Dietz inspired, called for a bilingual magazine, two-thirds of which would be in English.[50] When the *Central-Blatt and Social Justice* appeared, the social reform content was divided equally between English and German, but the section devoted to organizational news made it a predominantly German-language publication. Dietz was sufficiently aware of the highly charged nature of the language question that he devoted an article in the first issue to justifying the use of English. He argued very cogently that "The younger generation of German Americans, the sons and daughters of Germans, will eventually cease to recognize the hegemony of traditional ideals, unless they become incarnate in English." The German heritage he was most concerned to preserve was the tradition of leadership in Christian social reform. "In this area," Dietz wrote, "lies the principal contribution of the German Catholic world to modern civilization. . . ." If this German Catholic heritage was to make its influence felt in the United States, Dietz maintained, the Central-Verein had to use English in its social reform program.[51]

Dietz's position was perfectly reasonable: To influence Americans one had to reach them, and to reach them one had to use their language. He was also able to cite the authority of Dr. August Pieper, a leader of the Volksverein für das katholische Deutschland, who agreed that the Central-Verein's social program should be conducted in English. Still there was a dilemma, which could not be made to disappear even by calling on the prestige of Dr. Pieper. The German-American Catholics who were the most faithful supporters of the Central-Verein were much more deeply committed to the German language than to the social apostolate. For years they had been fighting to preserve it, and they were deeply suspicious of those who appeared to neglect it in favor of English. One can easily imagine the reaction of such persons when they read Dietz's statement that the Germans should "fraternize" with other American Catholics in the use of English, or when they pondered his question: "Dare we hope to have a shaping influence on the non-Catholic American mind and ultimately upon the destinies of the nation unless we have first shaped ourselves to American conditions and needs?" No doubt there were some for whom this sort of talk awoke recollections of the quarrels with the liberal Americanizers!

There is no evidence that Kenkel and Dietz clashed over language, but Kenkel was well aware that the Central-Verein could not abandon German, even to promote the social reform program. Such a step would have been suicide, considering the character of the organization and the sensitivity of German-American Catholics on the language question. Unlike Dietz, who never worked to preserve German or placed any intrinsic value on its use, Kenkel esteemed it highly and entered with passion into discussions about its preservation.[52] But Kenkel was not an unreasonable diehard about language, and it is likely that he saw in Dietz's eagerness for an all-English magazine merely another manifestation of weak judgment.

Inextricably associated with the differences over policy and procedure between Kenkel and Dietz there was a fundamental clash of personalities. Neither of them was the sort of person who could take orders gracefully, and the hazy relationship between the Central Bureau and the first editors of *Central-Blatt and Social Justice* made it rather uncertain who was in charge of what, thus aggravating the tensions between the two men. Besides the fact that they were both strong personalities, there were other similarities between Kenkel and Dietz.[53] Both were second-generation German-Americans; both had traveled and received part of their education in Germany; both had difficulty in finding their proper niche in life and suffered attacks of melancholy; both were profoundly apostolic; and when they found their vocation in Catholic social reform both dedicated themselves to it unreservedly.

But there were also important differences between them. Kenkel was fifteen years older than Dietz; he came from an upper middle-class family, and his cultural and intellectual background was richer than that of the young priest. His approach to the social question was conditioned by his deep alienation from the prevailing spiritual and intellectual tendencies of the age. His social theory reflected his admiration for the organic community of the Middle Ages, and he drew his inspiration primarily from the writings of Catholic social reformers in Germany and Austria. While he was aware of the need for trade unions and of other social and economic problems that required immediate reforms, Kenkel's ultimate aim was a corporative social order quite different from the prevailing American model.

Dietz's approach to the social question was more characteristically American. He came from a working-class family; his father was a varnisher, and Dietz himself was familiar with the trade union movement from his boyhood. He laid greater stress than Kenkel on the organization of labor as the key element in the solution of the social question. His approach was basically that of the "pure and simple" trade unionist, with special attention to the religious needs of Catholic workers. This emphasis on pragmatic unionism reflected Dietz's conviction that "the American realizes the social problems of the present with greater facility and thus far has solved them best, although it is generally known that the final solution is still, far distant." Where Kenkel dreamed of reconstructing American society from the ground up, Dietz's ambition was "to cooperate in giving direction" to the spontaneous forces at work in American society. To realize this ambition, Dietz perceived while still a seminarian that he needed to "*master* the the English language, literature, theology, and the character of the people."[54]

Although they were both of German descent, Dietz was in a sense considerably more "Americanized" than Kenkel. The two might still have gotten along together if each had been willing to bear with the other a little more sympathetically, and the cooperation might have been a good thing for the Central-Verein's social program. But each was born to command, and it proved impossible for the impetuous Dietz and the temperamentally conservative Kenkel to mesh their efforts. By September, 1909, Dietz was striving to free himself from any direction on the part of Kenkel, and within four months it was clear that further cooperation between them was out of the question.

At another special meeting in January, 1910, it was decided that Dietz would have to go.[55] After editing the English-language section of *Central-Blatt and Social Justice* for March, 1910, Dietz parted company with the Central-Verein forever.

The residue of ill-feeling that followed this unfortunate experience with Father Dietz hampered cooperation between the Central-Verein and other Catholic agencies with which he was associated, notably the Social Service Commission of the American Federation of Catholic Societies. Kenkel himself did not appreciate the true value of Dietz's work in Catholic social reform until after the latter's death. And Dietz carried with him to the end a sense of injury arising from the treatment he received. He was partially compensated, however, by the "not particularly supernatural" satisfaction he took in the thought that he had more to offer the Central-Verein than it got from any other source.[56]

Whatever justification Dietz may have had for feeling as he did, there can be no doubt that the Central-Verein chose wisely in preferring Kenkel's leadership. Dietz's rash and precipitous methods would have been disastrous for an organization where those in authority had to be sensitively attuned to problems of language, nationality, and the transition of generations. The Central-Verein was not prepared to pay so little attention as Dietz did to these ethnic considerations. Dietz himself moved on to the AFCS, where he had the encouragement of Archbishop Messmer but where his work did not depend on the support of any particular ethnic group. But Dietz's insistence on action may have been just what the Central-Verein needed at the outset of its social program. Too much caution at the beginning might have smothered the vital initial enthusiasm. The pressure brought by Dietz and the Cleveland delegation no doubt hastened the establishment of the Central Bureau and the appearance of the *Central-Blatt and Social Justice*. And his connections with Catholics in the labor movement brought the Central-Verein into contact with men who continued to cooperate with it. Dietz wanted to do too much, but he also showed that much could be done.

In looking back over the first year and a half of its activity, the Committee for Social Propaganda could take considerable pride in its work. It had led the Central-Verein into a new field of work that was timely and also in keeping with the religious and ethnic dimensions of the organization. Its Central Bureau was a going concern and was headed by a man of rare talent and dedication. It had established the first Catholic magazine in the United States devoted to the study of social problems. Although adequate financing was to remain a troublesome item, the other early problems had been reduced to manageable proportions, and the membership was responding to the new mission in a gratifying way. The Central-Verein was, in fact, well launched into its campaign of Christian social reform.

VI

The Work of the Central Bureau

Between the establishment of the Central Bureau in 1909 and America's entry into the World War in 1917 the Central-Verein experienced its period of greatest vitality and influence. This vitalization was intimately related to its involvement in the social question, and the Central Bureau was the indispensable dynamo in the social reform campaign. In keeping with Kenkel's belief that true reform required a socially enlightened populace, the Bureau's first concern was with social education, carried on principally through publications but also by means of lecture tours and special study courses. The *Central-Blatt and Social Justice* was the cornerstone of the educational program. Kenkel, who took full editorial charge after Father Dietz's departure in 1910, retained the bilingual format but increased the size of the magazine to some thirty pages within a few years and added new features, such as a section on the woman's role in social reform, in 1913, and historical notes on the German-American Catholics, in 1917. Many of the articles were by Kenkel or his assistants at the Bureau; two other frequent contributors were Father Charles Bruehl, a seminary professor, and Father William J. Engelen, S.J., who taught at a Jesuit college in Toledo. John A. Ryan, already the most well-known priest in the reform movement, contributed an occasional article and had a very high opinion of the magazine, praising it publicly in the Milwaukee *Catholic Citizen* for avoiding the "edifying and empty platitudes" that so often passed for social analysis.[1]

As Ryan's remarks indicate, Kenkel maintained an uncompromisingly high level of discussion; in fact he purposely eschewed popular articles because he hoped to create a Catholic leadership elite on social matters among the readers of the *Central-Blatt*. This policy elicited some complaints from the rank and file that the magazine was too rarefied for the average member of the Central-Verein. On one occasion a priest from Iowa reported that to the German Catholic farmers in this area "*Wirthschaft*" meant "saloon"; they were understandably baffled when they read articles on "*Wirthschaftslehre*" (economics) and encountered nothing at all on the subject of saloons.[2] The Central Bureau tried to meet this criticism by publishing a second, more popular magazine on social topics, but the attempt was abandoned after a few issues. Because of its rather specialized character and the language barrier for English-speaking Catholics, the *Central-Blatt and Social Justice* never attained a very large circulation. The peak circulation of just under eight thousand was reached in 1913; but since many of the copies went to pastors and local German societies, a much larger number of German-American Catholics were indirectly exposed to the magazine, and Catholic reform leaders like Ryan were aware of its position.

The Central Bureau supplemented the often abstract or technical analysis of social issues in the magazine through the publication of pamphlet literature. These more popular treatments were concerned primarily with the social question and extended from such broad topics as "The Social Problem and Its Solution in General" to "Gedenke, dass du früh einkaufst," an appeal for early Christmas shopping so that department store workers could enjoy Christmas eve with their families. Apologetical and religious pamphlets also occupied a prominent place, and among its most widely circulated pieces were critiques of *The Menace*, a virulently anti-Catholic newspaper published in Missouri. Occasionally the Bureau directed its efforts at a specific audience. In 1913, for example, a leaflet outlining Catholic objections to sterilization was sent to members of a state legislature that was considering a sterilization measure, and in the first year of its existence the Bureau mailed a copy of *Catholic Social Work in Germany*, by the English Jesuit Charles Plater, to every member of the American hierarchy. This aspect of the Bureau's work also won praise from Father Ryan, and its extent is suggested by the fact that within the first five years of the Bureau's life it had distributed over a million copies of its pamphlets and leaflets.[3]

Another activity of the Central Bureau, its press service, seems to have grown out of the practice of sending copies of pamphlets to Catholic newspapers. This soon became a separate operation of considerable proportions: In 1915 the Bureau reported that in the previous year it had sent out ninety-four press releases to thirty-one German-language and 123 English-language Catholic papers. By that time the tensions caused by the war in Europe were making themselves felt. The report notes that press letters dealing with the war were not welcomed by the English-language papers even though they were "purely factual" and "based upon Catholic ethical principles." These "circumstances of the time" led the Bureau in the following year to restrict its press releases to social and apologetical themes.[4]

This press service and a similar one instituted by Father Dietz for the Social Service Commission of the American Federation of Catholic Societies[5] thus anticipated the press bureau established after the war by the National Catholic Welfare Conference. The Central Bureau also became a kind of reference service as a result of numerous individual requests for information; Kenkel gradually built up a vast file on religious and social reform matters. One request for assistance from Bishop Joseph Busch, of Lead, South Dakota, prompted Kenkel to dispatch Louis F. Budenz, then an assistant at the Central Bureau, to cover the Lead hearings of the United States Commission on Industrial Relations. These hearings were concerned with labor problems at the Homestake Mining Company, owned by the Hearst interests. Budenz' findings provided material for two press letters on the Homestake situation, which was also discussed in a *Central-Blatt* articles on "The New Paternalism."[6]

Central Bureau personnel were much in demand as speakers before meetings of the member units of the Central-Verein and other groups. To supplement the work of these speakers, the Bureau made available a number of prepared lectures accompanied by lantern slides which could be borrowed by interested groups. Some of these *Lichtbilder* series were obtained from the German Volksverein at München-Gladbach, but the Central Bureau prepared others centering on such topics as housing conditions in American cities. The Bureau also rented out small traveling libraries dealing with social and religious matters.

Just as it maintained contact with the Volksverein and other European and American organizations interested in reform, the Central Bureau drew upon outside sources in its campaign of social enlightenment. The two most active lecturers sponsored by the Bureau were not members of the Central-Verein—David Goldstein, a Jewish convert to Catholicism and former socialist, and Peter W. Collins, prominent in the International Brotherhood of Electrical Workers until he resigned to devote his time to lecturing against socialism. Before they transferred their services to the Knights of Columbus, who offered them a more attractive contract in 1914, Goldstein and Collins had delivered a total of more than 250 lectures under the auspices of the Central Bureau. Both concentrated on the socialist menace and were very popular with the audiences who heard them.[7]

Although the socialist threat received a good deal of attention, the Central Bureau did not confine itself to antisocialist polemics. Socialism was but one of the four themes dealt with at the special social study course sponsored by the Central Bureau at Spring Bank, Wisconsin, in 1910. The speaker, Father William J. Kerby of the Catholic University, was a serious student of social problems who combined his treatment of socialism with a more general examination of reform. At the same Spring Bank course, John A. Ryan gave five talks on labor and wage problems; Bernard J. Otten, S.J., of St. Louis University, discussed the moral principles involved in the social question; and another priest who had visited München-Gladbach under the sponsorship of the Central-Verein described the work of the German Volksverein.[8] These social study courses, which had been pioneered by Dietz at Oberlin and even earlier by Gonner at Dubuque, were an important part of the Central Bureau's program of social education in the early years. In both 1912 and 1913 two separate summer courses were given: one at

Spring Bank and the other on the East Coast. The excitement caused by the European war perhaps contributed to a loss of interest in them, for in 1916 the study course comprised only three lectures given by Father Engelen and was held as an adjunct to the Central-Verein's convention. Thereafter the study courses were merely added features to the annual conventions.

Wartime distractions also played a part in frustrating the Central Bureau's most ambitious undertaking in the area of social education. This project, the Ketteler Study House, was especially dear to Kenkel, who always insisted that systematic study was an essential prerequisite to fruitful action. Since, in his judgment, there was no school where Catholics could get adequate theoretical grounding in social philosophy and field experience in social work, Kenkel hoped to establish one. Once in operation, the school would also become the home of the Central Bureau, thus providing in one consolidated headquarters a center for social education and an agency for social action. The school was to be named after the great Bishop von Ketteler, and it would champion the Central-Verein's "Ketteler-like view of the social question."[9]

An initial donation of five thousand dollars furnished the nucleus of the Study House fund, and as early as the fall of 1910 the officers were investigating the possibility of locating the school in Chicago, where it could work in conjunction with Loyola University. By 1913 sufficient funds had been collected to purchase land in Chicago worth sixteen thousand dollars.[10] Father Frederic Siedenburg, S.J., who had already begun to build up a program of sociology and social work at Loyola, was willing to collaborate with the Study House, and there was a good deal of enthusiasm among the Central-Verein's membership. In spite of this promising start, the Ketteler Study House was a goal that remained unrealized. Difficulties arising in 1913 over a suggestion that the AFCS participate in the establishment and direction of the Study House perhaps delayed the project,[11] but it seems likely that it was the outbreak of World War I that doomed it. The war brought new demands for contributions from German-American Catholics and turned their attention to new problems. When the war was over, the situation had changed drastically and the Central-Verein soon abandoned any hope of creating such an ambitious new institution. It sold the Chicago property in the early 1920's and bent its efforts toward strengthening the position of the Central Bureau.

However, one major new institution, the St. Elizabeth Settlement, was opened in 1915 despite the unfavorable climate brought on by the war in Europe. This undertaking illustrates Kenkel's twofold approach to social reform work. While it met an immediate practical need, Kenkel also thought of St. Elizabeth's as having an educational dimension, since he hoped it would serve as a model for similar institutions to be erected by other Central-Verein groups and he planned to give the students from the Ketteler school practical social work experience at St. Elizabeth's.

St. Elizabeth's was established after Budenz surveyed a parish on the south side of St. Louis in which about a thousand low-income German-Hungarian families were living. There were working mothers in many of these families, and some of them were leaving their children in the care of Protestant day nurseries. The Central Bureau therefore determined to open its own children's protectory in a two-story building belonging to the parish school. While St. Elizabeth's Settlement was primarily a day nursery, other features, such as citizenship courses for immigrants, were to be added in the course of time. Overall direction rested with the Central Bureau, but the settlement was staffed by three School Sisters of Notre Dame from Milwaukee. The work was supported principally by contributions, with the Bureau making up any deficit. Within six months of the dedication in September, 1915, the settlement was providing day-long care for some seventy children and handling many more for lunches and during the after-school hours. A laywoman was employed as a caseworker, and the first year's report notes that her home and hospital visits had done much to bring separated couples together and assist in other family problems.[12]

Although the example of St. Elizabeth's was not followed by other groups in the Central-Verein, its establishment in the troubled atmosphere of World War I and maintenance to the present time constitutes one of the major achievements of the Central Bureau. But the Bureau's significance was not confined to the projects which it undertook on its own. Equally important was the stimulus it lent to activities on the part of the member societies of the Central-Verein.

The Activities of the Member Units

Numbering some 108,000 members when the social reform program got under way, the Central-Verein reached its peak strength of about 125,000 in 1916. While the blossoming of organizational life was closely related to the social reform work, it would be mistaken as well as unfair to imply that the reform function was cynically exploited merely to keep the organization alive. Uneasiness over the advances of socialism was growing among the rank and file and there was a more sophisticated appreciation of the need for reform on the part of a number of leaders. In other words, there was genuine commitment to reform for its own sake. At the same time, the leadership was well aware of the invigorating effect that dedication to reform activities was having on the *Vereinswesen.* But if reform work was good for the organization, it was conversely true that organizational strength was necessary if the Central-Verein was to contribute energetically to the effort to correct the evils in American society. Hence dedication to reform and dedication to the organization meshed together perfectly.

One other element was present in this combination. Even after it launched into the reform campaign, the Central-Verein remained a society to which persons belonged because they thought of themselves as German-American Catholics. Thus ethnic consciousness was necessarily involved both in the reform commitment and in the drive to strengthen the organization. In 1910 special observances of the feast of St. Boniface, the apostle of the Germans, were made an integral part of the Central-Verein's program; similar "Ketteler-Windthorst" celebrations were more clearly related to the reform mission, but the fundamental purpose of these occasions was to quicken ethnic feeling. As president Joseph Frey put it in calling for special ceremonies on St. Boniface's Day, "What we need most is *Catholic German-American self-consciousness;* awakening and strengthening this feeling, especially among the younger generation, *must* be our chief task."[13]

Christian social reform was the cause to which the organized German-American Catholics were now dedicated, and the Central Bureau was the soul and center of the reform campaign. There were veteran priests who had labored zealously for "the German cause" in the past who now saw that the Central Bureau and its work were "everything" to the Central-Verein.[14] Support of the Bureau and the campaign it was directing was therefore identified with loyalty to the group and its heritage. And the Bureau, for its part, was tireless in assisting the member units of the national organization. It sent out organizers to form new societies, helped in the creation of new auxiliary societies for youth and women, and the example and stimulus it provided galvanized the state leagues into new life.

The formation of the Gonzaga Union for young men (1913) and the National Catholic Women's Union (1916) were the chief organizational innovations between the launching of the reform program and America's entry into the war.[15] The former was created to attract the younger generation, and it prospered moderately until after the war, when it collapsed completely. The *Frauenbund* was a response to the changing situation of women in American society and was primarily intended to educate Catholic women of German extraction to the role they could play in social reform. It was in the long run much more successful than the Gonzaga Union, and in the 1920's it became a major organizational bulwark to the Central-Verein.

While the Central-Verein was committed to the work of social reform, the Central Bureau did meet with a good deal of apathy in its efforts to promote reform activities among the member societies. On one occasion, the secretary of a local verein returned a packet of the Bureau's literature, demanding to be informed "What in hell has this to do with insurance?"[16] But Kenkel never gave way to pessimism, and he achieved a remarkable degree of success in guiding the national organization into the new work. Discussion of the social question became the focal point of the Central-Verein's yearly conventions; many regional or city federations were formed that arranged their own study courses or lecture series and agitated for such measures as progressive labor legislation in their own localities. Some of the state leagues had already done pressure-group work, especially in respect to school laws, but there was a great upsurge in their activities after 1909.

The state leagues were most active in New York, Pennsylvania, Illinois, Missouri, Minnesota, and Wisconsin. Analysis of the reports submitted to the Central-Verein convention in 1914 suggests a threefold classification of the sort of activities they undertook.[17] The first category includes projects that were primarily religious in inspiration and could have been undertaken by any group of American Catholics. Examples of such projects were the sponsoring of laymen's retreats, encouragement of the St. Vincent de Paul Society and other charitable work, and agitation against *The Menace* and other anti-Catholic movements. Support for censorship laws, opposition to teaching sex hygiene in public schools, and efforts to get Catholic representation on the Public Welfare Board of Chicago also reflected religious motivation, coupled with the American tradition of applying group pressure in public affairs.

A second category of *Staatsverband* activities was inspired by German ethnic feeling. In several states festivals were staged honoring St. Boniface, Joseph Görres, and in St. Louis the centenary of Germany's liberation from Napoleonic rule. In Ohio a society was formed to investigate the history of the German Catholic element in the United States; and the Illinois league was represented at a demonstration staged in Chicago in August, 1914, to protest the anti-German tone of the war news carried in the English-language press.

The third type of activity was more directly derived from the social reform emphasis of the Central-Verein. Included here were purely organizational matters such as the establishment of special women and youth sections, which were only indirectly related to reform, but this category also embraced more substantive reform efforts. Numerous study courses and lecture programs were reported; at least one state league set up a speaker's bureau. The Pennsylvania league had its own Social Propaganda Committee; the Illinois group published a journal called *The Christian Solidarist;* and there was widespread support for the Ketteler Study House project. An example of attention to local affairs was the very active Minnesota league's information bureau for those wishing to buy or sell farms; the Missouri group's support for a state workmen's compensation law illustrates the positive legislative preoccupations of the *Staatsverbände*.

Most of the state leagues had legislative committees. To increase their effectiveness they were linked together through the Central Bureau into a Conference of Legislative Committees. But by 1915, when the Conference made its first report, the tensions caused by the war were already quite noticeable. This factor contributed to the heavily negative orientation the legislative committees had adopted.

Opposition was the keynote of their activity—opposition to convent inspection bills, to eugenic marriage laws, to various educational measures, to women's suffrage, and to a bill in Congress that would have restricted the sale of intoxicants to minors. Agitation on behalf of workmen's compensation laws was about the only positive reform action the legislative committees could report. This negative stance was the traditional posture of American Catholics before legislative bodies, and some of the committees' negativism was doubtless justified by the character of the measures they opposed. But wartime suspicions intensified the defensive attitude, as the report read by Budenz in 1915 made clear:

There had been evidences that the great European War had somewhat distracted the attention of the German Catholic people of this country, and there was much reason to fear that this fact would be seized upon by those opposed to our ideas and interests to push through legislation this year which would prove harmful to us and our ideals. Accordingly the Director of the Bureau [Kenkel] suggested . . . that a joint letter be sent out to the Legislative Committees . . . calling the attention of the committees to the necessity of extra diligence this year.[18]

On the whole, while a critic might object that not all of the Central-Verein's social action projects were altogether positive, there was no denying that the organization had engaged itself deeply in the contemporary struggle to correct the abuses of American society and raise the tone of American life. Even attempts to quarantine offensive theatricals or to remove dangerous books from public libraries were part of the reform program,[19] despite the fact that such endeavors may seem misguided to reformers today. For the Central-Verein wanted to reconstruct society on a thoroughly Christian basis; the moral norms of the community were therefore integrally involved in the reform effort. These aspects of the program will fall more naturally into place when we survey the Central-Verein's position on some specific social issues and examine its underlying social philosophy.

Some Reform Attitudes

Fear of socialism was perhaps the most important single factor in turning the attention of the German-American Catholics to the social question, and as the socialist movement gained momentum in the first decade of the century there seemed no leeway for relaxation. So vigorously was the antisocialist campaign waged that in 1912 a Central-Verein speaker in Minnesota claimed that the organization was "the principal bulwark in this country against the red specter of revolution, socialism."[20]

The origins of socialism were traced back to the Reformation, with its subjectivism and denial of religious authority. The Enlightenment and the French revolution then paved the way for the individualistic liberalism that prompted the Communist Manifesto as a reaction. Central-Verein commentators laid great stress on the materialistic and antireligious aspects of socialism and its denial of the sanctity of marriage. Although the *Central-Blatt and Social Justice* carried an article in 1915 that distinguished very clearly among the varieties of American socialists and noted that most of them were very "tame" Revisionists,[21] the Central-Verein played no favorites in condemning socialism. All varieties were rejected, moderates like Victor Berger as well as doctrinaires like Daniel DeLeon. The very first issue of *Central-Blatt and Social Justice* in 1909 reproduced a piece by a Socialist Labor Party writer to prove that all socialists were committed to an antireligious position even though the "pussyfooters" of the Socialist Party of America might try to deny it.[22]

While relentlessly hostile to socialism, Central-Verein spokesmen would not be stampeded into opposing all reform measures advocated by socialists; they insisted, rather, that Catholics must distinguish between socialism and social reform and must work actively for the latter. For that reason the organization supported many progressive measures and greeted with satisfaction the awakening public interest in reform legislation. But as the major political parties threw themselves more actively into reform, the native conservatism of the Central-Verein reasserted itself. Partisan politics were never discussed in the conventions, but Kenkel dropped a remark in 1912 indicating that he thought Theodore Roosevelt's Progressive Party stood for a "radical" program. The Central-Verein's resolutions for that year noted that while the interest in reform on the part of the major parties was commendable, the approach they followed was apt to be dictated by political expediency rather than sound principle.[23]

Resolutions passed in the next few years, although strongly favorable to reform, repeated the warning against measures that were opportunistic, unsystematic, and of a merely palliative character. In 1916 Kenkel drew the explicit conclusion that followed from this line of thinking. Calling upon the Central-Verein to throw its "conservative energy" into the arena of reform, Kenkel added: "I see the day coming when we, who for 20 years have said *there is a social question,* who have been called socialists, may be forced to . . . protest against the radical tendencies of the day. I believe," he continued, "I will see the day when I will . . . [be] forced to say: 'This is the hour of state-socialism.' In fact, we have been doing this in Missouri already." He then explained that the Bureau had opposed a rural credit proposal in the state legislature, "considering it as tending to state-socialism."[24]

The danger of state socialism, no more than a cloud on the horizon in the Progressive period, became a major preoccupation after the war; in the earlier years the more immediate threat of socialism to the trade union movement caused the Central-Verein to devote much of its attention to the problems of labor. There was disagreement as to how near the socialists were to capturing the American Federation of Labor (AFL), but all concurred in need for preventive action. The resolutions therefore stressed the duty of Catholic workingmen to participate actively in union affairs to forestall the socialistic influence. The *Central-Blatt and Social Justice* also publicized instances in which the designs of "*die Herren Sozi*" were frustrated.[25]

The revolutionary, direct-action tactics of the Industrial Workers of the World made the IWW completely unacceptable to the Central-Verein; but it was quite sympathetic to the aims and activities of the more conservative AFL. It explicitly recognized labor's right to organize, and the *Central-Blatt* published many articles sympathetic to unions while castigating the National Association of Manufacturers and similar groups for their antiunion policies. Perhaps the most telling evidence of Kenkel's feeling for unions was the fact that he frequently likened them to the guilds of the Middle Ages, pointing out among other things that the medieval cathedrals were built under what amounted to a closed-shop arrangement.[26]

In 1911 Kenkel described the Central-Verein's program in a public letter to Samuel Gompers, stated its support for the AFL, and claimed it had "been instrumental in moulding public opinion in certain circles in a manner favorable to the real interests of Labor and to the cause of organized Labor in particular.[27] Following a precedent set by Father Dietz, the Central-Verein also attempted to cement its friendship with the AFL by sending "fraternal delegates" to the latter's conventions. In 1912, however, the fraternal delegate was refused a seat at the AFL meeting because some in the Federation's leadership were offended at the Central-Verein for publishing and circulating a defense of the Christian trade unions of Germany against criticisms made by one of the AFL's vice-presidents. This ended the sending of fraternal delegates, but in spite of the rebuff the Central-Verein refused to nourish a grudge.[28] Instead Kenkel argued that the incident showed how important it was that Catholics participate actively in union affairs, and the Central-Verein continued to take a very positive line in respect to union demands. It took the step, remarkable in a Catholic immigrant organization, of endorsing the AFL's demand that immigration be restricted to protect labor standards; the Missouri state league resolved that unions should be exempted from prosecution under the Sherman Antitrust Law; and the Wisconsin *Staatsverband* called for limitations on the use of injunctions in labor disputes.[29]

Besides its strong support for unions, the *Central-Blatt and Social Justice* interested itself in many other aspects of the labor problem. It discussed the causes of unemployment and various plans for unemployment insurance. The injustices visited upon seasonal migrant workers and others in the unskilled and unorganized labor force were also publicized, as were the evils associated with children's and women's employment. Although the Central-Verein later opposed the child labor amendment as a dangerous step toward statism, it consistently supported state legislation to regulate the labor of women and children. The magazine rejected the theory that labor was a commodity subject only to the laws of supply and demand, and strongly supported the right of the state to intervene in economic affairs to protect the workingman. It endorsed arbitration as a legitimate governmental function but also recognized labor's right to strike under certain conditions. The *Central-Blatt* likewise championed minimum wage laws, and several state leagues actively promoted their passage.[30]

Industrial safety legislation and workmen's compensation laws were the aspects of government intervention that the Central-Verein advocated most vigorously. The *Central-Blatt* carried many articles on industrial accidents and occupational diseases and on steps that could be taken to eliminate them. The Central Bureau and member societies actively cooperated with the American Association for Labor Legislation in the campaign to outlaw the use of poisonous white phosphorus in the match industry. The magazine also devoted much attention to workmen's compensation and insurance laws, and, guided by the Central Bureau, the *Staatsverbände* entered wholeheartedly into the agitation to put these laws on the books in their respective states.

While thus devoting full attention to those aspects of the labor problem involving natural justice, the Central-Verein did not neglect the specifically religious dimension of the Catholic workingman's situation. We noted in a previous chapter that a few workingmen's associations were formed under German Catholic auspices early in the century. In St. Louis the Central Bureau assisted in the organization of a federation of such societies that was called Arbeiterwohl, and Kenkel called upon other cities to follow this example. The "Militia of Christ" formed by Father Dietz when he was with the Central-Verein and shortly after was of a similar character. The Central Bureau also endorsed the work of the Kolping Journeymen's Societies which were roughly comparable to YMCA's for young workingmen of German Catholic descent. Societies such as these were intended to supplement rather than substitute for true labor unions. Like the later Association of Catholic Trade Unionists they were designed to meet the specific religious needs of Catholic workers and to school them in the application of Catholic teaching to their work situation and union activities.[31]

In 1912 a papal ruling on a dispute raging in Germany over the participation of Catholics in trade unions gave added impetus to the Central-Verein's efforts to encourage Catholic workingmen's societies. The point at issue in this quarrel, which was part of the larger battle between liberals and conservatives in the Catholic Church in Germany, was whether it was permissible for Catholics to join trade unions that were open to members of other denominations. The so-called Berliner Richtung of ultraconservatives rejected Catholic participation in the Christian trade unions, which were interconfessional in principle but largely Catholic in actual membership; the opposing Köln-Gladbacher

Richtung championed the Christian unions and argued that the Berliners' exclusively Catholic organizations could provide no real economic assistance or protection for the Catholic worker. After several years of bitter controversy, Pope Pius X ruled in the encyclical *Singulari Quadam* that Catholics could join the Christian unions provided certain safeguards were observed, one of which was that Catholics belonging to interdenominational unions were also to join Catholic workingmen's societies to offset the dangers to faith arising from association with non-Catholic unionists.[32]

Father Engelen's commentary on *Singulari Quadam* in *Central-Blatt and Social Justice* was rather rigorous. Engelen asserted that the Pope's directive applied in the United States as well as Germany; he concluded that the perils of interdenominationalism and socialism in the American labor movement made the "adoption of safeguards, yea, of special assistance [for Catholic workers], peremptory!" The sort of parish workingmen's societies Engelen envisaged might include nonunion workers and were to be closely supervised by the clergy. In the event Catholics were ever forced to withdraw from the AFL—a possibility by no means remote, according to Engelen—these societies could provide the framework for a Catholic labor union.[33]

Among the organizations that Catholics were not permitted to join according to Engelen's reading of *Singulari Quadam* was the Farmers' Educational and Cooperative Union of America. This unbending stand was in keeping with the Central-Verein's earlier severity on the question of secret societies, but it also illustrates the organization's interest in the agricultural aspects of the social question. Many of its members were farmers or lived in rural areas, and the *Central-Blatt* published many items on agricultural topics, giving special encouragement to cooperatives and stressing the need for more adequate credit for farmers. In fact, the Federal Farm Credit Act of 1916 was the only reform measure of Woodrow Wilson's administration that the magazine explained in full-length articles.[34] As we shall see, the farm problem assumed an even more prominent place in the Central-Verein's thinking in the 1920's.

The Central-Verein concerned itself with agriculture not only because its clientele included farmers but also because its social theory emphasized the importance of small independent producers. Indeed, it took pride in having a reform philosophy that took cognizance of more than socialism and the labor question. That reform philosophy was in truth very comprehensive.

Solidarism, the Central-Verein's Social Theory

Many of the proposals advanced by Progressive reformers seemed mere palliatives to Kenkel. What he had in mind was a fundamental reconstruction, for he considered liberalistic society to be as thoroughly unacceptable as socialism. The social ideal he formulated for the Central-Verein had as its ultimate aim the realization of a Christian corporative order; the name of his system, borrowed from the German Jesuit Heinrich Pesch, was "Solidarism." But while Pesch was considered the standard authority in the early years of the reform campaign, there were other influences as well, and we shall focus on the Central-Verein's version of Solidarism rather than trying to summarize Pesch's system as contained in his multivolume *Lehrbuch der Nationalökonomie*.[35]

The most convenient statement of the Central-Verein's social theory is a talk given at the organization's 1915 convention in St. Paul. A brief recapitulation of this speech offers the best entry to the subject for a number of reasons. The speaker, Father Engelen, was born in München-Gladbach and as a student had been acquainted with Pesch; Engelen also enjoyed Kenkel's full confidence as an interpreter of Solidarism, and his talk at St. Paul was regarded as an authoritative statement of the Central-Verein's social philosophy. Moreover, the speech is valuable because it reveals so clearly the general temper of the Central-Verein's theorizing in addition to outlining its substance.

"Was wollen wir" (Our Aims), as the lecture was titled, began with a prologue in which Engelen portrayed the war raging in Europe as the latest fruit of capitalism and lamented the weak grasp that many Catholic reformers had on the true principles of social reconstruction.[36] He disclaimed originality for the theory he was about to sketch, indicating that it more or less created itself from the teachings of history, philosophy, and theology. His was not a program designed merely to repair "the reprehensible system of liberalism"; rather it was a set of ultimate aims by which one could judge all reform proposals and thus guard against the errors made by "many quacks, including Catholic quacks."

Getting down to the discourse proper, Engelen launched into an analysis of the nature of man. God had created man limited and incomplete; man was therefore a social animal because he had to live with his fellows and be dependent upon them. But God had given man free will to use in his life in society; hence man was to be understood as dependent, first of all, on his own efforts for the success of his undertakings. If individual effort did not suffice, man was then to turn to his relatives, neighbors, and friends for assistance; and if voluntary mutual aid was still insufficient to accomplish what was intended, the state should step in to assist. "The divinely ordained purpose of the state," Engelen explained, "is that it should be the final assistance and support of all its children in the great national family."

This brought Engelen to his fundamental principle of all social life. First there was to be purposeful self-help; secondly, and united to the first, voluntary social assistance from others; and, as a last resort, energetic assistance from the state. "This hierarchy of activities," said Engelen, "will, to use Pesch's terms, necessarily lead to the freedom of order, the restraint of arbitrary self-will, the unification of forces, and the adjustment of interests." Freedom under this arrangement would be voluntarily self-limited in the interest of the common good and could truly be called "social freedom," changing men from self-seeking creatures to genuinely social beings. Under Solidarism friendship would replace hatred in the human heart, and the godless struggle for existence would be no more. If the individual did not learn to curb his self-will, those wronged by his selfishness would unite in voluntary associations for protection, or the state could step in to shield the weak from oppression.

A society functioning according to solidaristic principles would engender the growth of vocational organizations, said Engelen. These organizations would not be instruments of class warfare; rather, animated by a spirit of mutual cooperativeness, they would assist individuals and adjust divergent interests. The "solidaric person" would learn "social thinking" by "physical necessity," thus promoting the growth of vocational organizations and the reconciliation of interests. "Hence the state would again become an organism. . . ."

The state, which is built on classes and estates [*Ständen*], protects itself when it protects these organs. At the same time, it achieves through these organs that which is seemingly impossible—it penetrates into the furthest cottage without needing to embrace socialistic absolutism to accomplish this. Yet the state only lends assistance where assistance is required, for it respects liberty. As a result, the solidaric state is strong enough to overthrow the absolutism of liberty for the protection of the fettered and the afflicted without becoming a menace itself.

The permeating consciousness of the need to subordinate all activities to the common good would lead to a genuine national economy in which the welfare of the entire national community would be the dominating consideration. The "ripe fruit" of the solidaristic system would be a healthy *Mittelstand*—that is, a middle class of small independent producers.

With this set of glowing assertions, Engelen declared that the essential outline of Solidarism was complete, but he added a few remarks on immediate problems. He gave qualified approval to labor unions as vocational organizations, noting, however, that they were not yet truly "solidaric" because they lacked the feeling for social justice and remained *Kampfklassen*—groups organized for purposes of class competition. Elaborating somewhat on the role of the state, Engelen called for increased governmental action in the social and economic order, but he also warned that the state must not transgress upon the rights of the subsidiary organs, the vocational estates.

These vocational estates, the specifically corporative elements in the program, were to play an important role in the solidaric society. (In another discussion Engelen made clear they were to be "true social and moral organs of the state," and should be given "limited, subordinate and superintended self-government and legislative and judicial power.")[37] By belonging to a vocational organization, the individual would come to think of himself as an organic unit in an organic society rather than merely as a member of a class. Classes were unacceptable as social divisions because they were based solely on wealth and were therefore unorganic. Vocational organizations would also eliminate the evils of capitalism by controlling production and restricting unfair competition. Engelen did not specify how this was to be done, but he was an enthusiast for vocational organizations. "Organizations everywhere," he exclaimed. "What cannot these groups accomplish when protected by the state." Among other things, he pointed out, they could relieve the state of the need to concern itself with wages, safety legislation, and social insurance.

In concluding, Engelen appealed strictly to logic to show that the solidaric society was a practical possibility; he argued, for example, that Solidarism was based on God's law and God did not require the impossible. Earlier in his talk, however, he had cited historical evidence of its practicability. After describing the *"Gotteswelt"* or divine world that Solidarism would usher in, Engelen added that it had existed in its essential outlines "when the merry, smiling Middle Ages still constructed cathedrals and when religion still pervaded economic life." In those days, he continued, "the state governed in the true sense. The guilds bustled with activity; and the greatest of men was no more a slave of mammon than was the least of men a wage-slave." The dream had become a reality in the Middle Ages, and it was the task of Solidarism to reconstruct this reality with new materials under new economic conditions.

Thus did Engelen's authoritative statement outline the theory of Solidarism. His relatively short speech was not a complete exposition of the Central-Verein leaders' position; still less was it an adequate presentation of Pesch's elaborate social and economic theory. But it was an official statement and was quite representative of the social theorizing carried on in the Central-Verein.

The most striking feature of the talk was its speculative character. The first part was speculative in the technical sense—from a philosophical analysis of the nature of man Engelen deduced the correct socioeconomic order. And in his mind, it was the logical coherence of the argument that proved the practicability of the solidaristic system. The stress on logical consistency was quite in keeping with the belief, shared by Engelen and Kenkel, that a total system had to be formulated before one could be sure of avoiding mistakes in the particulars of reform. Indeed, their writing on social reform was strongly affected by that fondness for abstract speculation and system-building which Theodor Brauer called an essential characteristic of the German mind. "The innate need of system," wrote Brauer, who was an important Catholic social theorist himself, "makes the German . . . profound, but pedantic; comprehensive and rich in outlook, but rationalist and doctrinaire."[38]

But Engelen's St. Paul talk was speculative in the popular as well as the technical sense. Once the philosophical groundwork of the system was laid, Engelen turned immediately to describing what life would be like under Solidarism. He made not the slightest effort to explain how the abyss between theoretical construct and social reality was to be bridged; although he spoke as if the conditions to which he referred were established facts of experience, Engelen was simply speculating. In fact, speculation is too mild a term for his visionary presentation of a happy kingdom, a socioeconomic paradise where lion and lamb would lie down together. Many of his longer expositions in the *Central-Blatt and Social Justice* were pervaded by this utopianism to such an extent that one is taken aback by the occasional reminder that, because of original sin, society would not be perfect even under Solidarism.

A third feature to be noted in Engelen's discourse is the vagueness of the social system he described. The perfection he postulated of solidaristic society was of a highly generalized sort; and the effort to form a clear conception of what life would be like under Solidarism leaves the reader more frustrated than satisfied. The evils of liberal capitalism would be absent, of course; mutualism would replace self-interest as the animating spirit of society; and there would be vocational organizations, or corporative estates. But while the first two points are hardly precise, the extreme ambiguity of the corporative structures cries aloud for clarification.

The vocational organizations were, after all, critically important elements in the whole scheme. They were to serve a vital social-psychological function as the locus of human fellowship and communal solidarity, engendering in the individual the consciousness of being part of an organically unified society. They were also economic institutions that would play a key role in regulating production and the conditions of labor, and as "true social and moral organs of the state" they were unmistakably political in character. Indeed, it was by virtue of the political operation of the vocational organizations that the problem of freedom and order was to be solved: Upon them depended the "seemingly impossible" reconciliation of liberty with state regulation and assistance penetrating "into the furthest cottage." It would be unreasonable to demand of a short talk that it provide a detailed exposition of how all this was to be realized, but Engelen's failure even to hint at a solution of the many difficulties obviously entailed in such a scheme points to a fundamental weakness in the social philosophy of the Central-Verein. This failure to come to grips with complex problems invoved in the introduction of the solidaristic system and to describe precisely how it would function was characteristic of the social theorizing carried on in the organization.

The diffuseness of the solidaristic vision of society and the failure to specify the means of its attainment and mode of its operation sprang in large measure from the way in which Kenkel and the other Central-Verein writers handled certain analytical concepts—or, to put it less abstractly, the way they thought about society and the state, social life, politics, and economics. Their great emphasis was on the organic wholeness of human life. They deplored the tendency of liberal individualism to reduce society to a mere aggregation of atomistic units, and they deprecated the corresponding tendency to think of human existence in a compartmentalized way. Man was a unity, and his life should not be fragmented into a collection of unrelated roles—as citizen, as worker, as consumer, as worshipper. All the facets of human existence were to be organically connected; the various spheres of life should penetrate one another rather than assuming the character of separate, self-contained categories. True social reform, therefore, had to be total reform—it had to comprehend and integrate all the dimensions that were grounded in the unified life of man. This perspective added depth to the critique of liberalism; it also made the Central-Verein theorists sensitive to the social dislocations brought on by industrialism and to the mutilations of the human spirit that accompanied these dislocations. But at the same time the central preoccupation with organic wholeness almost inevitably led to an oversimplification of the real complexity of modern society and blurred crucially important distinctions.

The vagueness surrounding the corporative organizations was primarily traceable to the working of this holistic bias. The corporative estates were posited as restoring organic unity to modern society by amalgamating social-psychological, economic, and political functions. It was never made clear, however, just *how* all this was to be done— how the corporative organizations were to replace actually existing social, economic, and political institutions. To clarify these matters would obviously require detailed treatment of specific issues in several spheres of human activity. But it was precisely this dissection of human life through the isolation of problems in distinct conceptual categories that was most repugnant to those who favored the organic approach. While the Central-Verein's social theory thus made possible a penetrating critique of the ills of modern society, its emphasis on organic unity militated against the systematic analysis needed to discover an adequate remedy.[39]

Central-Verein spokesmen realized, to be sure, that their version of reform involved what is now called the "quality" of life—that it involved a transformation of social personality, a "new spirit" permeating the community. For this reason, they insisted that solidaristic reform would entail a renewal of religion and morals in addition to a restructuring of the institutions of society. Engelen scanted this aspect of the matter in his St. Paul talk, but in other discussions he gave more attention to the need for religious renewal. "No complete, no lasting reform . . . is possible," he wrote, "without the Church and without correct ethics; for a reform of moral ideas is required, and also an application of the moral law to our economic life; and this is impossible without the divine teacher of true morality."[40]

The specifically Catholic dimension of social reform was closely associated in Kenkel's thinking with the corporative features of Solidarism. He felt that Catholics were the only group of Americans who could appreciate the principle "that every society should be structured according to *estates*." "The American Constitution," Kenkel added, "completely did away with this principle, as with so many others. . . ." Consequently most Americans thought in terms of classes, which implied social antagonism; they had no grasp of the notion of social "estates," which implied an organic connection between the various parts of society in the same way that "the hand and foot, the eye and brain and stomach work with every other part of the body." The "old, healthy society of the Middle Ages" had been built upon the "*Lehrstand, Wehrstand und Nährstand*"—that is, the clergy or teaching estate, the nobility or governing estate, and the commons or producing estate. Lacking these functional estates, modern society was, in Kenkel's opinion, "therefore sick because it is *wrongly organized*."[41]

Kenkel did not explain why he thought Catholics were more likely than other Americans to appreciate the need for corporative social organization, but his and Engelen's references to the Middle Ages provide a very obvious clue. The Middle Ages saw the flowering of a great Catholic civilization, and the corporative social order was an integral part of this magnificent "age of faith." American Catholics responded enthusiastically in the Progressive period to the message of James J. Walsh's *The Thirteenth, Greatest of Centuries*.[42] Kenkel, who was personally devoted to medieval studies, undertook to explain how the desirable features of the medieval social order could be revived in the twentieth century. In a speech before the AFCS, Kenkel commented:

> You have undoubtedly heard of the guilds of medieval times. They were social organisms constructed on the lines of Christian ideas. It is sometimes said Catholic social action should lead to their renewal. But that is utopian. You cannot resurrect them. But what is not impossible is this: to resurrect the spirit that gave them life and strength. Why are the trusts obnoxious? The guild was a trust—the strongest kind of trust. But it was not founded upon the principles of capitalism . . . but on the principle that the producer was an officer of the public weal, that the guild as a whole and each individual member had a duty to perform toward the public . . . that to be a master artisan was to hold a public office. Justice and charity permeated these associations, their constructions and their members, and thus ramified that solidarity we so much admire but cannot imitate. . . . We would do well . . . to proclaim a social and economic system which avoids the errors of both individualism and collectivism: the system of mutual solidarity.[43]

Conflicting Influences from Germany

In explaining to Americans how a corporative order reminiscent of the Middle Ages could be reconstructed, Kenkel could draw on a rich tradition of German Catholic social theorizing; and his social philosophy reflected some of the crosscurrents at work among Catholic thinkers in Germany at the turn of the century. A review of the Central-Verein's program would therefore be incomplete without a brief sketch of the German background.

Corporatism emerged in Germany as a conscious social theory in the context of romanticism. It was part of the romantic reaction against the rationalism, liberalism, and cosmopolitanism of the eighteenth century;

it was also related to the conservative and nationalist reaction against the institutional changes introduced by the Napoleonic conquest of Germany. A number of romantics were admirers of the Germanic Middle Ages and several became converts to Catholicism as a result of their enthusiasm for things medieval. Among these romantic converts who preferred the organic social order of the Middle Ages to the ideology of the French Revolution was Adam Müller, one of the earliest theorists of the corporative state.[44]

By the latter half of the nineteenth century, the Catholic contribution to corporative thinking in Germany was so important that Ralph H. Bowen devotes a chapter to "Social Catholicism" in his study of *German Theories of the Corporative State*. As the title of this chapter indicates, corporatism loomed large in the reform tradition among German Catholics. Until about 1880 it was clearly the dominant influence; then a more melioristic approach assumed first position until after World War I, when there was a strong resurgence of strict corporatism. The career of the Westphalian priest Franz Hitze illustrates these cross-currents of reform thought in Germany. In 1880 Hitze published a book which Bowen calls the "most comprehensive theoretical elaboration" of corporatism to appear in Germany to that date. However, almost immediately thereafter Hitze abandoned his dedication to full-scale corporative reconstruction, feeling that piecemeal improvements and practically oriented reform organizations offered a more promising way of attacking the social question. Shortly before his death in 1921, Hitze reverted to rigid corporatism, but by that time he had become the outstanding champion of the meliorist approach. He was one of the founders of both the Volksverein für das katholische Deutschland and of the Christian trade unions.[45]

While the meliorist approach was dominant in the generation before World War I, there were also Catholic reformers in Germany who rejected it as a compromise with liberalism and held out for thorough-going corporative reconstruction. Karl von Vogelsang, a north German convert to Catholicism who settled in Vienna, taught a strict version of corporatism that was strongly redolent of romantic medievalism. His teaching had considerable influence in Austria and southern Germany. In 1894 "an unreconciled group of radical corporatists" attempted to commit the Center Party to a stringent formulation which called, among other things, for "*political representation of the vocational bodies,*" either in the existing legislative bodies or in separate corporative chambers of equal rank. The moderates in the party defeated this move, not wishing to be tied to such a rigid program, although its proponents insisted on calling the plan "*the* Catholic social program."[46]

In the first decade of the present century the Köln-Gladbach Richtung of meliorists, or "social realists," came under fire for deviating from what was described as "*the* Catholic position" on a number of points. Corporatism was not an explicit issue in these disputes, but the strict corporatists were naturally opposed to the meliorist approach and some of them urged the critics—the Berliner Richtung—to adopt a comprehensive corporative program. The dispute over Catholic participation in the Christian trade unions, which we have already noted, was one facet of the wide-ranging controversy; raging concurrently was a battle over the character of the Center Party. The key issue was whether the Center Party should remain interconfessional or whether it should become a *strictly* Catholic party, committed to a "Catholic viewpoint" rather than a "Christian viewpoint." The relationship between Catholicism and culture was disputed in another quarrel, but the *Literaturstreit*, as it was called, is peripheral to our interests.[47]

The controversies took place against the background of the Modernist movement and the reaction against it, and they were obviously related to this fundamental dispute over the response Catholicism should make to the contemporary world. The basic charge against the Köln-Gladbach faction was that it was minimizing Catholic doctrine in its devotion to pragmatic policies in the fields of labor and politics and in its desire to lead German Catholics to a confrontation of the problems of the age. In their effort to break out of the ghetto the progressive Catholics were said to be verging over into the condemned Modernism.[48] The Köln-Gladbach people, on the other hand, considered their indisputably conservative critics to be "Integralists" who were guilty of a superorthodoxy that was as un-Catholic and dangerous as ultraliberalism. They sometimes characterized this attitude as medieval, and they were particularly incensed by the Berliners' fondness for making their exaggerated ideas the touchstone of orthodoxy.[49]

The controversies in Germany were strikingly similar to the battles between conservatives and liberals in the American Church in the

1890's. The similarity was not lost on the German conservatives. In 1909 a critic of the German Volksverein pointed out that its version of "social Catholicism" was touched by "a little of the American spirit," for it emphasized "Catholicism of action" rather than "Catholicism of doctrine."[50] In commenting on the dispute over the Christian trade unions, Kenkel also gave evidence that he recognized the parallels between the German situation and the earlier American controversies. Criticizing the manner in which the friends of the Christian trade unions interpreted *Singulari Quadam* as an unqualified endorsement of the interdenominational unions, Kenkel reminded *Amerika's* readers of the school controversy in which an "American prelate" had translated the papal *"tolerari potest"* as "fully approved."[51]

But while the Central-Verein was firmly on the side of the conservatives in the American disputes, the situation in Germany was not so clear-cut. As it worked out, the thinking of the Central-Verein's reform leaders was influenced both by the German progressives and the conservatives. The progressive influence was predominant at first but was superseded in time by the stricter corporatism of the antimeliorist group.

The progressive Volksverein was the explicit model for the Central Bureau, which followed the eminently practical methods of social education and agitation that had been mapped out by its German counterpart. And after the Gladbachers had been under fire for over a decade, Kenkel still praised the Volksverein very highly.[52] Moreover, Heinrich Pesch is generally classified among the more practical and realistic of the German Catholic theorists, and his Solidarism was, of course, the Central-Verein's official philosophy. It is true that there was a strong dash of utopianism to Kenkel's and Engelen's thinking, but it was tempered by Kenkel's realistic attention to detail and the practical orientation of many of the Bureau's activities. In his speech quoted earlier, Kenkel distinguished between what was "utopian" and what was "not impossible"; and in publishing a detailed blueprint of a Christian corporative society, Kenkel added an editor's note saying that what it proposed was "of course, impracticable, at least at the present time and in this country."[53]

Kenkel certainly did not disdain practical reforms in his commitment to total reconstruction based on vocational estates, but neither he nor

Engelen wholly escaped the doctrinaire rigidity so easily engendered by adherence to an ideological system that is self-enclosed and intellectually consistent. The theoretical symmetry and perfection of Solidarism encouraged in them an attitude of superiority to those "quacks" who did not think "solidarically"; it also led them to call for ever more "fundamental" reforms. For example, Kenkel criticized the measures of the Wilson administration in 1914 as insufficiently fundamental and Engelen once characterized the AFCS resolutions on the social question as "Nothing but a sum of the present popular reforms, but no principles. Temporizing, another sign of the widest ignorance."[54] On another occasion, Engelen remarked that if he were to address a group of Catholics who had been considering reform matters it would be equivalent to saying to them: "'Gentlemen, you have busied yourselves in vain with trivial questions. Everything must take its proper place. After you have heard me, you may therefore revise all your plans again.'"[55]

The growing uneasiness about state socialism was related to the reservations Kenkel and Engelen felt toward nonsolidaristic reforms. Eventually they included the Köln-Gladbach Richtung among the opportunistic and dangerous class of reformers. This conversion to the position of the Berliners did not occur until after the war and was part of a general movement toward conservatism on the part of the Central-Verein. But there were indications from the very beginning of the social reform program that Kenkel was not entirely in harmony with the approach of the meliorist reformers in Germany. In view of his distaste for the "shattered, distracted" modern world, and his profound admiration for the Middle Ages, Kenkel was bound to feel some sympathy for the more radical corporatists who also rejected the modern world and based their system on the medieval order. Evidences of this sympathy are plentiful, most notably in Kenkel's veneration for Karl von Vogelsang, whose extreme corporatism had a pronounced medieval flavor and whose approach to the social question has been characterized as the precise opposite of the "social realism" of Franz Hitze and the München-Gladbach school.[56] Kenkel also referred frequently and favorably to Albert M. Weiss, a Dominican priest who wrote on social reform and became a prominent critic of the Köln-Galdbach group.[57]

The blending of practical and utopian elements in the Central-Verein's social program thus reflected in part the conflicting influences coming from Germany at a time of deep disagreement among Catholic social theorists. In the administration of the Central Bureau, in the activities it pursued, and in strengthening and guiding the member units of the Central-Verein, Kenkel showed a hardheaded realism; to the degree that these phases of the program had a European inspiration, that inspiration came from the meliorists who created the Volksverein. But Kenkel's social theory lent itself to visionary speculation of a highly romantic sort, and it proposed a restructuring of American society so radical and far-reaching as to be almost by definition impracticable. Peschian Solidarism differed from the more extreme teaching of Vogelsang in that, rather than rejecting the modern world out of hand, it accepted it as the starting point for reform. But Pesch's Solidarism also stressed corporative institutions and envisioned fundamental structural changes. Kenkel gave no indication that he saw any incompatibility between the thought of Pesch and that of Vogelsang; instead he cited both as sources of wisdom on reform and as equally reliable guides to the creation of a better society.

In combining elements of down-to-earth practicality and romantic corporatism, the Central-Verein's social program reflected not only conflicting influences from Germany but also the personality of Frederick Kenkel, the architect of that program. Kenkel's estrangement from the modern world, his love for the Middle Ages, and his fondness for corporative theory place him firmly in the tradition of German romanticism. But Kenkel was also a man who believed in laying solid foundations for ambitious projects and who insisted on attention to detail and making haste slowly. During the prewar era, the practical work at the Central Bureau and among the state leagues claimed most of Kenkel's attention, and perhaps the very palpable achievements of those years, on the part of the Central-Verein and Progressive reformers generally, encouraged him to believe that the melioristic approach would suffice. But the romantic corporative vision that implied a total rejection of modern society was just beneath the surface even in the Progressive period. In the 1920's it emerged into full view, while meliorism was repudiated. This shift in Kenkel's social thought will be examined in Chapter VIII, but first we must trace some aspects of the Central-Verein's experience in American society between 1909 and 1917, for this experience played a part in shaping Kenkel's thinking.

VII

The complex influence of Catholic theorizing in Germany upon the Central-Verein's social program shows that the organization was conscious of the links binding it to the old homeland. But another historical heritage also played a part in shaping its development in the Progressive period—its heritage as an organization of Catholics of German descent existing in American society, the new homeland. This heritage was also complex, reflecting the situation of a group having a tripartite identity: as Catholics, as Germans, and as Americans. The three constitutive elements were all essential to the nature of the group, and Central-Verein spokesmen prized each of them. As Father Heinrich Kunig put it in 1916: "We are of the Catholic religion and are fortunate in that. We are of the American nation and take pride in that. We are of German descent and rejoice in that."[1] However, the relationship between the three elements was constantly shifting in response to the experience of the group with Catholics who were not German, with Germans who were not Catholic, and with other Americans who were neither Catholic nor German.

As the major organizational vehicle for a group with a threefold identity, the Central-Verein had to define its unique position in respect to three symbolic referents: Catholicism, Germanness, and Americanism. It was profoundly committed to each of them; yet its commitment to each was qualified although not diminished by its commitment to the other two. Thus the Central-Verein was made up of men deeply loyal to Catholicism; but this loyalty was conditioned by their sense of being different from other American Catholics because of their German descent. Similarly, their loyalty to the German ethnic element in their identity was conditioned by the recognition that their Catholic faith set them apart from other German-Americans. And their loyalty as Americans was given a specific character by their distinctive ethnic-religious identity.

To say that the multiple loyalties of the Central-Verein members conditioned one another is not to say that they stood in opposition to one another. Central-Verein members would never concede that one could not be simultaneously a good German, a good Catholic, and a good American. Rather they would have agreed with Morton Grodzins, who argues in *The Loyal and the Disloyal* that national loyalty is based upon and synthesizes the subordinate loyalties that center around the multiple reference groups to which the citizens of a democratic society belong.[2] Grodzins also points out, however, that in conflict situations these subordinate loyalties can compete with national loyalty. Such a situation arose for German-Americans with the outbreak of World War I. But even before 1914 it was evident that the complex loyalties of the German-American Catholics profoundly influenced their relations with fellow Catholics who were not German and with fellow Germans who were not Catholic.

Getting Along with Non-German Catholics

Because of their German ethnicity, the members of the Central-Verein were Catholics with a difference. Exactly how this difference affected their relations with fellow Catholics of other national backgrounds is best illustrated in the relations of the Central-Verein with the American Federation of Catholic Societies. As we have seen, the German-American Catholics were early supporters of the Federation, but the fear of being absorbed also stimulated them to strengthen their own national organization. Although the Central-Verein joined the AFCS and cooperated with it, there was an element of tension between the two groups. The pattern of cooperation accompanied by friction did not change fundamentally from the inception of the social reform campaign to America's entry into the war.

The early years of the reform program were years of relative harmony with the Federation. The prospects for cooperation seemed especially hopeful to the Central-Verein men because a resolution safeguarding the rights of language and nationality had been adopted by the AFCS in 1906; in 1909 the Federation's secretary extolled the Central-Verein's contribution and drew attention to the fact that eight of the national officers of the AFCS were of German derivation.[3] And although Frederick P. Kenkel was not an officer of the Federation, he was prominently featured as a speaker before the 1910 convention.[4] This era of tranquillity, however, was short-lived. The tensions that soon appeared were centered around two principal issues—organizational rivalry and divergent approaches to the social question. Strictly ethnic factors were involved in each of these areas.

Organizational friction increased after 1911 over the Federation's efforts to bring the local societies of the Central-Verein into direct affiliation with subordinate branches of the AFCS. This was regarded by Central-Verein leaders as proselytization that would disrupt and undermine their own organization. In contrast to the policy of "amalgamation," Central-Verein president Joseph Frey championed the principle of true "federation." Frey claimed that all the Central-Verein's member societies were already part of the AFCS because the Central-Verein belonged to Federation as the national society of German-American Catholics. Moreover, he insisted that the federative principle should extend to the level of county and local organization. Individual German vereins should organize themselves into local or district unions, which would then establish a cooperative relationship with the city or county branches of the AFCS through their respective executive committees. The individual German Catholic societies were not to join the subordinate branches of the AFCS as single units because such "amalgamation" would be tantamount to the absorption of the German society.[5]

Experience had shown, according to Frey, that besides being disruptive, amalgamation was unworkable. Consolidated subunits of the Federation that had been set up tended to disintegrate within a short time because they lacked the unifying bond of common nationality. Believing that the nationality organization was a necessary link between the individual society and the Federation, Frey argued that the Federation should be organized according to ethnic derivation, even among third- and fourth-generation immigrant Americans. The resulting loose league of ethnic organizations, cooperating through liaison among the top echelons of leadership, would constitute the most desirable sort of federation for American Catholic societies. Frey held to this plan even when calls for greater Catholic unity were voiced by the German-American prelates Sebastian Messmer, Henry Richter, Joseph Schrembs, and Joseph Busch.[6] The emphasis of these churchmen, especially that of Messmer and Busch, implied a less "nationalistic" approach than that supported by Frey. F. W. Heckenkamp, who was both a Central-Verein member and a dedicated worker for the AFCS, also differed with Frey on this point and once characterized the policy of the Central-Verein's leaders as "fostering race prejudice that in my opinion is bordering upon fanaticism."[7]

By 1914 the executive committee of the Central-Verein had become so exasperated that it considered withdrawal from the AFCS unless proselytizing among Central-Verein affiliates was halted.[8] At the AFCS convention in 1914 an agreement was reached which mollified the Central-Verein, although it did not make ethnic background the main organizing principle of the Federation. According to this compromise, local societies of the Central-Verein were not to be solicited to join the state or county branches of the AFCS, but they were free to do so on their own volition. However, such societies would have to pay additional dues to the Federation; the national dues paid by the Central-Verein did not relieve them of this financial obligation. The provision was obviously intended to discourage individual societies from joining the AFCS. Thus there was no guarantee that Central-Verein locals would not be affiliated directly to the Federation, but the agreement specified that "Organization and propaganda among American Catholics of German birth or descent is the right of the Central-Verein."[9] This delimitation of the respective spheres of the two organizations cleared the air somewhat, and there was an imposing show of unity in 1916 when both met simultaneously in New York City in what was called a "Catholic Week." However, the idea of meeting together with the Federation was by no means universally acclaimed in the Central-Verein. On the contrary, there was so much opposition that the Central-Verein's official announcement of the convention included assurances that the organization was not about to surrender its independence and that joint meetings with the AFCS were not to become a regular occurrence.[10]

A second area of friction developed after 1911 when Father Peter E. Dietz persuaded the AFCS to enter the field of social reform by setting up a Social Service Commission. Dietz had ended his troubled association with the Central-Verein only the year before, and it was evident at once that some suspicion was carried over from the previous dispute to Dietz's new undertaking. Thus when the AFCS officers met to confirm the appointments to the Commission, Nicholas Gonner raised objections to Dietz's being made secretary of the Social Service Commission.[11] But Dietz got the job, and an informal agreement worked out in 1912 seemed to smooth the way for cooperation between the Central Bureau and the Commission. Peter J. Muldoon, bishop of Rockford, Illinois, and chairman of the Social Service Commission, broached the subject to Kenkel, who responded with a suggestion for exchanges of information between the two agencies concerned with Catholic social action. Kenkel also proposed consultation "for the purpose of arriving at an understanding toward harmonious cooperation" if such consultation was felt to be mutually desirable. The tentative character of the suggestion was quite acceptable to the Social Service Commission, several of whose members were opposed to any sort of compulsory cooperation with the Central Bureau.[12]

The need for caution was demonstrated in 1913 when attempts to include the Federation in the Ketteler Study House project brought on the most serious crisis in the history of the Central-Verein's relations with the AFCS. The trouble began innocently enough when several subordinate branches of the Federation discussed the possibility of supporting the Study House campaign, which was progressing so nicely that it seemed the Central-Verein would soon be able to realize Kenkel's dream of establishing a school for social study in Chicago. One of those who suggested Federation participation in the project was Adolf Weber, a former president of the Central-Verein; another German proponent of the plan was Father J. Meckel, a priest of Alton, Illinois, who in his youth had been personally acquainted with Bishop von Ketteler.[13] Kenkel learned of these initiatives earlier, but the idea was presented to him in a more formal way in a letter from Father Frederic Siedenburg, S.J., who was in charge of Loyola University's collaboration in the Study House venture.

In June, 1913, Siedenburg reported that the Study House campaign had been discussed at an Illinois AFCS gathering he had recently attended. Father Dietz and Bishop Muldoon of the Social Service Commission were present, and the latter praised the Ketteler school as "*the* need" of the day. Both Muldoon and Siedenburg felt that the Federation should cooperate in the project, and Siedenburg wanted to see other Catholic organizations like the Knights of Columbus brought into it so that a real unification of Catholic forces could be achieved in the realm of social action. Siedenburg agreed with Muldoon in thinking that all the groups that aided in establishing the Study House should be represented on its "governing board." Dietz had already indicated that he would oppose Federation support for the Study House unless the AFCS were given some voice in its management. Siedenburg asked for Kenkel's reaction so that he could inform Bishop Muldoon.[14]

The reaction was immediate and almost explosive.[15] "Your letter has caused me great concern," Kenkel began, declaring that if such "views and plans" became known they would cause the Central-Verein members to think that a movement was afoot "which tended to rob the German Catholics of their cherished hopes." "The mass of our people," he continued, "have no confidence in the English speaking Catholics. Nothing good has ever come to them from that quarter, they say. Honors and offices are for the Irish, they say; we are graciously permitted to work and to labor." Kenkel had heard such sentiments expressed "a thousand times," and he foresaw dissension rather than harmony among Catholics if Siedenburg's proposal were acted upon. For his own part, Kenkel wanted "the German Catholics . . . [to] perform this task by themselves."

I am convinced that we can do it better than others, because we are Germans. We are a people not alone of ideals, but of hard work, painstaking with *small things*, plain and unassuming, but 'opferwillig' when we know what it is all about, and only poor 'politicians.' And there is the nub! . . . Let us complete the Study House, formulate its plans of action, study and practice, and if then the Federation should desire to further same, let it erect *a chair* of something or other or create scholarships. I would welcome such generosity as a token of good will. . . . The very fact that *representation* is demanded from *the beginning,* is not to my taste. Therefore: Timeo Danaos et dona ferientes.

There was in addition, Kenkel noted, the very important question of social policy. The Central-Verein would "always take a Ketteler-like view of the social question and the remedies to be applied will look to some people drastic"; the Federation, however, would "try to meander its way through these problems without arousing antagonism." In conclusion Kenkel said that the former Apostolic Delegate had advised the Central-Verein to retain control of the Study House in its own hands, and he thought it wise to remember that counsel.

Siedenburg, who "never dreamt" that his letter was "so revolutionary and would cause so much concern," assured Kenkel he had done nothing indiscreet that might have harmed the cause of the Study House, and he reiterated that Muldoon had spoken most flatteringly of the Central-Verein's work.[16] Kenkel's position, however, was endorsed by Central-Verein president Frey, and Joseph Matt dwelt at length on the bickering that could be anticipated if other nationalities were brought into the Study House project.[17]

After receiving several letters from Father Meckel on Federation cooperation in the Study House, Kenkel asked for a full expression of his views. Meckel responded that the AFCS should be represented in the direction of the Study House if it was to have the full backing of all American Catholics; he felt that "an amalga[ma]tion of all the Catholics into one grand force" was desirable for the future development of the Church.[18] Although praising the past efforts of the Germans, he cautioned that they should not imagine "that they are the great nation, representing the Catholic strength of the U. St."

We Germans must be willing to join hands with all the Catholics of whatsoever nationality and embody in our program for our future action everything good and healthy, all the might and power characteristic of each individual nationality.

Hence I propose that the Central-Verein in a generous manner hold out its hand of fellowship to the federated Catholic Societies of the country, invite them to build up that grand institute, the Catholic School of Science, and readily grant them the privilege of being cooperators in the great cause and thus profit by their material help as well as also by their counsel.

Kenkel's reply has not been preserved, but he sent Meckel's statement to Frey, who positively erupted when he read it.[19] "It makes me feel hot under the collar," he snorted "to have these fellows prate about Catholic unity—*good fellowship—fair play*—etc.—and then, when a practical test is to be made of their professions they'll turn about and expect us to *swallow everything they choose to give us*." Frey was usually a kindly and good-natured man, but his irritation led him to speculate that Meckel's willingness to "amalgamate everything" was animated by personal ambitions for the episcopacy. In any event, Meckel had "let the cat out of the Bag and we *now know* what is ahead of us."

We will need all our firmness—coolness and tact to get through the breakers ahead of us! If we could only have some assurance that the Federation means to deal fairly with us we might consider some scheme of cooperation in re Study House. But all these backsliding Germans believe and tell everybody that our Organisations are merely *ephemeral* doomed to perish before long etc.—and in saying such they are merely echoing the sentiments of the Clan that govern[s] our *Church in America*. The only hope for relief that I can see for the future is the coming up of other races of Catholic people in this country . . . the Italians and the Poles etc. The Irish in this country are politicians all the time—both in the state and in the Church—and so many of our Germans are glad to have them walk all over them in exchange for some cheap flattery.

Frey found it "disheartening to be compelled to fight both front and rear," but he promised Kenkel that a way would be found at the coming convention to deal with the problem. When the Central-Verein gathered in Buffalo a month later, however, the Study House crisis had subsided; the principal Federation offense discussed there dealt with "*recruiting* among our people," as Frey once called it.[20] On hand for part of the convention festivities were prelates with the un-Teutonic names of Colton, Hickey, Burke, Fitzmaurice, and Garvey, but Frey had sufficiently recovered his "firmness, coolness and tact" to assert that this was a matter of special gratification. "We all know that blood is thicker than water," he declared, "but when we German-American

Catholics are with those of our faith we recognize no differences of birth and race . . . we know that our bishops, though they be of Irish race, are our bishops at all times." The occasional friction that arose Frey described as something that happens "in the best of families."[21]

The Central-Verein remained wary of closer cooperation with the Federation, but in 1914 and 1915 the reason advanced for this reserve was the incompatibility between Solidarism and the reform philosophy of the Federation.[22] At the joint meeting with the AFCS in 1916 the Central-Verein did pledge itself to cooperate, "in as far as the constitution and autonomy of the Central-Verein shall permit," with a new agency of Catholic social action that was being organized. There was ample justification for wariness on this occasion, for the instigators of the movement for a unified social service agency wanted "a working organization which would amount almost, if not quite, to coalescence, rather than cooperation. . . ." These men had reached the conclusion that cooperation by autonomous organizations was a "rope of sand"; they were working for an agency more directly under Federation control.[23] But the United States entered the war before the proposed body got beyond the planning stages, and the development of the groups involved was drastically influenced by this event. A completely new organization, the National Catholic War Council, was created in 1917; the Federation quietly died on the vine, and the German-American Catholics found themselves facing an altogether different situation in the war and postwar years.[24]

The relationship between the Central-Verein and the Federation was characterized by what we might call tense cooperation, and it reflected the situation of an immigrant group that was midway along in the process of assimilation. The Germans were sufficiently Americanized to associate themselves with Catholics of other backgrounds in an organization dedicated to general Catholic interests; their willingness to do so was an important factor in bringing the Federation into existence and in strengthening it during its relatively brief life span. At the same time, however, their strong sense of being *German* Catholics made them keenly sensitive to anything that infringed upon their ethnic interests or seemed to threaten the well-being of their own ethnic organization. The suspicions arising from ethnic feeling illustrate the lines of continuity between the controversial era of the 1890's and the evolution of the German Catholic group in the twentieth century. But the weakening of this ethnic feeling was manifested by the Central-Verein's cooperation with the Federation, and was dramatized by Frey's blast at "backsliding Germans" who seemed willing to sublimate all national differences for the sake of a more strongly consolidated Catholic organization.

It is impossible to say how many Catholics of German descent in the United States would have fallen into Frey's category of backsliders, but there is no doubt that the national organization of German-American Catholics was determined to maintain its autonomy and its German identity. The refusal of the Central-Verein men to merge themselves into any sort of undifferentiated unity with other American Catholics cannot be construed as a reflection on their dedication to Catholicism. Indeed, it would be presumptuous even to defend them from such an insinuation. It was simply that they were who they were, and their way of being good American Catholics was to be good German-American Catholics. The ethnic element in their identity conditioned the religious element—that is, it caused them to perceive themselves from a particular angle. Conversely, the religious element conditioned their relations with other German-Americans who were not Catholics. And the relations of the Central-Verein with the major national German-American organization were even more prickly than with the American Federation of Catholic Societies.

Getting Along with Non-Catholic Germans

The life span of the Deutsch-Amerikanische National-Bund (DANB), or National German-American Alliance as it was officially called in English, was almost exactly identical with that of the American Federation of Catholic Societies.[25] The preliminary organization of both associations began in 1899; each was constituted as a national federation in 1901, and the entry of the United States into the World War led to the demise of both. The purpose of the Alliance also was analogous to that of the AFCS: It was intended to bring about a unification of all German-Americans through a federation of existing societies. The Alliance was the most successful of all attempts to unite the German-Americans; at peak strength it boasted well over two million members.

Until shortly before the dissolution of the DANB in 1918, its president was Dr. Charles J. Hexamer, a Philadelphia engineer who had long been interested in German-American unification efforts. The program of the Alliance was an ethnic-cultural one. It aimed to further the unity of the group, stimulate the teaching of the German language and Turner gymnastics in the public schools, commemorate and win greater recognition for the achievements of the Germans in the development of the American nation, and promote amicable relations between the United States and Germany. It opposed restriction of immigration and urged all German immigrants to become citizens as soon as possible. Its constitution excluded partisan political activity but sanctioned the defense of political principles and called for the removal of "outmoded" laws limiting "personal liberty." The Alliance showed scant interest in social legislation of the type championed by the Central-Verein, but it was active in defending personal liberty against the prohibitionists. The antiprohibition campaign furnished the chief bond of unity in the DANB and accounted for its rapid growth; after 1913 it was "handsomely subsidized" by an association made up principally of the brewing interests.[26]

Although religious questions were to be "most rigorously excluded" from the Alliance,[27] it was not wholly successful in overcoming the old antipathy between the *Vereinsdeutsch* (the liberals of the Forty-Eighter tradition) and the *Kirchendeutsch* (those more closely identified with the churches). Some of the more liberal German churches aligned themselves with the Alliance and a Lutheran minister became its president a few months before it disbanded, but the main body of conservative Lutherans as well as the German Catholics remained aloof. To these groups it represented a continuation of freethinking anticlericalism of the earlier Forty-Eighters. On the other hand, the liberalism of the Alliance was too mild to suit the Turners or German Socialists and both criticized it, especially during the first few years of its existence. Some persistence of anticlericalism can be inferred, however, from the fact that the members of the Ohio Alliance were cautioned against always referring to clergymen in derogatory terms.[28]

In spite of the earlier hostility between German Catholic and German liberal immigrants, the Central-Verein's attitude toward the Alliance was not at first unfavorable. When the DANB was formed the

Central-Verein was in the throes of its reorganization and the matter arose only fleetingly. Beginning in 1904, Alliance president Hexamer made it a practice to send greetings to the Central-Verein's annual conventions. These messages were cordially received, and leaders like John B. Oelkers and Nicholas Gonner spoke positively of cooperation with the Alliance.[29] By 1907, however, a new note of caution was sounded. The convention lauded the DANB's efforts to preserve the German language and customs, but it asked in return that the Alliance respect the Central-Verein's religious purposes and activities. Direct affiliation with the DANB was rejected, but cooperation between the two groups on specific projects was not excluded and a committee was authorized to look into the possibility of closer relations.[30]

This committee never reported, but the relationship of German Catholics to the DANB became a more controversial matter after 1907. The *Herold des Glaubens* of St. Louis began to take a more critical attitude toward the Alliance, and in May, 1908, the *Central-Blatt* reproduced a sharp attack from Joseph Matt's *Wanderer* in which the group was branded as a decadent "epigon" of the liberal German-American movements of the nineteenth century.[31] Matt disliked the rationalism and anticlericalism of the Forty-Eighters, but he pronounced their aims much loftier than those of the Alliance; he was particularly scornful of efforts to make antiprohibition work "the task of German culture" in the United States.[32]

Not long thereafter, the Illinois state league rejected affiliation with the DANB, saying the organization was unacceptable to Catholics because there were too many "Sauls" and not enough "Pauls" among its membership.[33] In the city of St. Paul, however, Matt had his hands full to keep the Catholic societies from responding to the Alliance's appeals; the New Jersey *Staatsverband* reportedly favored affiliation with it, and in New York the state league authorized its executive committee to cooperate with the Alliance if such cooperation did not conflict with Catholic principles.[34] Serious qualifications were expressed about the DANB when the New Yorkers discussed this move, however, and some "fought tooth and nail" to prevent any fraternization; the dissidents were outvoted, "but their NEIN sounded like a thunderclap."[35]

No doubt because of these events and because Alliance officers had called upon Central-Verein president Oelkers urging cooperation, the convention in 1909 adopted a special resolution to clarify the organization's position with respect to the DANB. Hexamer had invited the Central-Verein to send a committee to the convention of the Alliance "to negotiate a basis upon which the two bodies could, in certain questions, work hand in hand." Joseph Matt read the resolution spurning this overture; it was sharply criticized by a few delegates but confirmed by a "great majority." The "difference in principles" was cited as the obstacle to affiliation with the DANB. "We stand in all things upon the basis of the Christian-Catholic weltanschauung, while the Alliance supports and furthers atheistic and humanistic ideas and ideals." Even where the two groups had similar aims, they employed different methods, according to the resolution. Both wished to preserve the German language, for example, but whereas the Central-Verein relied on the parochial school, the Alliance favored working through the public school. Hence the Central-Verein refused to acknowledge the Alliance as the spokesman for the American *Deutschtum*. It left the disposition of local relationships to the state leagues, but recommended the procedure followed in New York whereby local societies were required to get clearance from the state executive committee before participating in any functions sponsored by the Alliance.[36]

By quoting from the New Yorkers' statement the passage most critical of the Alliance, the resolution made the stand of that state appear tougher than it actually was. It is doubtful that this maneuver was pleasing to Joseph Frey, at that time president of the New York *Staatsverband,* for he later proved distinctly partial to the DANB. Oelkers of New Jersey was another Eastern leader who had "great hopes" for more friendly relations with the Alliance. Only after its officers in Newark attacked the Church in the controversy resulting from the execution of the Spanish anticlerical Francisco Ferrer did Oelkers regretfully conclude that "the hatred of religion, the old fanaticism" was still strong in the DANB. He acknowledged that the Alliance had "many Catholic members" in the East, but promised that "we will soon thin their ranks."[37]

Frey, who had been in contact with Hexamer, reopened the question at the convention in 1910. He read a message in which the Alliance president explained that no formal affiliation of the Central-Verein was sought, but an understanding that would permit the two groups to work together in "common German endeavors." Hexamer also denied that the Alliance was committed to an antireligious position; its aims were strictly ethnic and it welcomed German-Americans of all religious or political persuasions. Frey heartily seconded Hexamer's sentiments, saying that German-American Catholics should emphasize their common ground with the Alliance rather than those things which separated them. At this point Kenkel, who had already aroused the hostility of DANB leaders in Missouri, entered the debate. "We are not the ones who have widened the schism and stressed the divisive factors," he declared, adverting to shabby treatment accorded to Catholic societies at a "German Day" celebration in St. Louis to document his charge. Kenkel insisted that positive action on the local level must accompany protestations of friendship from Alliance officers, and the convention endorsed his stand.[38]

Frey became president of the Central-Verein in 1911, but the uncompromising policy championed by Kenkel and Matt remained in force in the next few years. However, in spite of Matt's opposition, Frey did succeed in getting the convention's authorization to respond in a friendly manner to Hexamer's greeting.[39] The Alliance persisted in its efforts to attract Catholic societies, concentrating on the rural areas since the state leagues and urban groups were more resistant to its propaganda. One reason it was interested in winning Catholic support was that the Central-Verein's stand on prohibition seemed shaky to the Alliance. In 1913 the Central-Verein took note of alcoholism as "a very grave danger to the welfare of our people"; it therefore recommended using "those means for combating this evil which our holy religion provides."[40] This declaration was far from satisfactory to the DANB, which later admitted it had "fought prohibition tooth and toenail."[41]

The outbreak of the war in Europe, which distracted attention from the prohibition issue, also affected the attitude of the Central-Verein toward the Alliance. A few days after the war started, Frey announced to the delegates to the 1914 convention that he had given a statement to the newspapers declaring the solidarity of the German-American Catholics "with all our *ethnic kindred [Stammesgenossen].*" He had also written to Hexamer endorsing the latter's protests against the anti-German tone of "Anglo-American press." In this context, the convention authorized Frey to reply "in a fitting manner" to Hexamer's annual greeting.[42] As the war went on German-American Catholics became more actively involved in the Alliance both because of their heightened consciousness of fellowship with other Germans and because the DANB was able to carry on more intensive organizational work through funds provided by the brewing interests.[43]

However, before the war injected a new element into the situation, the Central-Verein maintained a cool, almost icy, distance between itself and the national federation of non-Catholic German societies. The men most responsible for this policy were Matt and Kenkel, outstanding intellectual leaders deeply conscious of their own identity and of the tradition of antagonism between German Catholics and liberals. The membership at large sustained the policy of these two leaders—although not in its fullest rigor—thereby demonstrating that the awareness of internal cleavage in the German ethnic community was widely shared. But Frey spoke for those in the Central-Verein who wanted it to work more actively for a rapprochement with the Alliance. Frey came from the East, where the process of Americanization was thought to be furthest advanced among the German Catholics; he was not an intellectual leader of the organization, but was a businessman with a wide circle of friends in New York and a reputation for affability. We may, perhaps, regard him as representative of those German Catholics who were less sensitive than Matt and Kenkel to the ideological dimensions of their social identity and who hoped to see the old barriers between German-Americans broken down to make way for a unification based on common ethnic derivation.

The multiple loyalties of the German-American Catholics thus conditioned their relations both with fellow Germans and with fellow Catholics. The history of the Central-Verein's relations with the Federation of Catholic Societies and with the Alliance clearly indicates, however, that the consciousness of religious identity took priority over strictly national identity, insofar as the two can be isolated from each other. The Central-Verein affiliated itself with the AFCS and, although there was friction between the two, its official policy was one of cooperation. Its policy with respect to the German-American Alliance was just the opposite: It refused affiliation and discountenanced cooperation even on an ad hoc basis. It was unwilling to go as far in cooperating with the Alliance as some Irish-American Catholics did, for in 1907 the Ancient Order of Hibernians and the DANB pledged themselves to work together to prevent the United States from adhering to an Anglo-American alliance, to combat prohibition, and to oppose restriction of immigration.[44]

After 1914 "hyphenation" became a burning issue. War in Europe and disagreement over America's proper role as a neutral aroused slumbering fears and passions among a heterogeneous people. Terms like "German-American" and "Irish-American" were no longer regarded as designating distinctive ways of being American which could at least be tolerated. Rather the hyphen was branded as the mark of divided loyalties that were inconsistent with true Americanism. The German-American Catholics suffered along with other groups during this crisis, but because of their tripartite identity they were in a condition we can call "multiple hyphenation" when it began. Set somewhat apart from other Catholics by their nationality and more apart from other Germans by their religion, those who thought of themselves as German-American Catholics were peculiarly alone when their civic loyalty and patriotism was called into question.

Multiple Loyalties in Crisis, 1914–1917

Shortly before the German-American Alliance was disbanded in 1918, the Senate held hearings to determine whether its charter should be revoked. Former Congressman Richard Bartholdt of St. Louis explained on that occasion that to understand the attitude of German-Americans toward the war one had to "divorce from the word 'German,' etc., all political significance and regard it merely as a racial designation, which it really is."[45] Bartholdt oversimplified matters, but his contention is broadly applicable to the Central-Verein. The German-language Catholic press of course included Germany in its general news coverage and featured local notes from various regions of the homeland; the Central-Verein was also keenly interested in the social reform activities of Germany's Catholics and took pride in the accomplishments of the Center Party. Otherwise the organization paid virtually no attention to internal political affairs in Germany after the Kulturkampf, and until 1914 it showed even less interest in Germany's role on the international scene. When Central-Verein spokesmen used the terms *Deutschtum*, or *katholisches Deutschtum* they were referring either to the ethnic group in the United States or to the qualities that characterized the group. *Deutschtum* was primarily an ethnic-cultural phenomenon; the bald term "Germanism" does not translate it adequately and it could not be fairly equated with outright political nationalism. Kenkel's criticism of militarism and other aspects of the regime in Germany at the time of the Kaiser's twenty-fifth jubilee in 1913 showed that his feeling for *Deutschtum* sprang not from political sympathies but from the ethnic-cultural nationalism of an American immigrant group.[46]

But while we must distinguish between ethnic-cultural and political nationalism, the two are not totally unrelated. Germany did, after all, exist as a national state; it was there that the German ethnic stock, the German language, German virtues, and German culture presumably reached their fullest development. Enthusiasm for these cultural aspects of *Deutschtum* could easily engender some degree of German nationalism in the political sense. The chauvinistic letter which Kenkel received from an Illinois priest who had been "most deeply offended" by his criticism of the Kaiser in 1913 showed that some German-American Catholics had been touched by German nationalism in the political sense even before the war.[47] After the war began, concern for Germany's military and political fortunes undeniably colored the Central-Verein's feeling for things German.

It was perfectly natural that the Central-Verein's sympathies lay with Germany during the years of American neutrality; as Frey said, "We cannot help it—blood is thicker than water. . . ." Friends and relatives were still living in Germany or serving in her armed forces, and German Catholics wholeheartedly participated in mass demonstrations of sympathy for the fatherland like the one held in St. Louis on August 8, 1914. The annual Central-Verein convention which began in Pittsburgh the following day was also marked by expressions of sympathy for Germany: "The Watch on the Rhine" was sung at the first session, along with the national anthem and a religious hymn, and the hall thundered to *"Deutschland lebe hoch, hoch, hoch!"* when the resolution on the war was adopted.[48] The resolution itself deplored the resort to arms and welcomed efforts at mediation, including those of

President Wilson. The Central-Verein also pledged itself to assist the victims of war among "our German brethren across the sea," thus initiating a relief campaign that totaled $57,000 by 1917. And finally, the resolution strongly protested against "intentional malicious publication of flagrant falsehoods" in the handling of war news by "the Anglo-American press."[49]

Central-Verein members were particularly sensitive to the treatment of the war by English-language Catholic publications. "Is this a specimen of the Paulists' scientific method?" asked Father Engelen after reading a review of the first months of the war in the *Catholic World*. To him it was a classic example of "stupidity, malice, insinuation, distortion, half-truth, abuse, and misrepresentation."[50] In Illinois, German Catholics were calling for the dismissal of the editor of *New World* of Chicago; the Central-Verein group in Baltimore claimed to have influenced the editorial policy of the *Catholic Review* in that city.[51] When a committee of Catholic intellectuals in France published a work attacking Germany and linking religion with the Allied cause, Joseph Matt brought out the American editions of the rebuttals which the Catholics of Germany immediately produced.[52]

The German Catholic press followed the same general line on the war as other German-American papers. Most of their editors probably shared the feelings of Father Joseph Och of the *Josephinum Review*, who told Kenkel he was giving much space and "some *animus*" to discussions of "all the subjects upon which the German people have been slandered and misrepresented."[53] Even the printed proceedings of the Central-Verein's 1914 convention began with some remarks intended to put the war in proper perspective. The recording secretary explained that Germany had "*not* sought this fearful war" but that it had been forced upon her by enemies jealous of her achievements. Germany had never fought a "*juster war*," and "*lasting peace*" could come only when "the Russian bear, the Gallic cock, and especially perfidious England" were rendered incapable of threatening Germany ever again. One of the 1914 convention speakers pointed out that the war was a struggle for civilization against the hordes of Slavdom.[54] The following year another convention speaker was led to a consideration of the war in his treatment of the theme "Back to Christ." His conclusion was printed in boldface type: "The World War is at the same time a war between

Christianity and Antichrist." And it was "the land of the Teutons" which battled for Christianity.[55]

The Central-Verein maintained its strongly pro-German stand throughout the years of American neutrality. Just a month before the United States entered the war the *Central-Blatt and Social Justice* reported a "Singular Festival" staged by the German Catholic *Frauenbund* of Baltimore in honor of the Kaiser's birthday. American and German flags decorated the hall, a portrait of Wilhelm II was prominently displayed, a group from an interned German vessel provided music, and the chief speaker enthusiastically defended "the cause of Germany and the German army."[56] Two years earlier the Central-Verein group in Baltimore had boycotted an American patriotic demonstration to show their dissatisfaction with the pro-Allied tone of the press; its leaders also went on record as endorsing the view expressed in *Die Amerika* that the sinking of the *Lusitania* was an act of self-defense.[57]

In questions involving American neutrality the Central-Verein consistently took the position most favorable to Germany or, when the situation grew more tense, least likely to lead to a break between the United States and Germany. Thus it strongly supported the movement to lay an embargo on shipment of munitions to the belligerents, vigorously protested British violations of neutral rights, and disapproved of the American "preparedness" campaign in 1915.[58] In 1916 the president of the Illinois *Staatsverband* sent a letter to Illinois congressmen saying that armed merchantmen should be classed as warships and calling upon the government to instruct Americans to stay off the vessels of the warring nations.[59]

Central-Verein spokesmen were convinced that their stand was in keeping with strictly American interests and conformed to the requirements of true neutrality. They were equally convinced that the administration had departed from true neutrality and was following a pro-Allied policy. Father Engelen expressed the prevailing view when he told Kenkel that he had read President Wilson's comments on neutrality "with great hilarity." Wilson's sentiments were excellent, Engelen continued, except for his belief that he was guided by concern for neutrality while the German-Americans were not.[60] But by this time—October, 1915—neither the Central-Verein nor other German-Americans were in a strong position to assert that their neutrality was purer than Wilson's or to contrast their concern for American interests with the administration's "lick-spittle policy" toward Great Britain. On the contrary, they had forfeited all claim to impartiality by their strident support for Germany. It was perfectly legitimate for them to favor Germany during the years of American neutrality and for them to attempt to influence American policy along the lines of their natural sympathies. But given the predominant national feeling in favor of the Allies, it was inevitable that their position should be unpopular. And since they were so obviously animated by emotional ties to the old homeland, many Americans began to suspect that the loyalty of the German-Americans to their new homeland was not all that it should be.

The crisis over hyphenations which arose out of this conflict situation brought to light the tensions implict in the multiple loyalties of an immigrant-derived population. To understand why the antihyphen campaign was directed primarily against German-Americans and why their American loyalty was questioned as the debate over neutrality continued, we must look at several elements in the American reaction to the war. First of all, Germany was popularly held to be the aggressor. Whatever the responsibility may have been for the war, Germany appeared to be the nation that started the fighting, and American opinion was alienated at the outset by her invasion of Belgium.[61] Indignation over the violation of Belgian neutrality mounted with tales of German atrocities. These stories seemed to be confirmed in a report by Lord Bryce, the highly esteemed former British ambassador to the United States.[62] Americans found it easy to believe the Germans were following a policy of deliberate terror and intimidation, for the sinking of the *Lusitania* occurred only a few days before the appearance of Bryce's report. Twelve hundred passengers lost their lives on the *Lusitania*; the horror inspired in Americans by this departure from accepted rules of sea warfare made them less tolerant of those who supported Germany.[63] Hard on the heels of these shocks to American feeling, and even more disastrous for the good standing of German-Americans, came a series of sensational revelations of German intrigue, propaganda, and sabotage in the United States.[64]

Most of these reports in the summer and autumn of 1915 were exaggerated if not imaginary, and the principals in the clandestine activities were German nationals. But prominent German-Americans like George Sylvester Viereck, editor of *The Fatherland,* were implicated, and Captain Franz von Rintelen, a colorful German saboteur, was assisted in planting incendiary bombs on Allied munitions-carrying vessels by "hyphenates"—in this case, Irish-American longshoremen embittered against England. Rintelen later asserted that he had encountered some German-Americans who "were ready to do anything to help the Fatherland and injure its opponents."[65] Since many Americans imputed the same extremity of pro-Germanism to all their fellow citizens of German descent, the wildest rumors were given a ready hearing. German-Americans thus found themselves stigmatized as persons of doubtful loyalty, and a formidable "Swat the Hyphen" movement was under way.[66]

German-Americans, who reserved their patriotism for the United States although their nationalism was divided, were outraged by attacks on their loyalty.[67] Particularly offensive were Wilson's remarks in his message to Congress in December, 1915. He spoke of foreign-born citizens "who have poured the poison of disloyalty into the very arteries of our national life; who have sought to bring the authority and good name of our government into contempt, to destroy our industries . . . and to debase our policies to the uses of foreign intrigue. . . ."[68] In 1916 the Central-Verein took official note of the President's "preferring charges against a part of our citizenship who heretofore enjoyed the proud distinction of unquestioned loyalty and patriotism." "We regret this utterance and deplore its effects," the resolution continued, noting that it was "calculated to foster unfounded suspicion and mistrust of a large element of our American people. . . ." The protest was unsympathetically treated by the *New York Times,* which headlined the item "Germans Attack Wilson" and which editorially criticized "certain fanatics and alien propagandists" who "subordinate their religion to their transmarine idolatry."[69]

Attempts on the part of German-Americans to organize themselves as a massive pressure bloc to influence American policy only confirmed the fears of the antihyphenates. These efforts were branded as manifestations of Pan-Germanism rather than being accounted the expression of a legitimate American viewpoint. The German-American Alliance was the most prominent organization and the favorite whipping boy of the antihyphenates, but the Central-Verein also became involved in pressure group work, especially through the activities of Joseph Frey, who associated himself with a bewildering number of German-American movements. Several of these campaigns were conducted jointly with such Irish-American organizations as the American Truth Society, whose president, Jeremiah A. O'Leary, was dubbed "the arch-hyphenate" by the *New York Times*.[70] But even during the critical years 1914–1917 German-Americans found it impossible to overcome all their intramural animosities; if more had been known of the internal tensions the "Teuton Lobby" might have appeared less formidable and threatening.

A chronological sketch of the Central-Verein's participation in the confused succession of German-American efforts to influence American policy begins with Frey's declaration of "solidarity with all our ethnic kindred" in 1914. Frey followed up his statement by attending a conference called in Washington, January 30, 1915, to organize the German-Americans for the drive to enact an embargo on munitions.[71] The conference was arranged by Congressman Bartholdt, who also invited his fellow-Missourian Kenkel to attend. Kenkel could not get away from St. Louis, but he assured Bartholdt of his interest in the project. When it was over Bartholdt informed Kenkel of the steps taken and of the bickering that immediately broke out among the leaders of the American Independence Union, which had been organized at the Washington gathering.[72]

The American Independence Union was to be succeeded by a number of other ephemeral associations with similar names, but it remained in the field long enough to help in organizing a mass demonstration at Madison Square Garden in June, 1915, which passed resolutions demanding an embargo and defense of neutral rights on the seas. Frey attended "in the name of the Central-Verein" and later reported to the 1915 convention that a crowd of 100,000 had protested there against efforts to stampede the United States into war in the interests of "international capital."[73] The executive board of Central-Verein approved Frey's participation in the Washington and New York gatherings; the convention also resolved in favor of an embargo and endorsed another mass meeting being staged in Chicago in September, 1915, by a group called The Friends of Peace. Frey was one of the honorary vice-chairmen of the committee organizing this affair, and a number of Central-Verein units were represented at the so-called National Peace Convention, but the demonstration was less impressive than its sponsors had hoped.[74]

German-American organizational efforts grew even more feverish and complicated in the election year of 1916. In February, German-American journalists met in Chicago to form the National German Publishers Association. Ex-president Gonner of the Central-Verein and August F. Brockland, of *Die Amerika* and the Central Bureau, were among the Catholics at this meeting, but Kenkel did not think it accomplished very much. "The outcome has been as nil," he told Frey three months later.[75] Shortly after the journalists' meeting, German-American organizational efforts suffered a damaging public relations blow in a sensational exposé of the pro-German lobbying carried on in Washington by the German-American Alliance. Alphonse G. Koelble, who had been active in the Central-Verein before shifting his attention to the United German Societies of New York, was featured in this episode as the "Man Who Is Accused of Being Head of Lobbyists for Germany."[76] Later in the spring of 1916 the Central-Verein participated in a campaign to flood Congress with messages calling for peace during the crisis resulting from the sinking of the *Sussex*. Frey was one of a committee of German- and Irish-Americans which sent out telegrams saying the administration was preparing to go to war over the incident and calling for demonstrations in favor of peace.[77]

With the mounting passions of wartime so many German Catholics aligned themselves with the DANB that some Catholic leaders became concerned. In the spring of 1916 Bishop Vincent Wehrle of Bismarck, North Dakota, warned his people against joining the Alliance, many of whose members, he said, gloried in German nationalism and "the spirit of free-thinking [*Freigeisterei*]." While he sympathized with those who felt a quickening of ethnic feeling, Wehrle advised German-American Catholics not to be misled by agitators harping on "*Deutschland über Alles*." He suggested that contributions for the relief of war victims was the most acceptable way of showing one's love for the old homeland, and he cautioned against immoderate criticism of the American government or "speaking in a braggartly way, as though we want to, or can, dominate the politics of our state."[78] Both Kenkel's *Amerika* and the Texas *Staatsverband* agreed it was best to take a stand on political issues simply as Americans rather than as German-Americans.[79] Even before Wehrle's statement appeared, Joseph Matt was so troubled by the number of Catholics flocking to the Alliance that he began to negotiate with its leaders in Minnesota in the hope that establishing a loose official connection between the Central-Verein and the DANB would discourage German Catholics from joining it directly. Matt had in mind the creation of a "Conference Committee," made up of the leaders of Catholic societies and DANB units, which could formulate plans for common action and mobilize widespread support. Alliance president Hexamer opposed this plan, however, and, according to Matt's informants, he deliberately torpedoed it by arranging a meeting in Chicago to set up a different "German-American Conference Committee"—one that the national officers of the Alliance could be sure of controlling. Matt bitterly denounced Hexamer's action, claiming the whole undertaking was thereby "botched."[80] But when Joseph Frey, who was probably unaware of Matt's maneuvers, received an invitation to Hexamer's Chicago meeting he wrote immediately to Kenkel saying he was "definitely in favor" of Central-Verein participation. Kenkel also went along with the plan but had little enthusiasm for it. He warned Frey that "we must in no wise permit ourselves to be dragged into any situation in which such men as Sylvester Viereck and other 'hot spurs' and 'self-seekers' attain the leadership. We ought to look at things more sanely than do these men," he added, "because our ideals are higher and the consciousness of our duties of citizenship greater."[81]

Frey attended the Chicago meeting in May, 1916, and became a member of the "permanent Conference Committee" created there. The Central-Verein convention endorsed this action later in the summer and authorized Frey to continue such activities so long as they conformed to the organization's statutes and traditions.[82] Frey was convinced that all German-Americans must form a united front against the "calumnies and insults" that had been heaped upon them from the beginning of the war. The Chicago conference settled upon achieving this object by getting a satisfactory statement from one of the presidential candidates in the 1916 election and then mobilizing German-American support behind this candidate. Hence a delegation from the permanent Conference Committee called upon Republican nominee

Charles E. Hughes, satisfied themselves of the soundness of his views, and determined to support his candidacy.[83]

Frey was not among those who called upon Hughes, but he was far from idle. On September 16, 1916, he and several other German-American leaders had a conversation in New York with the Democratic senator from Missouri, William J. Stone, who had embarked on a "gumshoeing" expedition to salvage some of the German vote for Wilson. This meeting left Frey "with the conviction that Stone meant well enough but could do nothing for us."[84] Much more encouraging were the results of a conversation between Hughes and a delegation from the American Independence Conference. This organization—another of "the multiform, many-named combinations of 'the Germans and the Irish'"—included the German Conference Committee and O'Leary's American Truth Society (of which Frey was a charter member), but its real parent was an earlier association called the American Embargo Conference.[85] The Embargo Conference had been organized in the summer of 1915 and poured seemingly unlimited funds into the work of sending embargo and peace messages to Congress; much of its money had come from the German government, but that fact was unknown to the Americans who were the ostensible leaders of the organization. The Embargo Conference had organized upwards of two thousand branches, but they had fallen into quiescence after the *Sussex* crisis in April, 1916. As the election approached, however, the American Independence Conference—which was really the Embargo Conference transmogrified—sprang into life, sent the delegation to interview Hughes, established a "working agreement" with the Republican National Committee, and began to spend money with a suspicious prodigality in canvassing among German-American voters.[86]

One of the projects of the Independence Conference was to line up German-American clergymen and religious organizations to support Hughes. In Wisconsin, Indiana, and Ohio it invited clergymen and lay leaders to expense-paid meetings for this purpose. The meeting for Protestants in Milwaukee was held on October 24, 1916, on the same floor of the same hotel where the state Republican committee had its headquarters. The Republican organization was presumably the source of the funds the Protestant leaders were urged to spend for mass meetings and brass bands to promote the Hughes campaign. But the meeting for Protestants drew so much adverse publicity that the next day's meeting for Catholics was poorly attended, and those who did attend adopted a resolution against taking any stand on "party politics."[87] Although the president of the Central-Verein's Wisconsin *Staatsverband* endorsed the calling of the meeting for Catholics, it was he who offered the resolution that frustrated the purpose for which Independence Conference had brought them together. A few days later Archbishop Messmer forbade any priest of his diocese to take part in political activities.[88] Catholic meetings in other states were also unproductive from the viewpoint of the Independence Conference. Henry Seyfried, president of the Central-Verein's Indiana branch, refused to cooperate and was probably the author of a letter quoted in *Amerika* protesting the "rash and un-American activity" of the Conference. In Ohio the Catholic meeting again refused to come out for any candidate; Archbishop Henry Moeller of Cincinnati also expressed strong disapproval of priests' engaging in political activities.[89]

The unwary Joseph Frey, however, was deeply enmeshed in the activities of the American Independence Conference. He attended a meeting of its national executive board in Chicago on September 30, which he said was called to decide upon a plan of action and "prepare an authorative [sic] Statement for publication."[90] A stunningly authoritative report soon appeared: The Democratic National Committee somehow got hold of the minutes of the Chicago meeting and released them to the *New York Times*. The documents revealed the story of the Independence Conference's secret conversations with Hughes and their decision to back him; they also made public the working agreement with the Republican National Committee and the plan to use German-American religious leaders to beat the drums for Hughes. The result of these revelations was, of course, that both Hughes and the American Independence Conference were discredited. Hughes suffered the greater loss: His negotiations with what the *Times* called a "cabal of aliens" fastened the opprobrious "hyphen vote" irretrievably around his neck.[91]

Before all of this came out, Frey was confirmed in his conviction that Hughes was the man the German-American Catholics should back for president. Accordingly he addressed a printed letter to his "Dear Friends" in which he quoted Central-Verein resolutions critical of Wilson because of his handling of the Mexican affair and his policies in respect to the European war. His conclusion was that "Patriotic duty and the best interests of our Country demand the decisive defeat of the present incumbent of the office of President. . . ."[92] Frey maintained that he sent the letter out at his own expense, and it is hard to say precisely what happened. But, probably through the agency of the American Independence Conference, people all over the country received his letter in the official envelope of the Republican National Committee![93]

Frey deeply regretted that his confidence in others had been abused, making his letter seem an "appendage" of the Republican party. In addition to Kenkel and Matt, Central-Verein leaders in Indiana and Maryland were seriously upset by the turn of affairs.[94] Both Matt and Kenkel were very cool toward Hughes; Kenkel's *Amerika*, a traditionally Democratic paper, in fact advised its readers to abstain from voting for either presidential candidate in 1916.[95] The fiasco of German-American efforts at solidarity in the election was regarded by Matt and Kenkel as evidence of the backward state of the American *Deutschtum*. But it was Henry Seyfried of Indiana who arrived at the most judicious evaluation of the situation. Only a nonpartisan movement could have served the "real welfare of our people," he wrote; but the German-American Catholics were "filled with anger and feelings of revenge overrode good judgment; hate supplanted reason." "Following their feeling they quit thinking," Seyfried continued, and thus became "easy prey" to schemers who "used them for purely partisan purposes." He feared that the result of "such indiscreet action" would be "anti-German and anti-Catholic propaganda."[96]

After the feverish activities of 1916, the months intervening between Wilson's reelection and America's entry into the war were somewhat anticlimactic in spite of the worsening relations between the United States and Germany. Frey no doubt summed up the feelings of all German-American Catholics when he wrote in February, 1917, that "The critical aspect of our Foreign relations have [sic] depressed me greatly."[97] But deplore it though they might, war between the new homeland and the old mother country became a reality in April; and whatever their inward travail, the members of the Central-Verein, as loyal Americans, had to adjust themselves to the new situation.

America's declaration of war ended an era for the Central-Verein, as for all organizations of German-Americans. It is true, as H. C. Peterson has remarked, that multiple loyalties "are not necessarily exclusive" and that only "provincial people" so regard them;[98] but it is equally true that they almost inevitably entail tensions and that they can come into opposition in a period of crisis. Even before the war broke out in Europe, the multiple loyalites of the German-American Catholics required the preservation of a delicate balance between the elements of ethnic, religious, and American identity. The years of controversy over neutrality, followed by the bitter trial of war itself, came near to shattering the old balance completely. Unlike the German-American Alliance, the Central-Verein survived the war; but it would never again be a "German-American Catholic" organization in quite the same proud, bold, and fruitful way that it had been before 1914.

VIII

The Impact of War and Fading Ethnicity

America's declaration of war against the Central Powers began a period of "inner martyrdom" for German-Americans and marked a turning point in their history. The war alone did not cause the dissolution of the group, for that process had begun much earlier; but when it was over, as Kenkel put it, "the strength of the American *Deutschtum* was broken." Newspapers and societies were "scoured away" in the storm of anti-German feeling that swept over the country; in many families sons turned against their fathers and against the feeling of kinship with things German that their parents treasured.[1] Because their old homeland was the national enemy, portrayed as the embodiment of everything evil, the self-confidence and self-esteem of German-Americans was, if not extinguished, at least seriously undermined. German Catholics suffered along with their ethnic brethren, and the psychic damage of the war is discernible in many aspects of their postwar development.

In the very week that Congress declared war, Kenkel received a letter from "One who knows" characterizing his editorials in *Amerika* as "treacherous." "If you continue wrighting [sic] and publishing such unloyal and damned stuff," warned the anonymous patriot, "you may rest assured you will be boy-ed-ded and bernstorffed, possibly shot dead."[2] These peculiar threats—which referred to the ejection from the country of Karl Boy-Ed and Johann von Bernstorff, German naval attaché and ambassador respectively—were never carried out, but *Amerika* and other German Catholic publications did have their mailing privileges temporarily suspended because their enthusiasm for the war fell short of wartime standards. And the anti-Catholic *Menace* could hardly be expected to pass up an opportunity to attack the Central-Verein as an "aggregation of disloyalists and papal henchmen" who deserved deportation to Germany where they could "work under the direct supervision of their real bosses, the pope and the kaiser."[3]

More distressing to German-American Catholics, however, was the lack of sympathetic support from their fellow religionists and attacks on things German by other Catholics. Here and there Catholics protested the use of the German language in sermons; almost two years after the war ended the Central-Verein had to ask other Catholics to stop using the terms "Boche" and "Hun."[4] The legend that Cahensly's efforts on behalf of German Catholic immigrants were inspired by Pan-Germanism was revived during the war and immediately afterward.[5] These allegations, which reopened the wounds of the 1890's, were deeply resented and sharply repudiated. In 1918 Kenkel said, "We have been so discriminated against by even our own co-religionists that we have but scant reason to feel overly friendly toward them." He would personally "never forget" that neither the hierarchy nor the American Federation of Catholic Societies had defended them "at a time when every wretched Knownothing in this country considered it brave and honorable to vent his spleen on all Americans of German blood."[6]

But the resentment of the German Catholics did not spring exclusively from the indignities they suffered in the period of anti-German hysteria. Kenkel's dissatisfaction with the hierarchy's wartime attitude, for example, dated back to April, 1917, when he criticized the archbishops' letter to Wilson pledging Catholic loyalty because it spoke of the American cause as "the great and holy cause of liberty."[7] The sympathies of the German-American Catholics lay overwhelmingly with the Central Powers during the whole period of American neutrality, and their convictions did not change overnight when the United States entered the war. They supported the war effort because they were loyal Americans, and their sons flocked to the colors as they had done in all of America's wars.[8] But loyalty notwithstanding, it was difficult for German-Americans to regard the nation's course of action as anything but a mistake—a mistake into which it had been led by a pro-Allied administration seduced by British propaganda and pressured by munitions makers and Wall Street bankers who had staked their fortunes on an Allied victory.[9]

In stressing the role of propaganda, the munitions trade, and Wall Street, the German-Americans anticipated the later "revisionist" analysis of America's entry into the war.[10] Like the revisionists, they regarded it as a deviation from the true national interest dictated by the special interests of certain groups. To many German-Americans, as to the revisionists, the war seemed a great national blunder in which the people were duped and democracy perverted. In view of this highly "realistic" interpretation, it is hardly surprising that the German-Americans developed a cynical attitude about the nobility of American intentions even before that attitude became fashionable among American intellectuals. And when wartime patriotism took the form of an irrational anti-Germanism, it tended to confirm their belief that something basic had gone wrong in the national life. Thus Monsignor Max Wurst spoke scornfully of how we claimed to be bringing the blessings of liberty and democracy to the oppressed peoples of Europe while at home laws were passed to prevent children from being instructed in the German language. And in 1919 the Central-Verein lamented the "ambition and avarice, the lust for power and vengence" that the war had aroused in the American people. It also intimated that the influenza epidemic of 1918 was a divine punishment for the excesses of warlike passion and the hatred of "all things German."[11]

To some, the war against Germany seemed the final proof of the depravity of capitalism; it corroborated the need for a fundamental restructuring of American society. This line of reasoning was explicitly set forth by Frank J. Eble, an occasional contributer to *Central-Blatt and Social Justice*. In May, 1917, Eble informed Kenkel of a change in his social views: "In brief, the entrance of America into this horrible European war . . . has so radically changed my purpose and mind on the Labor Question and the entire social question, that I shall henceforth support every radical measure that is proposed in the interests of the workers . . . be they radicalism in the form of Socialism or Syndicalism or Trades-Unionism." To Eble, who held "Capitalistic Militarism" responsible for the war, the greatest source of anguish was "that a few men in the plutocratic governments of the world (outside of the Central Powers, whose cause I deem to be just before the bar of future history as well as of God) have the power to execute millions of the poor and workers among their subjects or fellow-beings."[12] Eble's case was extreme in that the violence of his reaction to America's entry into "the ranks of the enemies of the Fatherland"[13] carried him all the way over to left-wing radicalism. But it is instructive because it shows how ethnic loyalties spilled over into the seemingly unrelated area of social policy and how German Catholics who were interested in such matters were likely to react to the war by becoming more bitterly alienated from a system which could go so grievously awry.

Shifts in social theorizing were not the most obvious psychological results of the war among German-American Catholics. The waning sense of ethnic identity and the deterioration of the German language were much more widespread and unmistakable; moreover, they demanded immediate attention as serious threats to the maintenance of the group. The demise of twenty-three German Catholic publications between 1917 and 1927 furnishes dramatic evidence of the situation.[14] Eight of these went out of business in 1917–1918 and can be considered direct victims of the war; but the condition of the German Catholic press had been unhealthy since 1900, and the continued losses of the twenties show that its real nemesis was not external hostility but indifference among Catholics of German descent. The erosion of the language was further demonstrated by the negligible demand for Central Bureau pamphlets in German. In 1921 Kenkel regretfully informed the Social Propaganda Committee that although English-language materials circulated briskly, "there is virtually no demand for Brochures in the German language any longer." Four years later the Bureau distributed almost 85,000 English leaflets on request, but in the same three-month period only 1,725 German leaflets were requested.[15]

English made rapid strides in the Central-Verein after the war. It was used very prominently at the Ft. Wayne convention in 1921, and three years later the name of the organization was partially anglicized to "Catholic Central-Verein of America." In 1928 the convention proceedings were published in English for the first time. The secretary did include a brief note in German in which he tried to soften the blow, suggesting that if any old timer was unable to read English he should get his son to read the proceedings to him. This device seemed to please the secretary very much, for it would kill two birds with one stone—the oldsters would be kept up to date and learn English better while the young men would become acquainted with the Central-Verein's program.[16]

The linguistic transition was of course intimately related to the generational transition, but the divergence of interest between old and young was not to be overcome by such artifices as the secretary had in mind. In most areas, the "older element" was said in 1922 to be watching "with unfeigned suspicion every move in the language question," and the "gulf" between the generations led to a number of disputes over the shift from German to English.[17] Late in the decade such a quarrel in Illinois prompted one of those who favored using English to write to other state leagues inquiring how they had handled the language question. This informal survey showed that by 1930 English was the predominant language throughout the East and Midwest, even in states like Minnesota, which had been strongly German through the war years. In Texas, the Dakotas, and Oregon, German was still in fairly widespread use, but English was quite commonly used there too. The replies also showed that by 1930 most Central-Verein men were persuaded that the shift to English was essential to the preservation of the organization.[18]

Although the displacement of German was generally recognized as inevitable, German Catholic spokesmen insisted that their ethnic distinctiveness would persist through the linguistic shift. Kenkel touched on this subject in hailing the appearance of the English-language version of *The Wanderer* in 1930. The standard type of English-language Catholic newspaper was not congenial to the character and thinking of the German Catholics for a number of reasons. Germans, said Kenkel, were serious-minded and demanded a more thorough treatment of issues than these papers offered. Moreover, Germans were conservative; they rejected the sort of liberalism that he implied was to be found in the English press. Hence papers like *The Wanderer* were needed to give expression to the German Catholic spirit and to maintain it among the English-speaking generation.[19]

This line of argument was not new. Arthur Preuss and other publicists who used English had earlier insisted that the German qualities that were worth preserving could "become incarnate" equally well in English.[20] But the language shift meant the loss of the most specific and tangible element in the German ethnic identity. With language gone it became rather difficult to pinpoint what the distinctive "qualities" of the German Catholics were or to explain just why they were distinctive. The widespread shift to English among the second and third generations therefore radically changed the proportional weight of the German, the American, and the Catholic elements that constituted the group's traditional tripartite identity. With the disappearance of German among generations who had no personal recollections of the fatherland and whose attitudes were colored by the experience of the war, the self-consciousness of the Germans as a distinctive group within American Catholicism was drastically reduced.

A speech on the immigration question in 1924 illustrates the changing dynamics of German Catholic ethnic consciousness. The speaker, Henry B. Dielmann, a Central-Verein leader in Texas, restated the classic threefold identity of the German-American Catholics, but his approach was unprecedentedly assimilationist in tenor. He endorsed restriction of immigration and the exclusion of immigrants who could not assimilate because of their racial characteristics. Then he went on to point out the moral for German-American Catholics. They should wholeheartedly adapt themselves to American culture, he declared, for the experience of the war had shown that Americans would not tolerate in their midst groups who held aloof from the national community. This, Dielmann conceded, was what the Germans had done in the past. Too often in speech and thought they had divided *"die Amerikaner"* from *"wir Deutsche"* as though they did not really consider themselves American. Henceforth, Dielmann insisted, German-American Catholics should enter without reservations into American life.[21]

Sentiments such as Dielmann's and the galloping anglicization of the twenties drove some of the more traditionally nationalistic among the German Catholics to extremes of intransigence. Partially because of this ultranationalistic spirit among some in the Central-Verein, a talk on the dangers of nationalism was included in the 1927 convention. Father Aloisius J. Muench, who was later to be raised to the cardinalate, treated the subject in generalized terms, but he was privately troubled by the connection between nationalistic feeling and rigid insistence on the German language. Aside from other objections to nationalism, Muench was sure that such inflexibility was harmful to the Central-Verein's work. Organizational weakness in several states he attributed to "the fact that some of our stubborn Germans, who lack tact, prudence, and vision, insist on carrying on their meetings in a language which no longer has any attractive force with our younger generation." "Why must these men seek to keep alive a by-gone past?" he asked. "They certainly must see that there is no future for the German tongue in this country, and the quicker we take the facts as they are and weld them to our purpose so much the better."[22]

By the end of the twenties, most German-American Catholics had reached the same conclusion as Muench.[23] This represented a significant change; whereas preservation of German had previously been considered a praiseworthy act of loyalty, it now became a disservice to the cause of organized German-American Catholicism. German was finished, and those who identified group loyalty with language loyalty were in effect sentencing the group to extinction with the language. The Central-Verein, however, could live if it was able to attract the English-speaking second and third generations; and since the organization itself symbolized and mobilized the group, it could, by perpetuating itself, perpetuate the German Catholic heritage and tradition. Language was therefore to be sacrificed for organizational survival, and the organization was left as the last major symbol of the group consciousness of the German-American Catholics. But even the continued existence of the organization seemed problematical in the 1920's.

The Struggle for Organizational Survival

The Central-Verein stayed alive during the war years in spite of the unfavorable circumstances and adapted its program to the extraordinary needs of the day. It cooperated with the National Catholic War Council established in 1917; it supplied chaplain's materials and reading matter for servicemen; and it promoted Liberty Bond drives. The Central Bureau also tried to cultivate reform interest among the membership and to alert them to the problems of postwar reconstruction. These efforts, however, were only partially successful. The atmosphere was so oppressive by the summer of 1918 that the annual convention had to be cancelled—for the first time since 1859. The executive committee, which did meet, lamented "the despondency of so many of our members and the lack of interest in so many places."[24]

Areas that were weak before the war had the greatest difficulty recovering in the twenties; states like Ohio and Michigan failed to become active centers in spite of heroic efforts to resuscitate them. Conversely, some states, such as Minnesota, where the society flourished before 1917 seemed to bounce back quickly from the immediate effects of the war. But overall, the war aggravated the Central-Verein's problem by hastening the pace of assimilation. The decline in membership among men from more than 125,000 in 1916 to some 86,000 in 1930 reflects both the impact of the war and the waning consciousness of ethnic identity among the American-born generations.[25] While the younger men showed so little interest, the ranks of the faithful elders were relentlessly thinned by time. The passing of Joseph Frey in 1919 and three other ex-presidents in 1923 brought a sense of discouragement as well as bereavement. But Kenkel stayed on at the Central Bureau, devoting his full time to the work after 1920, and in Charles Korz, of New York, the organization found an energetic and capable president.

The general outlook was perhaps most depressing in 1919. The delegates to that convention recalled the hatred which forced the cancellation of the previous year's meeting. Joseph Frey, who died a few months before the 1919 convention, seemed a sacrifice to the wartime intolerance that was still by no means spent, and the treatment of defeated Germany presaged more suffering for the mother country. In this discouraging context, the message sent to the Central-Verein by Pope Benedict XV had a most revitalizing effect. The Pope praised the German-American Catholics for their loyal support to their new homeland during the war, and he appealed to them to demonstrate their charity by sending aid to the Catholics of Germany and Austria who were still suffering from the privations and destruction of war. After reading the appeal, Archbishop George Mundelein of Chicago spoke eloquently of how the German Catholics had proved their loyalty in spite of the obloquy heaped upon them and of how they were uniquely suited to lead other American Catholics in the noble work of reconciliation and relief. A powerful emotional reaction surged through the crowd and only the sacredness of the ecclesiastical surroundings prevented an outburst of cheering. Later, when the delegates clustered in front of the church, they contrasted the words of the Pontiff with the slanders of their fellow citizens. This mark of confidence and affection from the Pope himself was deeply consoling to the German Catholics, and it gave a great psychological boost to the Central-Verein.[26]

An incident connected with the launching of the relief campaign was symptomatic of the German Catholics' recovery of their old independent spirit. When the appeal was being discussed, Archbishop Messmer cautioned that since whatever Germans did would be misinterpreted it would be advisable to foward the Pope's letter to the American hierarchy and wait for them to set a relief program in motion. Messmer's suggestion was favorably received by the convention, but when the executive committee met a few hours later it determined to set about the campaign without waiting for direction from the bishops. They would merely send a copy of the Pope's letter to the hierarchy along with the information "that *we* undertook the relief work immediately."[27]

The relief campaign also served a valuable purpose in giving the Central-Verein an appealing cause to work for at a time when many of the members were quite dispirited. Reports from observers in Arkansas and Minnesota indicated that societies were active, money was coming in, and in general the campaign was having a beneficial effect on the *Vereinswesen*.[28] But there was a limit to the benefit that could be derived at home from money and time expended to improve conditions in Germany. The half-million dollars that the Central-Verein collected could have been well employed on its own projects.[29] Although the leaders did not begrudge sacrifices made to aid their brethren in Central Europe, they did mean to draw a line somewhere. By late in 1922 the time had come, Kenkel felt, to remind the Social Propaganda Committee that "charity begins at home and that we should not permit sentimentality or the begging proclivities of the Germans to get the best of us."[30]

The belief that contributions for European relief drained off funds needed at home seemed confirmed by the slowness of the Central Bureau's endowment drive. The lack of a secure source of income had long handicapped Kenkel's planning, and in 1919 the Social Propaganda Committee set ten thousand dollars as the amount the Bureau should be guaranteed annually. The following year an endowment drive was formally initiated with the aim of collecting a quarter of a million dollars. Henry Seyfried of Indianapolis served as an aggressive chairman of the drive, and the work of the Central Bureau was endorsed by Archbishops Glennon and Messmer. Yet the progress was disappointing. After four years of campaigning, only about half the amount had been collected, and Kenkel lamented the lack of interest among "so many in our ranks.[31] By 1925, president Korz spoke openly of "how poorly" the endowment fund was doing; it was "almost unbelievable," he said, "how little some states have done."[32]

Although the fund drive fell short of the leaders' hopes, the endowment had climbed to more than $215,000 by 1930. The sale of the Chicago Study House property several years earlier brought in an additional $44,000, which was funded in a separate amount.[33] The prudent investment of these sums in bonds and other conservative securities that weathered the depression guaranteed a modest income in spite of the hard times and declining membership.[34] Based on this limited but solid financial foundation, the Central Bureau could keep going so long as there was even a minimum of interest in maintaining it. In Kenkel it had a tireless and self-sacrificing director who was able to continue most of the Bureau's activities and even add to its facilities. A substantial old brick residence had been purchased in 1921, which still serves as the home of the Bureau, and in the thirties the adjoining carriage house was remodeled as a library for the Bureau's valuable collection of Catholic German-Americana and works on social reform.

But while the permanence of the Central Bureau was being assured, the Central-Verein itself steadily lost ground and a distressing indifference to the Bureau's activities was noted. Most discouraging was the failure of the Central-Verein's youth affiliate, the Gonzaga Union. Since it was "useless and hopeless" to expect young men to "work up an interest" in the Central-Verein through the benevolent societies or fraternals their fathers belonged to, activities of a different sort were needed to attract them.[35] Efforts were made along these lines, but the older men were not prepared to reshape their organizations entirely to suit the taste of the jazz generation. There were also those who argued that the young men ought to be brought directly into the Central-Verein rather than segregating them in the Gonzaga Union. This sort of thinking was perhaps an example of making a virtue of necessity, for by the mid-twenties the Gonzaga Union had obviously collapsed. In 1925 it was declared "obsolete and inoperative"; the provisions touching on it were eliminated from the Central-Verein's constitution.[36]

Revision of the constitution was one of the expedients by which president Korz hoped to galvanize the Central-Verein into new life. Complaining of apathy on the part of the members, in 1924 he served notice that the lack of united effort would be remedied through "constitutional obligation."[37] His hopes were, of course, not realized; indeed, the belief that local officers and members could be obliged by formal requirements to become enthusiastic workers for the cause indicates how far the judgment of the leaders had been disoriented by their problems. The revised constitution provided for direct personal membership in the Central-Verein. Previously, the only way one could belong to the national organization was through membership in one of its affiliated societies. Korz hoped that enough individual "life" and "sustaining" members could be won to offset the losses stemming from the erosion of the old organizational base. Some areas had fairly good success with these devices, but overall the individual memberships came nowhere near replacing the losses caused by the deterioration of the German Catholic Vereinswesen.[38]

A number of special committees on organization, emergency proposals, and a constant drumfire of reproaches from the officers failed to stem the tide. By 1928 the formerly active state of Illinois reported that "our numerical strength not only has decreased, but also our prestige and our influence has considerably diminished in the past ten years." The following year president Willibald Eibner compared the Central-Verein to an aged man who could still perceive what needed to be done but lacked the strength to do it.[39]

The only bright spot in this bleak picture was furnished by the women's affiliate, the National Catholic Women's Union (NCWU). Established in 1916, the women's auxiliary was well supported from the first, and by the middle twenties it was showing much more life than the parent organization for men. Its increasing importance was recognized in the constitutional revision of 1926, which changed it from an adjunct to an integral part of the Central-Verein and elevated its president to the stature of fourth national vice-president. The NCWU *Bulletin* gained subscriptions rapidly and soon had almost as many readers as the *Central-Blatt*. With some 56,000 members in 1930 the NCWU was approaching the men's society in numerical strength.[40] In Wisconsin the women's society "in fact . . . overreached the men in membership as well as activities," and Missouri reported, "We glory in their achievements; they accomplish so much more than does the men's branch."[41]

Why should the NCWU prosper while the Gonzaga Union collapsed and the Central-Verein itself was suffering demoralizing reverses? Two clues suggest an explanation for this seemingly paradoxical state of affairs. The first is that although *das Deutschtum* was usually more easily preserved in rural areas, the NCWU was primarily a city-based organization. The second is that while Minnesota was perhaps the strongest state from an organizational viewpoint, the women's society was relatively slow in taking root there.[42] The explanation toward which these two facts point is that Americanization, which weakened the Central-Verein and destroyed the Gonzaga Union, had the contrary effect of awakening Catholic women of German descent to the attractions of participation in associational activities. In other words, the process of assimilation tended to move the men completely out of the orbit of the ethnic society, but it moved the women out of the strictly domestic sphere and into organizational life of their traditional group.

The NCWU represented a sort of first phase in the emancipation of German Catholic women from the time-honored "*Kirchen-Küchen-Kinder*" sphere of activities—to which, incidentally, some of the "old guard" among the men thought they should remain confined.[43] It can be considered as an early phase of emancipation for three reasons. First, it took place within the associational life of the ethnic-religious group. The women who devoted themselves to the NCWU were not turning their backs on the past but manifesting their solidarity with their tradition. Second, the sort of activities it promoted involved no radical departure from the type of work that was customarily thought of as being the special concern of women. The NCWU took as its mission support of day nurseries, assistance to working girls, hospital aid, collections for the missions, and other sorts of social service. Finally, the NCWU explicitly rejected radical "emancipation" and adopted a very conservative theoretical stance on the role of women in the modern world. It repudiated "False and Perverted Feminism," and championed "first and foremost . . . the mother, the homemaker, the guardian of the fireside at which children are reared for the glory of God and the honor of the Christian name." It also rejected birth control, immodest dress, beauty contests, corrupting literature, and the trend to remove religious images from the home. In short, it stood squarely behind the most conservative traditional attitudes.[44]

But while it might seem that these women had stepped demurely forth from the family circle for the sole purpose of exalting the Christian home, there was more to it than that. They also proclaimed that "women should have new privileges in an age of democracy," and they advocated nothing that "cripples the unfolding of [the woman's] personality."[45] Those who became active in the NCWU found themselves involved in work that took them outside their homes and identified their activities with a national organization with the broadest social and cultural aims. Holding office in the NCWU offered a number of gratifying roles that had little direct relationship to the domestic sphere of activity. There were programs to plan and speeches to give; there was a private audience with the Pope for the national president in 1927, and there were papal decorations for her and the president of the Wisconsin state branch.[46] This move into the great world of extra-domestic life was made by an increasing number of women of German Catholic descent in the 1920's, and it was part and parcel of the overall process of Americanization.[47] The Central-Verein profited organizationally from this variety of Americanization because the NCWU provided an ideal vehicle for these women, who were sufficiently assimilated to long for something constructive to do outside their immediate family circle but who retained an identification with their traditional group and loyally supported the traditional value-system.

Raising the women to the level of full partnership and making the transition to English were the major accommodations to Americanization made in the twenties. Both adjustments were salutary, but they were less creative than the Central-Verein's reponse to the earlier challenge of Americanization in the first decade of the century. Then there was both an important structural reorganization and the development of a new mission in keeping with the times and appropriate to the interests of the younger generation. In the twenties, however, no new mission was elaborated to provide a more compelling raison d'être for the organization, in spite of the fact that social reform had lost much of its appeal and timeliness. Moreover, the two major adjustments to Americanization came about as unplanned reactions to existing circumstances rather than resulting from deliberate policy choices. The shift to English was merely a reluctant bowing to the inevitable; the enlargement of the women's role was not so much consciously intended as simply recognized, accepted, and welcomed. The Central-Verein could hardly have survived at all without these adjustments; but the manner of their introduction suggests that events were rapidly moving beyond the control of the leadership and that the possibility of their shaping the future of the organization was quite limited.

By 1930 the Central-Verein could look for support to three groups. First, to those we might call "ideological converts"—that is, individuals without any connection with the organizational life of the German-American Catholics who were attracted to it because of its social philosophy and dedication to reform. The device of individual membership was introduced in 1926 to enable such persons to join; but in 1930 there were only sixty of these life and sustaining members.[48] Even if all of them were ideological converts, which is doubtful, the number was much too small to add anything to the Central-Verein's life expectancy.

A more promising source of strength was the NCWU. For reasons already discussed, the participation of women held out a good deal of hope. But it was problematical whether the women's branch would continue to flourish or whether it would be a transitory phenomenon associated with a stage in the process of Americanization. Already in 1931 the Women's Union took particular note of the need to involve "young ladies" in their work—language which might have had an ominously familiar ring to old-timers in the Central-Verein.[49]

The third group were those whose ethnic loyalty had been translated into organizational loyalty. Both men and women might be classified here, but probably more of them were men. The group comprised that ever-diminishing number of American Catholics of German descent who looked upon the Central-Verein as *their* organization and supported it because it was a symbol of their ethnic heritage—or perhaps merely because family tradition linked them to it and they considered it a society worth preserving.

All in all, the prospects of the Central-Verein were not very bright. It was fighting a rearguard action, and the outlook grew progressively more discouraging through the 1920's. The root of the trouble was that it was fundamentally an ethnic organization for German-American Catholics; but as German-American Catholic ethnicity became more and more attenuated, there was correspondingly less justification for a distinctive ethnic organization. The Central-Verein had to Americanize itself as its clientele Americanized. It therefore became an organization of vestigial ethnicity that appealed primarily to the remnant of the *katholisches Deutschtum* who still retained some sense of their peculiar identity or a connection with the organizational tradition of the group.

New Interests and Old Problems

Although the Central-Verein did not develop any wholly new mission during the twenties, its area of interest was modified by shifting emphases and the elaboration of certain elements. Likewise, the old problem of getting along with other Catholic organizations cropped up in new form after the creation of the National Catholic Welfare Conference. The process of shifting emphases is well illustrated in the Central-Verein's growing absorption in the farm problem and matters related to rural life.

The Central-Verein had devoted some attention to agriculture in the prewar years, but there was a much greater concentration on this area in the 1920's. Several considerations help explain the new emphasis. The first is that although popular interest in "the social question" evaporated amid the distractions of the jazz age, the farm problem was one issue that could not be ignored, because the farmers were sufficiently clamorous to keep it before the public. Even the casual reader of newspapers knew the farmer was discontented. And those acquainted with the statistics on the flight from the land and the rise in tenancy were likely to be disturbed. The sturdy yeoman farmer, portrayed as the backbone of democracy for a century, was becoming an extinct species.[50] In view of this popular concern over the farm problem, the Central-Verein's new interest was timely; it made contact with the public mind at the point of greatest receptivity to the message of social and economic reform.

Secondly, interest in the farm problem was organizationally appropriate, indeed necessary, because so many Central-Verein members were country people. The two organizational bastions of the twenties, Minnesota and Missouri, had very strong contingents of German Catholic farmers who were intensely interested in agricultural problems. They scheduled their own meetings on the *Farmerfrage,* and Bishop Vincent Wehrle of Bismarck, who was worried by the growth of the radical Non-Partisan League in North Dakota, addressed the Central-Verein's national convention on "The Farmer Question."[51] Even during the prosperous war years Nicholas Gonner asked urgently for lectures for farmers in Iowa, and the drop in prices after the war was damaging to the organizationally weak Iowa *Staatsverband.* Later in the decade the *Central-Blatt and Social Justice* expressed special concern that rural depopulation was even affecting areas settled by German Catholic farmers.[52] Since its members were so intimately involved in this problem, the Central-Verein's interest would be understandable on these grounds alone.

A third factor is that the Central-Verein's interest was in keeping with the widespread Catholic concern over rural life in the 1920's. There had been numerous efforts to colonize Catholics on the land in the nineteenth century, but the organized rural life movement did not develop until after the World War. Its leading promoter was Edwin V. O'Hara, an Oregon priest who was bishop of Kansas City at his death in 1956.[53] After working through other organizations, O'Hara founded the National Catholic Rural Life Conference (NCRLC) in 1923. He and other Catholic ruralists argued that the "warehousing" of people in the cities produced conditions unfavorable to religious development. They also asserted that urban Catholics failed to reproduce in sufficient numbers to maintain a stable Catholic population without infusions from abroad or from the farms and small towns. Country life, on the contrary, was naturally conducive to piety, and rural Catholics had large families. Since American Catholicism was overwhelmingly urban, it would be doomed to slow extinction without continuous reinforcements of country-bred Catholics. This wellspring of vitality would be prematurely depleted, however, if the relatively small numbers of rural Catholics were not dissuaded from joining the precipitous flight to the cities. Hence decisive action was needed to minister to the needs of rural Catholics, to make their life more attractive, and to reduce the migration from farm to city.[54]

American Catholic ruralists found allies among the English Distributists, and their message had great appeal for the Central-Verein. Shortly before the NCRLC was organized, the *Central-Blatt and Social Justice* carried an article describing the city as a "goddess, bedecked in pinchbeck finery . . . who strikes dead at the nearest approach."[55] Kenkel and his staff at the Central Bureau played an indispensable role in the preparations for the first meeting of NCRLC, which took place in St. Louis, and the silver jubilee history of the organization stresses Kenkel's continuing contribution. "His influence," Raymond Witte states, "can be traced throughout the early years and his counsel, which was sought by most of the leaders, saved the Conference from many embarrassing moments. Of all the lay people present at the first meeting, he was the only one whose interest lasted through the full quarter of a century. His active participation as an officer and as a member lasted just as long as his age would allow."[56]

Kenkel's dedication to the Catholic rural life movement rested in part on the considerations already enumerated, but it was also related to his Christian-corporative social philosophy. One of the fundamental points of his teaching was that a healthy organic society required a vigorous *Mittelstand* (middle class), and this aspect was given special emphasis in the twenties. In 1921 Kenkel began an almost endless series of articles under the general title "*Mittelbesitz und Mittelstand*," and Father Engelen dealt with the same subject more briefly in English.[57] The *Mittelstand* was composed of independent owners of small units of productive property; it included tradesmen and shopkeepers as well as farmers. The concept tallies closely with the petty bourgeoisie, except that the stress laid upon the situation of the farmer focused attention on a petty bourgeois who did not live in a town. But the plight of the farmer—a small operator suffering from the advances of capitalism and large-scale industry—was symptomatic of the danger besetting the *Mittelstand* as a whole, and Kenkel considered it very serious. Once "a veritable yeoman" and "the backbone of a virile middle class," the American farmer in 1929 faced the prospect of degradation to the status of a latifundia worker.[58]

All this seems to fit together nicely, but it issued in some highly paradoxical consequences. For to speak of farmers as "yeomen" and "the staunchest supporters of Democracy" was to use the language of Jeffersonian individualism; it was precisely the same rhetoric as that employed by businessmen in the twenties who opposed doing anything to help the farmer. Moreover, opposition to individualism and the bourgeois spirit that destroyed the medieval corporative order was the cornerstone of the Central-Verein's social philosophy. Yet Kenkel and other contributers to the *Central-Blatt* extolled self-help and the middle-class virtues and insisted on the crucial importance of a healthy *Mittelstand,* even though they repudiated the American dream of middle-class success.[59]

So far as agriculture was concerned, the Central-Verein regarded the cooperative movement as the most hopeful development. Cooperatives not only offered a partial answer to the farmer's immediate needs, they might also prepare the ground for a full-scale reconstruction of society. The Central-Verein's solidaristic philosophy called for voluntary mutual assistance as well as vigorous self-help; the widespread enthusiasm for cooperatives in the 1920's seemed to indicate that Americans were beginning to appreciate the importance of such activity. The credit union movement, which the Central-Verein also heartily endorsed, was further evidence of the growth of a solidaric sentiment out of which a completely corporative social order might eventually develop. Thus a resolution espousing cooperatives in 1921 added the hope that they would point the way "to organizations along the lines of occupation and estate which, properly fitting themselves into the structure of civil society and guided by Christian principles, will become representative of the interests of agriculture."[60]

But even if cooperatives continued to prosper, there was no guarantee that they would develop in this direction. Everything depended on the spirit that animated them and many varieties of socialists had dreamed of a "cooperative commonwealth." Kenkel warned as early as 1919 that cooperatives could not be used as a screen for transferring ownership to the state. He emphasized that "The cooperative spirit [*Genossenschaftsgeist*] and not cooperative techniques [*Genossenschaftswesen*] is what we need above all." Kenkel was interested in cooperatives as economic instruments only in the most secondary way. What he really hoped for was a spiritual revolution, and cooperatives were desirable in proportion as they led to a quickening of the "social spirit," awakened a sense of community among men, and aided in the restoration of an "economy among brothers."[61]

The emphasis on the spritual transformation they could assist in promoting links the Central-Verein's enthusiasm for cooperatives to another new interest that may seem far removed—the liturgical movement. For the liturgical revival that began to stir in the 1920's meant more than an emphasis on Gregorian chant and a return to more primitive forms of worship. Rather the liturgical reformers' fundamental concern was to instill in American Catholics an understanding of the Church as a spiritual community, the Mystical Body of Christ, whose official public prayer, the Mass, should be approached as a corporate act of thanksgiving and sacrifice offered in common by all the faithful. Hence they stressed the necessity of active participation by the laity in the Mass, and they labored to overcome the individualistic orientation of American Catholics in their devotional and spiritual life.

German Catholics, especially in rural districts, had preserved among the folkways brought over from Europe many popular liturgical practices, and the American liturgical revival flourished earliest in such German Catholic centers as Minnesota and Missouri. Most of the early leaders of the movement were of German background, and the Benedictine priest Virgil Michel made St. John's Abbey in Minnesota the principal fulcrum of liturgical reform in this country.[62] The Central-Verein was therefore culturally situated to become aware of the movement at a very early date, but in addition there was a natural affinity between its social philosophy of solidarism and the liturgists' stress on the corporate character of Catholicism. Two years before Virgil Michel returned from Europe and breathed life into the movement, Kenkel's article on "The Parish Church, a True Community Center" suggested some of the social reform implications of the liturgical approach.[63] In

1925 the *Central-Blatt* featured a discussion of the liturgy as "the key to the solution of the Social Question." The argument advanced at that very early date by two liturgical pioneers in Missouri and elaborated more fully by Michel in the 1930's was that the social evils growing out of capitalistic individualism could be overcome only through a spiritual transformation. Modern man had to be converted from viewing society as the battleground of antagonistic interests to a conception of society that recognized its corporate character. This could best be accomplished through the liturgical renewal, for "If the religious life of a people is solidarically and socially oriented, their political, economic and social life will also assume a solidaric social form."[64]

Although the Central-Verein advocated cooperation in agriculture and emphasized the communal element in religion, it had difficulty working smoothly with other Catholic bodies on the practical level. The new element in this picture was the National Catholic Welfare Conference (NCWC), which grew out of the organization set up in 1917 to coordinate Catholic participation in the war effort.[65] The relations of the Central-Verein with the NCWC were much like its earlier relations with the Federation of Catholic Societies. Central-Verein representatives were present at several of the meetings to organize various departments of the NCWC, and it was officially affiliated to the subsidiary National Council of Catholic Men; yet there was also considerable tension between the Central-Verein and the NCWC. Since we must explore these tensions, we should note here that there were positive aspects to the relations between the two organizations. Kenkel, for example, served as the second president of the Catholic Conference on Industrial Problems, which was organized under the auspices of the NCWC Social Action Department to stimulate interest in social and economic matters.

In spite of such fruitful instances of cooperation, the strains between the Central-Verein and the NCWC were definitely present. They arose from matters of personality, from organizational fears, and from ideological differences; these three causes were often intertwined, and the factor of ethnic sensitivity cut across all of them. German-American Catholics were especially outraged by the revival of the old bogey of Cahenslyism in the official history of Catholic participation in the war written by Michael Williams, an employee of the NCWC. Charles

Korz blasted the book in an article that was widely discussed in the German Catholic press. He also forwarded a copy of his critique to Bishop Joseph Schrembs, one of the episcopal directors of the NCWC, asking that Schrembs use his influence to prevent further disregard of the feelings of the German Catholics. Schrembs promised to "take it up with the Department in Washington," but he added that "our German 'Gemütlichkeit' will have to do service in the future as it has in the past." The Irish-American Catholics, Schrembs thought, were unaware just how narrow their own perspective was; Williams, as a recent convert, had absorbed this point of view and "he easily forgets that there is anybody else in the Catholic Church besides the Irish."[66]

Other officials of the NCWC dealt with certain issues relating to school legislation and the civic education program (part of the postwar "Americanization" crusade) in ways that displeased German Catholics. Moreover, Kenkel felt that the press service of the NCWC did not give adequate coverage to the protests of German churchmen when the French occupied the Ruhr in 1923.[67] Besides the tensions resulting from individual actions of NCWC officials, there was also some personal resentment springing from the feeling of being neglected and ignored. This resentment is a dominant theme in the letters of Father Engelen to Kenkel in the postwar years. One of the earliest examples shows that it was associated with the embitterment caused by the war. "But like you," Engelen wrote in December 1918, "I felt very much the attitude of our Catholics. Not only no help, no word of encouragement, when we could not talk out; but often open hostility, an undercurrent of quiet satisfaction." Engelen felt little inclination to join wholeheartedly in endeavors with such Catholics, and he was uneasy about rumors that the Bishops were to set up an organization for social action "reaching into our own circles." He also remarked on "the arrogance and ignorance" of those who talked of reform and reconstruction using John A. Ryan as their only authority and with never a word about the Central-Verein.[68]

By the spring of 1921 Engelen was certain that his work and Kenkel's was being systematically ignored by the Social Action people at NCWC and other Catholic writers. "Well," he observed, "it is not only Dr. Ryan who ignores us. There is system behind it. And the more they ignore us, or rather neglect to call attention to the Centralblatt, the more they can copy, after some time has elapsed. Have you ever been able to find the time for a comparison of Husslein's program, which made him famous . . . and the one we published years ago? You have only to read mine backward. . . ."[69]

Engelen's sense of personal injustice, which was rather unfair to other Catholic reformers,[70] was allied to his conviction that the others, with the NCWC's Ryan at their forefront, were unsound from the theoretical viewpoint. And we should note that Engelen's uneasiness over a new organization "reaching into our own circles" was widely shared by those in the Central-Verein more conversant with the organizational situation. As in the case of the American Federation of Catholic Societies, the Central-Verein resolved to cooperate fully with the NCWC. But when the latter undertook to coordinate laymen's societies through the National Council of Catholic Men, an old problem reared its head: how to reconcile meaningful unification with respect for the autonomy of existing societies. German Catholic leaders in Indiana felt that "if the National Welfare Council is permitted to continue as they are doing it will mean the disruption of our State League and also of the Central-Verein."[71] Similar difficulties arose in Illinois, but the Central Bureau was informed that it seemed to be the strategy of the German pastors there to acquiesce in the formation of the new organization "then let it go to pieces."[72] Kenkel presented the viewpoint of the Central-Verein to the leaders of the laymen's organization and was assured that they had no intention of undercutting existing societies. He felt that this was the best that could be hoped for and recommended a policy of wary cooperation. "We must watch developments closely," Kenkel wrote, "and assert our rights . . . as they may seem in danger of being violated here and there from time to time."[73]

Kenkel could hardly have been surprised at the practical strains of coexistence, for they were not only the old story of the AFCS repeated but they might have been predicted merely from his analysis of the NCWC's weaknesses from the viewpoint of social theory. The basic trouble was that the NCWC had been established and was being run from the top down, rather than from the bottom up. It had not grown naturally but had been devised; therefore, it was not "organic" but "mechanical." Its subordinate units could not develop harmoniously together, for they were only parts of a mechanism; they did not share the common life of a true social organism. In Kenkel's opinion, the organization itself could not be squared with the correct Catholic social theory. And since the NCWC was flawed by the same fundamental defect as modern society in general, it could scarcely guide the reconstruction of society along the proper lines.[74] Given this background, it is easy to appreciate that much of the reform program of Ryan and the Social Action Department seemed mistaken and even dangerous to Kenkel and Engelen.[75] The NCWC reformers were too "liberal"; they accepted the prevailing system and hoped only to ameliorate its worst features. But to adopt such an approach was to abandon the hope of true social reconstruction; moreover, Kenkel maintained, it abetted the dangerous tendency toward state socialism.

State Socialism and True Reform

Kenkel's first postwar warning against state socialism was published a month after the appearance of the famous "Bishops' Program of Social Reconstruction" in February 1919, and it was very likely prompted by this document, which was written by Ryan. Kenkel followed Pesch in defining state socialism as that situation in which the traditional "state," rather than the socialistic "society" of the future, absorbed all hitherto private economic functions. To guard against this danger, Kenkel set up two criteria for measuring all reform proposals. First, all proposed reforms should meet the actual needs of the "transitional" period; secondly, they should introduce no practice or institution that would be inappropriate to the corporatively structured society which was the ultimate aim of social reconstruction. It seems probable that Kenkel had the Bishops' Program in mind when he added: "If the last state of things is not to be worse than the first, no Catholic program of social reform or reconstruction should be drawn up which does not make reference to this peril we have discussed and to the safeguards to be set up against state socialism."[76]

A quick review of the Bishops' Program makes clear why it might have seemed defective to Kenkel. Ryan had always believed in government intervention to secure social justice, and in the Bishops' Program he allowed the state a very broad sphere of action. He wanted federal work projects for returning servicemen, the retention of the

War Labor Board, and the expansion of the U.S. Employment Service. He suggested using the federal taxing power to end child labor; he endorsed state minimum-wage laws and comprehensive social insurance, and he also approved "substantially universal" vocational education. Although Ryan recognized that government housing programs and price fixing could not be continued, he rejected neither of them on principle. As a means of controlling the cost of living he hinted that the government should enter into competition with monopolies that could not be restrained by antitrust laws. By comparison with these sweeping proposals for government action, Ryan gave scant attention to the desirability of making wage earners at least part owners of the means of production through cooperatives, copartnership devices, and so on. His concluding paragraph on the need for a "new spirit" on the part of workers and owners alike was something of a *pro forma* appeal and received nothing like the emphasis Kenkel and Engelen would have thought necessary.[77]

The *Central-Blatt's* formal treatment of the Bishops' Program was by Father Charles Bruehl, a regular contributor on reform matters. His discussion was generally favorable, although he noted that the Program failed entirely to consider the *Mittelstand* problem and that parts of it would undermine the energy and initiative of the middle class.[78] More pertinent here, however, is that Bruehl's introductory remarks revealed a profound uneasiness at the "radicalism" of the times and a diffuse sense of instability.[79] The tremendous shock of the war, coupled with the revolution in Russia, the postwar uprising in Germany, and the labor unrest in the United States, had engendered in the American people a deep feeling of insecurity. The foundations of society seemed to be moving underfoot, and the future was uncertain. This widespread malaise disposed the people to respond to President Harding's call for a "return to normalcy," but it also set the stage for the frantic programs of Americanization and the hysteria of the "Red Scare."[80] The general unsettledness affected the German-American Catholics also, and among the social reform theorists of the Central-Verein it manifested itself in an exaggerated fear of state socialism.

In retrospect it seems almost absurd that anyone should have feared state socialism in the era of Harding, Coolidge, and Hoover, when rugged individualism was the order of the day. But if we approach the matter from the viewpoint of the German Catholics of that time it becomes more understandable. Even before America's entry into the war they had detected in Wilson's actions a trend toward dictatorship, and the war itself had brought a prodigious expansion of federal power. Not only were men drafted into the service, but public opinion was manipulated, prohibition introduced, the industrial and transportation systems of the country placed under government direction, prices regulated, labor-management relations supervised by one national board and the production and consumption of food by another. After the war there were many, like John A. Ryan, who thought that at least part of the apparatus of federal control should be retained. But the expansion of federal power had accompanied a war the German Catholics deplored, and they suffered grievously from the "hundred per cent Americanism" it stimulated. The survival of their schools was directly threatened by educational legislation: Between February and July of 1919, fifteen states passed laws which required that English be used as the medium of instruction and included other features unacceptable to the German Catholics.[81] The same year saw the beginning of a long struggle over federal aid to education, which the Central-Verein regarded as tantamount to federal control of schools throughout the country, and there were many other proposals that the national government undertake new concerns. Seen against this background, the Central-Verein's fear of state socialism does not appear wholly a matter of fighting fantasms. Even the quondam liberal Walter Lippmann warned against the aggrandizement of federal power in the heyday of Coolidgeism.[82]

The Germans were not the only Catholics who feared the growth of centralized government and opposed measures like the Smith-Towner proposal for federal aid to education. The majority of American Catholics shared this opposition; but the Central-Verein's stand was especially inclusive and uncompromising.[83] Its refusal to countenance state interference in the schools extended even to the question of antievolution laws, which it opposed even though its generally conservative position might have disposed it to regard such laws more tolerantly.[84] Fear of state socialism also determined its stand on the child labor amendment. In spite of its long-standing opposition to this abuse, the Central-Verein campaigned actively to defeat the ratification of the amendment that would permit the federal government to legislate against child labor. Aggrandizement of federal power was seen as a greater danger than ineffective regulation of child labor by the states. According to Vincent McQuade, who studied the Catholic reaction to this issue, the Central-Verein's opposition was a major determinant of national Catholic sentiment on the child labor amendment.[85]

John A. Ryan was the most prominent Catholic champion of the child labor amendment, and he debated Kenkel on this question at the third meeting of the Catholic Conference on Industrial Problems in 1925.[86] Two years later Ryan declared that this was the only "social subject" on which he was conscious of disagreeing with Kenkel "in any considerable degree." Ryan made this statement in response to an article in the Dubuque *Daily American Tribune* lamenting the existence of two divergent schools of Catholic social teaching, one headed by Kenkel and the other represented by Ryan and the NCWC. The *Tribune* was founded by Nicholas Gonner and reflected the German Catholics' view of the matter; Ryan, however, read of the divergence between himself and Kenkel "with a great deal of surprise."[87] Ryan was not the only Catholic writer on social questions who had this experience. Several years earlier the Jesuit, Henry S. Spalding, wrote to Kenkel that "I was surprised to read that our differences [on social theory] were of a *fundamental nature*."[88] But to Kenkel and Engelen, Ryan and other American Catholic reformers were "liberals" who prescribed mere stopgap measures and had no understanding of what true Christian social reform involved. They were certainly correct in thinking that their own social philosophy was different; anyone who read the *Central-Blatt and Social Justice* attentively in the twenties would have discerned in it a temper and approach quite different from Ryan's.

Engelen noted in 1920, in speaking of the differences of opinion among Catholic reformers in Germany, that the question that divided them—"how far we should go in practical reform proposals"—also had application in the United States. He added that if Ryan were in Germany he would stand among the extreme left wing of Catholic reformers. "And everyone follows after him. Defective in principles, extreme in practice."[89] As these remarks suggest, Kenkel and Engelen were following affairs in Germany with interest; their attitudes toward the different schools of thought there offer a revealing insight into their own beliefs concerning the nature of true social reform. In brief, what happened in German-speaking Europe was that the shock of the Central Powers' collapse and dissatisfaction with the postwar arrangements seriously discredited the approach of the meliorist group of Catholic reformers, who had accepted the existing social order and attempted to work within it for piecemeal improvements. In reaction there was a powerful resurgence of extreme corporatism among Catholic social theorists. Writers of this persuasion, who were especially entrenched in Vienna, turned their backs on the modern world and harked back to the romantic or even mystical corporatism of Vogelsang and other champions of the organic state.[90]

Kenkel had always been deeply attracted by romantic medievalism and was a devoted admirer of Vogelsang. The war deepened his estrangement from modern liberal, individualistic, and democratic society in its American form and made him more receptive to the romantic corporative vision of Vogelsang and the Vienna school. Vogelsang's authority was cited repeatedly, and when he was most alienated from the life around him Kenkel even used Vogelsang's term "*Gleichheitssumpf*" (morass of equalitarianism) to describe modern society.[91] The Central-Verein had modeled its prewar social reform work explicitly upon the meliorist approach of the Volksverein at München-Gladbach, but after the war the Gladbachers were stigmatized as having promoted state socialism, and Engelen flatly stated that "we represent the anti-Gladbach Richtung."[92] Numerous articles appeared in the *Central-Blatt* by representatives of the various corporatist schools in Vienna, the most extreme of which could only be described as frankly reactionary.

Kenkel opened the pages of the *Central-Blatt* to writers who rejected all political parties and movements as tainted with the Protestant and Modernist spirit and who held up as a model a system of "Catholic autarchy" in which each parish would be a self-contained economic unit organized on a handicraft basis.[93] However, these incredible prescriptions were not representative of the magazine's usual social teaching. Instead the *Central-Blatt* characteristically concerned itself with the description of current evils and explained the need for fundamental reforms and the desirability of a corporative "organic society." It pointed out the dangers of state socialism, extolled the virtues of the

Mittelstand, presented idealized pictures of the Middle Ages, and called repeatedly for the conversion of modern man to a new "social spirit" to replace the self-interested individualism of the age. Only a society that had become truly "solidaric" and "organic" could satisfy the requirements for true social reconstruction, but such a society could never be legislated into existence. One had to work from the bottom up through such institutions as cooperatives and credit unions, and even these were defective unless animated by the right spirit of mutualism and charity.

A Conservative Critique by Alienated Utopians

Clearly, something strange had happened to the social reform program of the Central-Verein. The organization still made reform its primary reason for being, and its resolutions touched upon a wide spectrum of social issues, ranging from international peace to yellow-dog contracts. Criticism of contemporary evils was passionate, and the crash and depression at the end of the decade only confirmed the conviction that modern society could not be healed by "poultices."[94] By comparison with other Catholic reformers, Kenkel and Engelen felt that only they understood the nature of thorough-going Christian social reconstruction. Their disaffection from modern society was sometimes expressed in almost violent terms. In contrasting his "real reconstruction" to the "makeshift" proposals of another Catholic writer, Engelen once described the program he was outlining as one that would "[hit] modern society straight in the face."[95]

But while it claimed to make no compromises with "the chaos which we call modern life,[96] the Central-Verein's viewpoint actually had much in common with the ideology of the most conservative elements in American society. Indeed, the organization's social philosophy seemed a bundle of contradictions. It stood for reform and rejected liberal capitalism and the laissez-faire state; yet it agreed with American businessmen in opposing reform proposals because they were paternalistic and would lead to bureaucracy and centralization. It abhorred all forms of radicalism and was self-professedly conservative but called for a fundamental restructuring of American society. It insisted that society had to develop "organically" but held up as a model a corporative order that had no historical roots in the American past. It championed the middle class but rejected with vehemence the most middle-class society in the world.

These inconsistencies become more understandable, however, if we interpret the Central-Verein's ideology as a conservative critique formulated by alienated utopians. Industrialism and urbanization were transforming American society at a fantastically rapid pace. Traditional values and ways of life were profoundly unsettled by these changes, and the psychic disruption of American life was aggravated by the great war, the postwar disillusionment, and the penetration of new currents of thought in the 1920's. In common with many other elements in society, the German Catholics were deeply disturbed by these changes; the social theory of the Central-Verein represented their critical reaction. The German Catholics accepted many of the same traditional religious, moral, and social beliefs as other Americans; hence it should not be surprising that the Central-Verein's ideology coincided in some respects with that of other conservative groups. Since the organization's membership included so many farmers, Kenkel's stress on the indispensable social importance of the small producer and the virtues associated with the *Mittelstand* conformed to the actual social and economic interests of the group represented by the Central-Verein.

Kenkel was the key man in shaping the ideology of the organization; the social theory of the Central-Verein was in fact the social theory of Frederick P. Kenkel. There had always been elements of alienation and utopian romanticism in Kenkel's approach to the social question. The war deepened his rejection and sharpened his critique of modern society, making him more receptive to utopian alternatives. Kenkel was not alone in being hostile to American life in the twenties. On the contrary, the note of alienation was a dominant one among American intellectuals. The philistinism and materialism of the times inspired the satire of Sinclair Lewis and the ridicule of H. L. Mencken; it also drove many of the most talented writers into self-imposed exile. Among critics of American social and political life there was widespread questioning or outright rejection of the doctrine of equality, the belief in progress, and other presuppositions of liberal democracy. Some of the remedies proposed for the ills of modern society—such as guild socialism and various schemes of occupational representation—sought to give institutional expression to man's craving for solidarity and community.[97] The architect Ralph Adams Cram was a writer whose social criticism, like Kenkel's, was explicitly related to his admiration for the Middle Ages.[98]

The European Catholic social theorists on whom Kenkel relied most heavily were even more deeply unsympathetic to liberalism and democracy, and from the first, Kenkel's attraction to the Middle Ages was intimately related to his spiritual estrangement from modern society. In addition, in the 1920's a spokesman for the German-American Catholics had much more reason than other intellectuals to be alienated from contemporary American life. Consider the situation of the group with which Kenkel identified himself and which he hoped would lead the way in healing society's sickness. Without adequate justification, the United States had fought a war against the mother country, and a humiliating peace had been imposed upon her. The German-American Catholics had suffered indignities at home because of the intolerant nationalism aroused by the war. Their language declined precipitously in the 1920's; their organizations were decimated by losses among the younger generation. They had become "a people without spiritual descendants"; they found no joy in working for the future and were afflicted by "a certain weariness, a gloomy hopelessness."[99] Their importance had diminished in the American Catholic Church; their contributions did not receive due recognition among Catholic social reformers; and interest in reform had almost disappeared among the American people at large.

Merely considered in the abstract, modern society was moving in the wrong direction according to Kenkel's social philosophy; but in its immediate effects upon the German-American Catholics, the course of American life might well appear calamitous. When the social criticism of Kenkel and Engelen is situated in this context, it becomes more readily understandable as a reaction to all the wrong turnings of recent American history. The Central-Verein writers endorsed some of the values of other middle-class Americans, but they felt that these values were being overwhelmed by the tendency of events and that they were partially vitiated in the American ideology by association with the philosophy of individualistic liberalism. To Kenkel and Engelen the middle-class virtues of independence and self-help could be properly realized only when the *Mittelstand* took its rightful place in an "organic" society structured along the lines of vocational "estates." In a healthy corporative order, individual initiative and self-reliance would be complemented by voluntary mutual assistance. Selfish individualism would be replaced by concern for the common good; brotherhood and cooperation would prevail and the antagonistic "classes" of a society pulverized by the atomistic philosophy of liberalism would be done away with. A society animated by solidaric communal feeling would not only guarantee social harmony, it would also answer man's deepest spiritual needs and permit the full flowering of human personality.

This was the utopian vision of Kenkel and Engelen. They projected it back upon the medieval past in much the same manner that the early German romantics idealized the Middle Ages as a reaction to the Enlightenment and its offspring, the French Revolution. Indeed, one can find in Novalis' essay "Die Christenheit oder Europa," a classic romanticization of the Middle Ages, almost the exact language that Engelen used in describing the halcyon times when "In happy cities happy guilds, filled with a social spirit, spread true happiness to the smallest home and shop."[100] To Kenkel, medieval society was good because it was "organic": It was a living social unity in which each individual fitted into a group having some functional role to fulfill. By performing its proper function, each "estate" contributed to the health of the whole; the health of the total organism was in turn transmitted to all the member parts and individual constituents of society. But as Reinhold Aris remarked of the corporative theory of Joseph Görres, the German Catholic publicist of the nineteenth century, the "organic metaphor" can best be understood "as a poetic transcription of his desire for unity" rather than as an attempt to grapple with the problem of reconciling the conflicting forces in society.[101] For in spite of the wealth of social analysis in the *Central-Blatt and Social Justice*, Kenkel never explained just how the corporative order was to be applied in American society or how the immense political complications it would involve were to be overcome.

No doubt Kenkel did not conceive it to be his task to enter into these details regarding the application of corporative theory. Judging from the discussions in the *Central-Blatt*, he envisioned his role as that of one who points out the inadequacies of the present system, describes in broad outline the alternative scheme, warns against developments that militate against it, exhorts to the spiritual change its introduction will entail, and encourages movements that hold some promise for future development. Kenkel was not primarily interested in the technicalities of social questions; he was even less interested in strictly economic or political questions. Rather he was passionately concerned with religious, moral, intellectual, and aesthetic matters—with the spiritual side of man's existence. Because of the personal alienation he felt in modern society and because of the social factors affecting the group with which his fate was linked, Kenkel found the life around him oppressive in the 1920's. Hence the critique he presented became more negative and at times a note of querulous embitterment crept into it. Existing society was abominable; a fundamental reconstruction was needed. Yet the reform proposals that seemed most popular would only compound the evil. The new order had to grow from small beginnings among a people converted to a new consciousness of solidarity; it could not be imposed from above, and all forms of revolution were inadmissible. In these circumstances there was little Kenkel could do but maintain his criticism of American society, keep his utopian vision before the people, and point out the shortcomings of all other reforms.

IX

The Pattern Is Maintained

In 1930 the Central-Verein marked its diamond jubilee. The convention in Baltimore, the same city where representatives from a handful of German Catholic societies created the national federation in 1855, was "an occasion of warranted rejoicing."[1] The organization could take pride in its long and fruitful career. Messages of congratulation poured in from all over the United States and from Germany, and Frederick P. Kenkel was honored by the presentation of the Laetare Medal— an award conferred annually by the University of Notre Dame on an outstanding Catholic layman for distinguished service to Church and country.

In spite of the rejoicing and the honors, the great days of the Central-Verein were over. Ex-president Charles Korz, the jubilee speaker, promised a bright future if the present generation kept faith with their fathers; he could not forbear pointing out, however, that fewer men belonged to the organization than in the year of its fiftieth anniversary. In 1955, when Joseph Matt wrote the Central-Verein's centennial history, he devoted only a few paragraphs to the years after 1930 and claimed no more than that "a permanent weakening of the organization" was staved off in that period.[2]

The loss of membership that began in the twenties could not be reversed. The Central-Verein still numbered some 86,000 men in 1930; that figure had dropped below 40,000 by 1942. The affiliation of several Catholic fraternal insurance societies in 1942 swelled the numbers carried on the rolls of the organization but did little to strengthen it financially or in terms of committed members. As in the twenties the women's branch remained active, but efforts to win young men to the cause were largely unavailing. Since the original benevolent and fraternal society basis has been so deeply eroded, both women and men are presently concentrating on recruiting individual memberships. But in 1966 the men's organization listed almost as many names (302) on the "In Memoriam Honor Roll" of distinguished deceased members as in the various categories of individual memberships (311 names).[3]

The changing attitudes accompanying the Americanization of the younger generation are suggested by the remarks of a speaker before the convention in 1933. This priest noted that although it had once been "considered an act of gross disloyalty" even to mention the Knights of Columbus, the Texas branch was then giving its full support to a historical project undertaken by the Knights of Columbus in that state.[4]

Another indication of the changing psychology of the membership mentioned by the same speaker was the almost universal use of the English language.[5] Changing the name of the magazine from *Central-Blatt and Social Justice* to *Social Justice Review* in 1940 was the last great landmark in the linguistic transition. But ethnic consciousness continued to manifest itself in the form of interest in the history of the German Catholic element in the United States. When the final remaining German-language section was eliminated from the journal in 1946, one of the reasons given was to permit the inclusion of more notes devoted to the history of the German-American Catholics.[6] Kenkel had been featuring such items since 1917, a year of critical importance in the relationship of German-Americans to their adopted homeland, and the file of the magazine contains a wealth of historical information. Kenkel's personal love for history was also largely responsible for the creation of a library specializing in Catholic German-Americana and socioeconomic studies. The housing of this mass of newspapers, organizational records, and books was undertaken in the difficult days of the Depression; in the 1960's many of the most valuable items were made more widely available on microfilm. The library, established as an adjunct of the Central Bureau, contains the finest collection of its kind and may well stand as the most lasting monument to the organized efforts of the German-American Catholics and to the vision of their greatest leader.

Strengthened by the endowment drive of the 1920's, the Central Bureau withstood the hard times and played an indispensable role in holding the national organization together in spite of declining support. Kenkel's heroic dedication to the cause kept him on the job as its active director until his death in 1952, at the age of eighty-eight. Besides enhancing its value as a repository of historical source materials, Kenkel and his successors carried forward the Bureau's other activities. The St. Elizabeth Day Nursery was maintained, and the Bureau also continued to supply the needs of missionaries in many parts of the world. After World War II it again undertook a program of relief for war sufferers and assisted in resettling displaced persons in the United States. It has likewise continued to publish pamphlets on social and religious topics; the publication of the *Social Justice Review* and the *Journal* (earlier *Bulletin*) of the National Catholic Women's Union has been uninterrupted in spite of their limited circulation. Today the *Social Justice Review* has a circulation of about 2,300; the organ of the women's society approximately 1,800.

Just as the organizational trends that emerged so clearly in the 1920's dominated the later period, so also did the Central-Verein's ideological development follow along lines marked out in the years after World War I. Its spokesmen remained highly critical of American society and called repeatedly for fundamental reforms, but its position was deeply conservative. Kenkel's overriding fear of state socialism and his distaste for federal paternalism had more in common with the laissez-faire conservatism of the business community than with any school of American reformers, although he rejected the classical liberalism of the former along with the new-model liberalism of the latter. During the first months of the New Deal, Central-Verein leaders shared in the enthusiasm generated by Franklin Roosevelt's personality and were encouraged by his administration's bold assault on the Depression.[7] But as early as June, 1933, Kenkel detected a drift toward "the bitter end of State Socialism," and he could not discern in the New Deal the approximation of the social order prescribed in *Quadragesimo Anno* that other Catholic reformers hailed.[8] His reservations on both scores were strengthened by the passage of time. In 1938 he condemned "so-called Liberals" who were leading the country toward the authoritarianism of contemporary European states, and in later years he remained bitterly critical of the centralization that had been so greatly augmented by the New Deal.[9]

Totalitarianism was completely repugnant to the Central-Verein, and World War II did not cause the same sort of psychological earthquake as the first World War, but in the 1950's the *Social Justice Review* defended the German people against the charge of being collectively guilty of all the crimes of the Hitler regime.[10] After the atomic era was well begun, Kenkel still regarded Karl von Vogelsang and his romantic followers in Vienna as the most satisfactory authorities in social criticism and reform. The meliorist school of German Catholic reformers, whose center at München-Gladbach provided the original model for the Central Bureau's activities, he dismissed as "appeasers of the existing political, social and economic order."[11] But the European experience of the thirties did make Kenkel more cautious and discriminating about corporative reconstruction and its application. He not only rejected Fascism and Nazism but also denied that such a "corporate state" as Portugal corresponded to the "corporative order" that Pope Pius XI had in mind in *Quadragesimo Anno*. It certainly was not what Kenkel thought of as a truly organic order, but, as the *Central-Blatt* noted several times, it was extraordinarily difficult to get across to Americans the notion of a corporative society structured according to vocational "estates."[12]

Perhaps in an effort to present the complexities of the business, the magazine even published one article in 1939 that showed the utter unworkability of corporatism as a political system! But this critique by the political scientist F. A. Hermens was exceptional, for the corporative order remained Kenkel's ideal.[13] It was not systematically promoted in the 1940's, however, and as the corporative goal grew ever more remote and vague, the conclusion is reinforced that it served for Kenkel not as a real alternative to the prevailing system but as a romantic vision of social harmony which could be contrasted to the ugliness and inequities of the modern world. After Kenkel's death it ceased to serve even that function. Since 1952 discussions of the corporative order have virtually disappeared from the *Social Justice Review;* it has concentrated instead on the dangers of communism and secularism, on educational questions, and on the general cultural crisis of our times. Thus has the situation of the German-American Catholics changed dramatically since the first decade of the present century. In 1910 they were still a large and self-assertive group; their national organization was newly invigorated, gaining in members, and plunging into the liveliest currents of Progressive reform. A half-century later the group can hardly be said to exist at all. The language is but a memory, and the dynamism is utterly gone from their associational life. A surviving remnant remains loyal to the old ethnic organization, but the Central-Verein (now called the Catholic Central Union) no longer stresses its German character, and the accent in which it speaks seems more a matter of ideological conservatism than of German nationality.

A fuller examination of the years since 1930 would shed more light on the final phases of this development, but it would not change the story essentially. The first three decades of the century are the crucial period, and since we have covered those years in detail we can now inquire what the Central-Verein's involvement with the social question reveals about the evolution of a Catholic ethnic group.

The Creative Moment

The Central-Verein's dedication to social reform is inextricably connected with the Americanization of the German Catholic group, and it began as part of a brilliantly creative response to a critical phase of this process. The emergence of the more assimilated second generation at the turn of the century, coupled with the collapse of the Widows and Orphans Fund and the creation of the American Federation of Catholic Societies, threatened to fragment the German Catholic *Vereinswesen* and thereby to accelerate the dissolution of the group. By judicious adjustments in respect to language and organizational form, the Central-Verein not only forestalled the disintegration of the *Vereins-*

wesen but also brought within its fold virtually all the German Catholic societies in the country, making itself *the* organizational symbol for the group. Although this in itself was a very considerable achievement, more was needed; the enlarged and rejuvenated federation had to have a mission that could focus the energies of its constitutent societies and give them meaningful activities to pursue. Nicholas Gonner had tried to use social reform for this purpose before the organizational problems were solved. That effort failed, but when the structural reorganization was complete and the Central-Verein began casting about for some task to assume, it moved more successfully into the field of reform.

The Central-Verein's selection of social reform as the mission that would furnish its raison d'être was an inspired choice. It was admirably suited to command the support of a second generation that was attuned to the prevailing temper of American life. As members of the working and middle classes, the men of the Central-Verein were subject to the same influences that turned the attention of other Americans toward the social question. And because of the socialist threat to traditional religion, the issue of social reform had relevance even to the most conservative segments of the German Catholic population. It appealed to personalities as diverse as the Americanized activist, Father Dietz, and the scholarly romantic, Kenkel. In short, it opened up a field of action in which a broadly attractive organizational program could be mounted, and this was precisely what the Central-Verein needed after its reorganization.

But while it had relevance to the American scene and enlisted the support of the younger and more Americanized element, social reform was also an activity that allowed the Central-Verein to draw on a new strain of its German heritage and forge new connections with the Catholic life of Germany. Moreover, it was presented in such a way that it seemed a new modulation of the German Catholics' earlier opposition to the liberal Americanists, who were said to deny the existence of the social question in the United States. Thus there were strong links between the social reform mission and the German Catholic past, both in this country and in the old homeland. Because of this continuity, social reform could be portrayed as a task the German-American Catholics were especially well qualified to take up and for which they should feel a special responsibility. Since it was a task to which they were particularly called, it permitted a reformulation of the symbolism of ethnic loyalty—that is, dedication to the Central-Verein's social reform program offered a means of manifesting one's loyalty to the German Catholic group and its traditions, even though the language and customs of the homeland had been largely abandoned. The sociologist Nathan Glazer has characterized the evolution of immigrant ethnicity in the United States as moving from "national culture" to "ideology," by which he means that the sense of nationality endures as an idea even after the disappearance of the language and other concrete cultural forms in which it was originally embedded.[14] Reformulating the symbolism of German-American Catholic ethnicity in terms of dedication to social reform represented a process of this general sort, and it was at least partially self-conscious. In the 1880's and 1890's "the German cause" was understood as involving the defense of language and nationality against the onslaughts of the Americanizers. But after 1908 the German Catholic cause was deliberately associated with the Central-Verein's reform program and its social philosophy of Solidarism. The older espousal of mother tongue and cultural distinctiveness was not suddenly abandoned; rather it was gradually relaxed. But alongside these traditional objects of loyalty, devotion to social reform furnished a new and more universalistic mode of expressing ethnic loyalty that was accessible to the American-born generations whose "cultural" ethnicity was already attenuated.[15]

Reformulating the symbolism of ethnic loyalty on a higher level of abstraction was an impressive achievement, and it added years to the normal life-expectancy of an organization like the Central-Verein. But social reform was also an intrinsically worthwhile and needful activity. This is the final reason for characterizing the new mission as a highly creative response to a crisis of Americanization. By plunging into the social question, the Central-Verein was not merely giving itself something to do that appealed to the second generation; it was widening the scope of its activities to include the whole of American society and placing itself directly in line with the most dynamic and progressive currents of American life. It responded to the challenge of assimilation by "Americanizing" the focus of its activities in the most positive way. There were problems in American society crying out for attention and rectification, and the Central-Verein allied itself with the forces committed to doing something about these problems. While its work was of only peripheral significance in the Progressive movement as a whole, the Central-Verein was nonetheless part of that high-minded effort to improve social, economic, and political conditions in our national life. Within the subculture of American Catholicism, the Central-Verein played a more noteworthy role. Its activities placed the German group in the vanguard of those who contributed to the awakening of American Catholic sensitivity to social problems in the twentieth century. It provided a vehicle and forum for individual leaders like Dietz and Kenkel; it stimulated the social awareness of a traditionally withdrawn sector of the Catholic population; and its efforts heartened other Catholic reformers like John A. Ryan, who always regarded the Central-Verein as an ally in the campaign to mobilize the Church behind the banners of reform.

The Failure of Creative Response

In staving off what seemed to be disintegration and in forging a program that served group needs while at the same time establishing positive contact with the most progressive forces of American society, German Catholic leaders had turned in a brilliant performance. The high promise of the beginning, however, was not maintained. Perhaps nothing better could have been devised even with the most inspired leadership, for the difficulties were intricate and great. However that may be, the fact is that as the assimilation of the German-American Catholics continued the Central-Verein lost ground steadily, its influence in American Catholicism was reduced, and its ideological alignment with the forces of progressivism was replaced by a negative rejection of American society that brought it more in line with ultraconservatives than with any reform group on the national scene.

One reason the Central-Verein lost touch with progressive forces in the 1920's was that those forces largely disappeared. There was some persistence of reform energies after World War I, but it was no longer a cause with great popular appeal. The theorists of the Central-Verein also isolated themselves ideologically from other reformers, and they repudiated the means favored by most others to achieve social improvements: reliance on government power. The society continued to identify itself as one devoted to working for social reform, however, and the point to be stressed here is that this mission was less functionally useful in the doldrums of normalcy than it had been in the heyday of Progressivism. The temper of the people had changed; they were not so disposed to react favorably to appeals for support issued in the name of reform. In stressing agricultural problems, the Central-Verein was hitting on what was perhaps the timeliest issue of the 1920's. But, in spite of its timeliness, this emphasis was more closely related to the interests of those who were already members of the Central-Verein than it was to the interests of those whose support the organization needed to attract. Young Catholics of German descent, like other Americans of their generation, were drifting away from farming; they were not apt to be swept into a society increasingly preoccupied with agricultural problems and rural-life enthusiasms.

More damaging to the organization than the diminished attractiveness of the social reform mission was the erosion of German Catholic self-consciousness. The primary appeal of the Central-Verein was to those who thought of themselves as German-American Catholics, and the process of assimilation steadily weakened this sense of ethnic identity. The removal by death of more of the older generation; the decay of the German language; the detachment of the younger generation from exclusive identification with German Catholic friendship groups, neighborhoods, schools, parishes, and other institutions of group life; the progressive adoption of American norms in all spheres of life—all of these trends reduced the number of those who still retained a strong enough sense of being German-American Catholics to prompt them to join an organization whose primary function was to represent the ethnic group and mobilize its energies. A tradition of belonging to the Central-Verein on the part of a family or local society doubtless reinforced the loyalty of many of the members, but in the twenties, increasing numbers—especially among the younger generation—no longer were interested.

These developments made the Central-Verein's task more difficult in the postwar era. But in its period of greatest success it was unable to enlist the full support of *all* Catholics of German descent, even among those most concerned over the social question. One of the principal sources of difficulty with Father Dietz, for example, was that he was too Americanized. His consuming ambition was to get a large-scale action program under way in the area of labor reform, and his lack of sensitivity to the special needs and limitations of an organization like the Central-Verein amply justified the decision to remove him from any policy-making position. The Jesuits Frederic Siedenburg and Joseph Husslein were two other priests of German Catholic descent committed to social reform and sympathetic to the goals of the Central-Verein who chose to work through different and non-German agencies. Archbishop Sebastian Messmer was primarily committed to the American Federation of Catholic Societies, although he was always friendly to the Central-Verein. And F. W. Heckenkamp perhaps fell into the category of Joseph Frey's "backsliding Germans" since he felt that the Central-Verein pursued too nationalistic a policy in its relations with the Federation.

The first World War hastened the process of assimilation and made membership in German organizations less inviting to many of the younger generation than it might otherwise have been. This development, along with the diminished attractiveness of the reform mission, created a need for imaginative and flexible leadership comparable to the need that existed in the first decade of the century. Postwar leadership, however, did not display these qualities. Instead a certain rigidity overtook the Central-Verein. No new mission was formulated; the new activities and emphases of the period were essentially derivations from the pattern previously established; and there was an almost harsh insistence on the rightness of what the Central-Verein was doing and the things it stood for. The relative absence of flexibility and creativeness, and the hardening of the Central-Verein's position, were at least partially consequences of a historical contingency, the traumatic experience of the war. This great national aberration from sound policy deepened the conviction of theorists like Kenkel and Engelen that American society was fundamentally defective. It embittered them and reinforced their tendencies toward alienation; their views of modern American society became almost wholly negative and critical. In reaction, they turned more sharply toward corporative theories of a profoundly conservative sort. The ideological commitment to utopian corporatism offered few points of contact with the realities of American life. Rather it added to the difficulties of formulating a positive program that would be attractive to American-born generations, whose outlook was shaped by the society in which they had always lived.

The Paradox of Conservative Reformers

The conservatism of the Central-Verein's ideological position emerged clearly in the 1920's, but it was not really new. That element had been present even in the organization's most progressive moment before the war. One aspect of conservatism was reflected in the fact that combating the socialist threat was the cause with the widest appeal in the prewar years. Kenkel, of course, insisted that it was not enough merely to fight socialism, and he agreed with the socialists in much of their criticism of existing society. But in criticizing American social evils, Kenkel was inspired by a vision of preindustrial harmony and solidarity.

Kenkel's conviction of the need for drastic social reconstruction sprang from an intense personal experience of estrangement from the modern world. His depression and sense of isolation in the 1890's he attributed to the meaninglessness of life in an age that had lost all consciousness of spiritual order and unity. Together with sensitive Americans of his own day such as Josiah Royce,[16] and much like the alienated student radicals of the 1960's, Kenkel longed passionately for a great, a "beloved" community—a condition of human fellowship in which the liveliest awareness of human solidarity would permeate all of society, reducing the tendencies toward egoistic individualism while at the same time permitting the fullest development of personality. He found in the Christian Middle Ages the model for such a social order. Although this might seem an unlikely source of inspiration to a modern reformer, it was quite in keeping with Kenkel's personal historical interests, with the widespread Catholic nostalgia for the European ages of faith, and with the tradition of German Catholic social thought that was most accessible to him.

In the prewar years Kenkel's inclination toward romantic medieval corporatism was counterbalanced by divergent influences from the meliorist school of German Catholic social thought centered at München-Gladbach. Moreover, the stringency of Kenkel's criticism of existing social abuses, which accorded so closely to the prevailing currents of Progressivism, masked the basically conservative character of his thought. Even then, however, he called for fundamental social reconstruction along corporative lines, and he drew attention to the dangers of centralization and state socialism. The shattering experience of the war, the growth of federal power, the conservative temper of the times, the accelerating disintegration of the group with which he associated himself, and the discouraging organizational situation of the Central-Verein all played a part in giving a negatively conservative cast to Kenkel's thinking in the 1920's and later. Everything around him was moving in the wrong direction, and the corporative ideal seemed by contrast all the more alluring. The revival of organic theories in Germany and Austria also provided a warrant for his rejection of modern society and reinforced his predilection for romantic utopian corporatism.

Although it was conservative, Kenkel's ideological position (and that of the Central-Verein) was radically reformist in the sense that it envisioned fundamental changes in the social order. It looked to a restoration in some new form of the old organic society made up of functional vocational estates such as had existed in the Middle Ages. Modern individualism, capitalism, secularism, and political centralization dissolved the medieval organic order and destroyed or seriously weakened the traditional institutions of family, guild, and church that played so important a role in the functioning of medieval society. Robert A. Nisbet argues brilliantly that these developments are at the root of the contemporary malaise of alienation and that the disappearance of subordinate social institutions in which the individual could find a solidaric community paved the way for twentieth-century nationalism and totalitarianism.[17] Kenkel experienced alienation, but he resisted with all his strength the tendency to magnify the state. His version of what Nisbet calls "the quest for community" envisioned, rather, a reconstitution of subsidiary social groupings (vocational estates) that could reclaim some of the power that had improperly devolved upon the state and provide alternative centers of moral authority, communal solidarity, and human loyalty.

In prescribing vocational corporations as a remedy for the disorder and anomie brought on by industrial capitalism, Kenkel agreed with

Emile Durkheim, who added a preface on the desirability of such institutions to the second edition of his *Division of Labor in Society* in 1902.[18] Kenkel's alienation and insistence on community also provide points of contact with today's social critics of a "new left" persuasion. But the restoration of the organic corporative society runs directly counter to some of the most powerful trends of the modern world, and it obviously would require a drastic restructuring of social life. As an ideology, romantic corporatism furnished an admirable platform from which to criticize the weaknesses of American society, but there were enormous obstacles in the way of its practical application. The ideology itself forbade reliance on the government to promulgate reforms, and revolution or other forms of violence were out of the question. Hence there was little that could be done in a positive way except to buttress the institutions of family and church, encourage such movements as cooperatives and credit unions, and reiterate the need for a renewal of the social spirit and a fundamental reorientation of social life. The patent inadequacy of the means suggested for achieving their goals lent an air of unreality to the whole social reform message of the Central-Verein. Its voice, which had been timely and pertinent in the prewar era, became less relevant and compelling in later years. Like many another reformer of the Progressive period, the organization subsequently settled into the role of conservative critic.

The Ambiguities of Americanization

There has been a good deal of talk in recent years about American Catholicism's "emergence from the ghetto," but the precise nature of that process has neither been clearly described nor investigated in depth. Somewhat similarly, the terms "assimilation" and "Americanization" are not as clear as they might be and are often used rather loosely by writers on immigration—as, indeed, they are in this book. But our study does offer some basis for a clarification of these notions, directly in respect to the German-American Catholics and indirectly for other groups and for the American Church as a whole. We shall not try to formulate precise definitions but to distinguish different aspects of Americanization and point out a fundamental problem implied by the process.

In general, the terms "Americanization" and "assimilation"—and, by extension, the expression "emergence from the ghetto"—are understood as designating the process by which individuals and identifiable social groups shed the characteristics that mark them as foreign, adopt the cultural norms of American society, become fully integrated into American life, and come to think of themselves simply as Americans. The individual and group levels of the process, although conceptually distinguishable, are in practice inseparably interwoven—as individuals are assimilated the foreign groups they comprise are necessarily affected by the changes taking place among their membership. Americanization at the level of the organized group refers to adjustments made by ethnic organizations in the effort to keep pace with the changes wrought by assimilation among their membership.

Ethnic organizations, such as the Central-Verein, come into being because a certain segment of the population thinks of itself as having a distinctive identity; to use Milton M. Gordon's term, it has a sense of its "peoplehood."[19] These formal institutions make possible a common associational life for the members of the ethnic group; they also serve as symbols for the distinctiveness of the group and as objects of common loyalty. To the degree that it is a structured body rather than a formless collectivity of individuals, ethnic organizations actually *constitute* the group.

Since they institutionalize and embody ethnic consciousness, these organizations appeal primarily to those with the liveliest awareness of their own distinctiveness, and they move toward Americanization more slowly than many of the individuals who share the common heritage. But as more members of the group Americanize, the ethnic organization must adjust to the changing situation or it will die when there are no longer enough old-timers to maintain it on the former basis. Such an organization must find a way to enlist the support of those whose self-identification differs only in a very marginal way from that of other Americans. In appealing to this element, however, it must avoid the appearance of betraying its own distinctive heritage, for it is precisely the preservation of this heritage that is its basic purpose and the surest grounds of its appeal. When the theoretically ultimate stage of assimilation is reached—that point at which *all* sense of ethnic distinctiveness has been lost—the organization must either die or justify itself as a strictly American association, making no claims for support on the basis of its peculiar heritage. But until that ultimate stage arrives, the problem for an ethnic organization (which is also the problem for the group as a group) is twofold. How, on the one hand, is it to preserve an inherited distinctiveness in American society without cutting itself off from society, becoming isolated, irrelevant, and unable to play a meaningful role? And how, on the other hand, is it to place itself in contact with and play a constructive role in American society without being completely absorbed by that society, thereby disappearing as a group distinguished by a heritage and identity of its own?

Let us apply these considerations to the history of the Central-Verein. Assimilation on the level of the individual members of the German-American Catholic group is most clearly reflected in two developments frequently mentioned in these pages: adoption of the English language and declining support for the Central-Verein. Use of the mother tongue and participation in the national organization of the German-American Catholics were at the same time expressions of ethnic loyalty and important means of preserving the identity and coherence of the ethnic group. Changes in these two spheres therefore required corresponding adjustments on the part of the Central-Verein; these adjustments constitute the group level of Americanization for the German-American Catholics.

One example of Americanization at the group level was the structural remodeling of the Central-Verein in the years 1900 to 1905. This adjustment permitted the inclusion in the national federation of more modern types of fraternals in addition to the original parish benevolent societies, and by unifying the *Vereinswesen* it shored up the ethnic group from the organizational viewpoint. The establishment of a bilingual journal and similar concessions to English that continued after the period of reorganization also registered on the institutional level the assimilation that was proceeding apace among the members. A third example of Americanization at the organizational level was the enlarged scope provided for women's activities, especially in the 1920's.

The most positive and original step in organizational Americanization was the assumption of the social reform mission, which widened the focus of the Central-Verein's activities to embrace—at least in intention—the whole of American society. The reform mission seemed ideally suited to allow the German-American Catholics to preserve their ethnic distinctiveness while simultaneously keeping them in fruitful contact with the most progressive currents in American life. By preserving identity without isolation and allowing participation without absorption, the reform mission triumphantly climaxed the Central-Verein's response to the challenge of Americanization in the Progressive period. But success once achieved did not perpetuate itself automatically. Steering between the Scylla of self-isolation and the Charybdis of total absorption required a constantly self-correcting reconciliation of divergent tendencies. After the war, the Central-Verein could not adequately meet the renewed and even more serious challenge of Americanization unless it made new adjustments as creative as those of the Progressive era. Equally creative adjustments, however, were not forthcoming; and as more individuals moved toward absorption into American society, the organization moved in the direction of self-isolation. The social reform mission could not prevent the steady erosion of the group through assimilation on the individual level, but it assumed an ideological form so critical of American society and so out of touch with the American spirit that it offered little scope for positive participation in the national life by the Central-Verein. Involvement in the social question helped bring the organized German-American Catholics out of an ethnic ghetto and into the mainstream of American society in the Progressive period. By 1930, however, commitment to social reform meant a rejection of American society that came close to shutting Central-Verein within the walls of an ideological ghetto.

The Central-Verein was led by dedicated and intelligent men, it stood for many worthwhile values, and it achieved some notable successes. But it did not find a permanently satisfactory solution to the problem of Americanization. Its failure was not without an element of tragedy and the efforts of its leaders deserve our respect. The experience of the organization may also have an exemplary value for the Catholic Church in the United States because assimilation has become a general problem in the 1960's. On the individual level, assimilation has made Catholics more like other Americans than they have ever been before, both in respect to social status and in respect to attitudes, beliefs, and self-image. With the decline of their self-consciousness as a distinct social group, Catholics have begun increasingly to question the desirability of maintaining separate Catholic schools or other "ghetto" organizations. Mounting demands for freedom and democratic structures in the Church give further evidence that Americanization will soon make itself felt with new intensity at the institutional level. The history of the Central-Verein demonstrates that institutional adjustments must follow upon changes in the social composition of the group that constitutes the clientele of an ethnic organization. Its history also illustrates how difficult it is to weather these changes successfully. There are important differences, to be sure, between the members of an ethnic group and Catholics considered as a social group, and between an ethnic organization and the Catholic Church. Allowing for these differences, there remains an underlying similarity between the situation of the Church and that of the Central-Verein. For the Church, as for the Central-Verein, the positive aim is to participate in a meaningful way in American life while preserving a distinctive identity that permits critical detachment from American society and judgment of it from a perspective not defined exclusively by the surrounding social milieu. To achieve this aim, the Church must steer between two perils, neither of which the Central-Verein wholly avoided. On the one hand, the Church's effort to adjust to the changing character of its clientele and to make itself relevant to American society must not be allowed to verge over into total absorption of the Church by society. But on the other hand, excessive concern to preserve the distinctive identity of Catholicism and to bring a critical judgment to bear on society must not be permitted to drive the Church into a false opposition to society, thus isolating her and making her totally irrelevant to the concerns of Catholics and other Americans.

The relationship of the Christian to the world and of the Church to society are perennial problems, but they must be pondered afresh by every generation. We confront them in this time and place as problems of Americanization. The long struggle of the Central-Verein stands as a witness to the difficulties involved; if its history has a lesson for American Catholics, it is to be sought in reflection on the ambiguities of Americanization.

ABBREVIATIONS USED IN THE NOTES

ACV

Archives of the Central Bureau of the Central-Verein, St. Louis, Missouri

AUND

Archives of the University of Notre Dame. Unless otherwise noted, all citations to this source refer to the papers of Frederick P. Kenkel.

CBSJ

Central-Blatt and Social Justice. In 1940 the name of this magazine was changed to *Social Justice Review* (see below, *SJR*).

CV Centennial

Joseph Matt, "Centenary of the Catholic Central Verein of America, Its Foundation and History," in *Official Program, Centennial Convention, The Catholic Central Verein of America* (Rochester, New York, 1955)

PAFF

Provincial Archives of the Franciscan Fathers, St. Louis, Missouri

SJR

Social Justice Review

55. General-Versammlung . . . 1910

Offizieller Bericht über die Fünfundfünfzigste General-Versammlung des Deutschen Römisch-Katholischen Central-Vereins gehalten in Newark, N.J., vom 11. bis 16. September 1910 (St. Louis, 1911). All of the Central-Verein convention proceedings are cited in the manner indicated, specifying the number of the convention and the year.

NOTES

Chapter I

1. Arturo Gaete, S.J., "The Paradox of North American Catholicism," in *Through Other Eyes: Some Impressions of American Catholicism by Foreign Visitors from 1777 to the present,* ed. D. Herr and J. Wells (Westminster, Md., 1965), p. 226.

2. Barry's book was published in Milwaukee in 1953. Georg Timpe, ed. *Katholisches Deutschtum in den Vereinigten Staaten von Amerika* (Freiburg im Breisgau, 1937) is a collection of essays of uneven value. The standard works on German immigration, Albert B. Faust, *The German Element in the United States,* 2 vols. (New York, 1909), and John A. Hawgood, *The Tragedy of German-America* (New York and London, 1940), contain very little on German Catholics. Much of the work of recent historians of American Catholicism bearing on the German Catholics is summarized in Robert D. Cross, *The Emergence of Liberal Catholicsm in America* (Cambridge, Mass., 1958). For the eighteenth and early nineteenth centuries see Lambert Schrott, O.S.B., *Pioneer German Catholics in the American Colonies (1734–1784)* (New York, 1933), and Emmet H. Rothan, O.F.M., *The German Catholic Immigrant in the United States (1830–1860)* (Washington, 1946).

3. Edward R. F. Sheehan, "Not Peace, But the Sword," *Saturday Evening Post,* Nov. 28, 1964, p. 39.

4. Thomas Beer, *The Mauve Decade* (New York: Vintage paperback ed., 1961), p. 114; Sheehan, *op. cit.,* p. 25, quotes Niebuhr; for Hofstadter see his *Anti-intellectualism in American Life* (New York, 1963), p. 138.

5. Cf. Paul Marx, O.S.B., *Virgil Michel and the Liturgical Movement* (St. Paul, 1957), and "Catholicism Midwest Style," *America,* CXIV (Feb. 12, 1966), 221–30.

6. Cf. Karl J. R. Arndt and May E. Olson, *Deutsch-Amerikanische Zeitungen und Zeitschriften, 1732–1955,* 2nd rev. ed. (New York, 1965), pp. 231–32, and Joseph Kreuter, " 'Der Wanderer' und sein Redakteur," in Timpe, *op. cit.,* pp. 82–84.

7. *Catholic Fortnightly Review,* XVI (1909), 685–87; *ibid.,* XVII (1910), 20–21, 113–114.

8. Father Joseph Kundek, an active promoter of German Catholic settlement in southern Indiana, obviously considered the German Catholics as quite a distinct group from other Americans when he advised them in 1846 to present a united front in politics. The "German Catholics never do well at an election," he wrote, "except they hold together—Jasper, Ferdinand, Celestine, One; and it'll go—else the German Catholic vote will not be regarded and I can not effect any good for you with the Americans once they find out they can divide us and set us against one another. . . ." Quoted in Albert Kleber, O.S.B., *Ferdinand,*

Indiana, 1840–1940 (St. Meinrad, Ind., 1940), p. 77. For other comments on German Catholic self-consciousness around the same period see Joseph Salzbacher, *Meine Reise nach Nord-Amerika im Jahre 1842* (Vienna, 1845), p. 189, and Gilbert J. Garraghan, S.J., *The Jesuits of the Middle United States,* 3 vols. (New York, 1938), II, 46–47.

9. Cf. Heinz Kloss, *Um die Einigung des Deutschamerikanertums* (Berlin, 1937), *passim,* esp. p. 36 ff.

10. Carl Wittke, *Refugees of Revolution* (Philadelphia, 1952), Ch. X; M. Hedwigis Overmoehle, F.S.P.A., "The Anti-Clerical Activities of the Forty-eighters in Wisconsin, 1848–1860" (unpublished doctoral dissertation, St. Louis University, 1941); F. P. Kenkel, "Subjected to an Acid Test," *CBSJ,* XVIII (Aug.-Sept., 1925), 163–64, 198–200.

11. Thomas T. McAvoy, C.S.C., argues persuasively for the basic Anglo-American character of American Catholicism in his essays, "The Catholic Minority in the United States, 1789–1821," *Historical Records and Studies,* XXXIX-XL (1952), 33–50, and "The Formation of the Catholic Minority in the United States, 1820–1860," *Review of Politics,* X (Jan., 1948), 13–34. Barry, *op. cit.,* explores the difficulties of German Catholic adjustment in the nineteenth century.

12. *Pastoral-Blatt,* XXII (Nov., 1888), 123.

13. *33. General-Versammlung . . . 1888,* p. 45; *53. General-Versammlung . . . 1908,* p. 11; *61. General-Versammlung . . . 1916,* p. 108 ff.; *68. General Versammlung . . . 1924,* p. 67. The same kind of tripartite identity was also characteristic of the Franco-Americans. See George F. Theriault, "The Franco-Americans of New England," in *Canadian Dualism . . .,* edited by Mason Wade (Toronto, 1960), p. 393. In 1924 the "Testament" of the recently deceased Bishop John E. Gunn of Natchez was quoted as follows: "In life and death I am proud of three things: my Irish birth, my Catholic faith, and my American citizenship. I tried to translate my love for all three into service and sacrifice." *CBSJ,* XVII (Apr., 1924), 30.

14. Barry, *op. cit.,* discusses the Priester-Verein and the St. Raphaels-Verein. For examples of other types of societies see Rothan, *op. cit.,* p. 108 ff.; Kleber, *op. cit.,* Ch. XV; Theod. Brüner, *Katholische Kirchengeschichte Quincy's . . .* (Quincy, Ill., 1887?, pp. 70 ff., 165, 227 ff., 301 ff.; and *Gedenk-Buch der St. Franziskus Seraphikus Gemeinde in Cincinnati, Ohio . . .* (Cincinnati, 1884), pp. 153–79. In 1861 the Jesuit vice-provincial in St. Louis wrote to his superior: "A general meeting of the conferences of St. Vincent de Paul took place . . . among our Germans [in St. Joseph's parish, run by the Jesuits] with wonderful fruit and to the lessening of that miserable spirit of nationality. The rest of the Germans have societies only for those of their own race." Quoted by Garraghan, *op. cit.,* II, 47.

15. This interpretation of ethnic consciousness and its relation to organizational activity was suggested by Joshua A. Fishman, "Organizational Interest in Language Maintenance," which is Chapter V of Fishman *et al., Language Loyalty in the United States,* a massive mimeograph report submitted in 1964 to the U.S. Office of Education. Cf. also Vladimir C. Nahirny and Joshua A. Fishman, "American Immigrant Groups: Ethnic Identification and the Problem of Generations," *The Sociological Review,* XIII (Nov., 1965), 311–26.

16. The evidence for this point and others that follow in the remainder of this chapter will be provided in succeeding chapters.

Chapter II

1. *Catholic Fortnightly Review*, XVI (1909), 685–86.
2. Bureau of the Census, *Special Reports: Religious Bodies: 1906* (Washington, 1910), pp. 18–19.
3. Derived from Johannes N. Enzlberger, *Schematismus der katholischen Geistlichkeit deutscher Zunge in den Vereinigten Staaten Amerikas* (Milwaukee, 1892).
4. Cf. Emmet H. Rothan, O.F.M., *The German Catholic Immigrant in the United States (1830–1860)* (Washington, 1946), p. 29 ff.; Anthony H. Deye, "Archbishop John Baptist Purcell of Cincinnati: Pre-Civil War Years" (unpublished doctoral dissertation, University of Notre Dame, 1959), Ch. V. In 1881, Cincinnati was the birthplace of forty-four German-speaking priests; Baltimore, with sixteen German vocations, was the closest any other American diocese came to this record. See W. Bonenkamp, J. Jessing, and J. B. Müller, *Schematismus der deutschen und der deutsch-sprechenden Priester . . .* (St. Louis, 1882), p. 156. A decade later, more of the German-speaking priests in the city were born in Cincinnati itself than in Europe. Derived from Enzlberger, *op. cit.*, pp. 56–61. Frederick Rese, who was the first German-speaking bishop, left his see city (Detroit) in 1841, after eight years as bishop, and spent the rest of his life in retirement.
5. Lambert Schrott, O.S.B., *Pioneer German Catholics in the American Colonies (1734–1784)* (New York, 1933), pp. 94–95; Francis J. Hertkorn, *A Retrospect of Holy Trinity Parish* (Philadelphia, 1914), p. 6 ff.
6. Schrott, *op. cit.*, p. 57 ff.; Hertkorn, *op. cit.*, pp. 11–20.
7. Many of the documents of the Holy Trinity affair are reprinted in Hertkorn, *op. cit.;* the quotation above is from p. 22. The account that follows is based on this work; on Patrick J. Dignan, *A History of the Legal Incorporation of Catholic Church Property in the United States (1784–1932)* (Washington, 1933), p. 79 ff.; and on Vincent J. Fecher, S.V.D., *A Study of the Movement for German National Parishes in Philadelphia and Baltimore (1787–1802)* (Rome, 1955).
8. Schrott, *op. cit.*, p. 60, refers to the purchase of the cemetery in 1768 as resulting from "the first signs of friction between the German and English-speaking Catholics"; and Hertkorn, *op. cit.*, p. 36, says that in 1789 Heilbron complained rather sharply to Carroll about "the antipathy and animosity existing between the German and English-speaking Catholics. . . ."
9. Fecher, *op. cit.*, p. 96.
10. Dignan, *op. cit.*, p. 266.
11. There is no comprehensive study of trusteeism. See the works of Dignan and Fecher cited above, and Peter Guilday, "Trusteeism," *Historical Records and Studies*, XVIII (1928), 7–73; John Tracy Ellis, *Catholics in Colonial America* (Baltimore, 1965), p. 444 ff., and Ellis, *Documents of American Catholic History* (Milwaukee, 1956), pp. 164–66, 219 ff.
12. Colman J. Barry, O.S.B., *The Catholic Church and German Americans* (Milwaukee, 1953), p. 6.
13. Edmund J. P. Schmitt, *Lose Blätter aus der Geschichte der Deutschen St. Marien Gemeinde von New Albany, Indiana . . .* (Cincinnati, 1890), p. 84; John B. Wuest, O.F.M., *One Hundred Years of St. Boniface Parish, Louisville, Kentucky . . .* (Louisville, 1937), pp. 50–53; William L. Lucey, S.J., *The Catholic Church in Maine* (Francistown, N.H., 1954), pp. 124–35.

14. Quoted in Rothan, *op. cit.*, pp. 115–16. Cf. Schmitt, *op. cit.*, pp. 82–84.

15. Cf. James F. Connelly, *The Visit of Archbishop Gaetano Bedini to the United States of America* (Rome, 1960), pp. 95–115; Deye, *op. cit.*, pp. 369–78.

16. A. F. Brockland, "Fr. Weninger's Encounters with German Atheists," *CBSJ*, XXIII (Jan., 1931), 347–48; Peter M. Abbelen, *Die Ehrwürdige Mutter Carolina Friess* (St. Louis, 1892), pp. 107–08; and *Mother Caroline and the School Sisters of Notre Dame in North America*, by "A School Sister of Notre Dame," 2 vols. (St. Louis, 1928), II, 92–93. Cf. also the citations given above in Chapter I, note 10.

17. *Berichte der Leopoldinen-Stiftung im Kaiserthume Oesterreich*, XXVII (1855), 84–85.

18. Peter Leo Johnson, *Halcyon Days: Story of St. Francis Seminary Milwaukee, 1856–1956* (Milwaukee, 1956), p. 52; F. P. Kenkel, "Die Thätigkeit der Volks-missionäre unter den deutschsprächigen Katholiken Amerikas," *CBSJ*, XIV (Sept., 1921), 187; Kenkel, "Die Stellung der deutsche Radikalen in Amerika zur Kirche und ihren Stammesgenossen," *CBSJ*, XIII (Dec., 1920), 274–76; Kenkel, "The Benevolent Society of Old vs. the Anti-Catholic Lodge," *CBSJ*, XX (Mar., 1928), 393; Rothan, *op. cit.*, p. 109 ff.

19. "Ziele des Centralvereins nach einem Einblattdruck des Jahres 1860," *CBSJ*, X (June, 1917), 73–74. On mutual aid societies, see William C. Smith, *Americans in the Making: The Natural History of the Assimilation of Immigrants* (New York and London, 1939), p. 96 ff., and Robert A. Park and Herbert A. Miller, *Old World Traits Transplanted* (New York and London, 1921), pp. 124–32.

20. *Berichte der Leopoldinen Stiftung*, XXVII (1855), 57.

21. *Four Historical Booklets Regarding the American Province of the Most Precious Blood Written by Francis DeSales Brunner* (Carthagena, O., 1957), p. 295; Michael J. Curley, C.SS.R., *The Provincial Story* (New York, 1963), p. 45; Albert Kleber, O.S.B. *Ferdinand, Indiana, 1840–1940* (St. Meinrad, Ind., 1940), p. 87.

22. Kleber, *op. cit.*, pp. 89–97; Wuest, *op. cit.*, pp. 48–50.

23. F. L. Kalvelage, *The Annals of St. Boniface Parish, 1862–1926* (Chicago, 1926), pp. 39–42; J. C. Bürgler, *Geschichte der kathol. Kirche Chicagos* (Chicago, 1889), pp. 57–58, 90; Mary Gilbert Kelly, O.P., *Catholic Immigrant Colonizing Projects in the United States, 1815–1860* (New York, 1939), p. 141.

24. "Aussöhnung einer verirrten Gemeinde mit Gott und der Kirche," *CBSJ*, XII (Nov.–Dec., 1919), 253–55, 287–89; *Annals of the Franciscan Province of the Sacred Heart*, No. 9, 1933 (n.p., n.d.), pp. 577–78; Curley, *op. cit.*, p. 53; F. G. Holweck, "Abbé Joseph Anton Lutz," *Pastoral-Blatt*, LI (Sept., 1917), 137–38; Hertkorn, *op. cit.*, pp. 100–01; Michael J. Curley, C.SS.R., *Venerable John Neumann, C.SS.R., Fourth Bishop of Philadelphia* (Washington, 1952), pp. 221–27.

25. On Trusteeism in New York, see Curley, *Provincial Story*, p. 48; Thomas Donahue, *History of the Catholic Church in Western New York* (Buffalo, 1904), pp. 141–89; Connelly, *op. cit.*, Ch. V; M. Felicity O'Driscoll, S.S.M., "Political Nativism in Buffalo, 1830–1860," *Records of the American Catholic Historical Society*, XLVIII (Sept., 1937), 279–319.

26. The quotation is from Thomas W. Mullaney, C.SS.R., *Four-Score Years: A Contribution to the History of the Catholic Germans in Rochester* (Rochester, N.Y., 1916), pp. 60–61; see also the account from the Buffalo *Aurora* in *Katholische Kirchen-Zeitung* (New York), Apr. 27, 1854. For the Rochester background, see Frederick J. Zwierlein, *The Life and Letters of Bishop McQuaid*, 3 vols. (Rochester,

N.Y., 1925–27), I, 197–222; John F. Byrne, C.SS.R., *The Redemptorist Centenaries* (Philadelphia, 1932), pp. 126–29.

27. *CV Centennial,* p. 46.

28. *Ibid.,* pp. 46–47; Mary Liguori Brophy, B.V.M., *The Social Thought of the German Roman Catholic Central Verein* (Washington, 1941), pp. 1–3.

29. Brophy, *op. cit.,* p. 3 n.; *CV Centennial,* p. 47.

30. These concepts are adopted from Robert K. Merton's well-known discussion, *Social Theory and Social Structure,* rev. ed. (Glencoe, Ill., 1957), p. 60 ff. Cf. also William I. Thomas and Florian Znaniecki, *The Polish Peasant in Europe and America,* 2nd ed., 2 vols. (New York, 1927), II, 1575 ff., esp. 1590–91.

31. The following account is based on the unpaged silver jubilee history of the society entitled, *1872–1897, Souvenir Programm des St. Bonaventura K. U. Vereins von Milwaukee, Wisc.* (n.p., n.d.), except for the item about optional life insurance which is taken from Joseph G. Grundle, *A Story of Pioneer Catholic Social Action* (Milwaukee, 1943), p. 10.

32. Quoted from F. X. Weninger, S.J., *Centennial Address to the Catholics of the United States* (New York, 1876), a pamphlet reprinted from the New York *Catholic Review.* See also A. F. Brockland, "What Fr. Weninger Wished the C. V. To Do," *CBSJ,* XIX (May, 1926), 58.

33. Brophy, *op. cit.,* p. 2.

34. For more details on the expansion of the CV's activities and the period of controversies, see John Philip Gleason, "The Central-Verein, 1900–1917: A Chapter in the History of the German-American Catholics" (unpublished doctoral dissertation, University of Notre Dame, 1960), pp. 20–73. The quotation is from p. 49. Cf. *New York Freeman's Journal,* Oct. 1, 1892.

35. The state of the *Vereinswesen* is discussed in more detail in Chapter III. For the national organizations mentioned above, see Barry, *op. cit.,* pp. 39–41, 98 ff., and Gleason, *op. cit.,* p. 36.

36. *New York Freeman's Journal,* Oct. 1, 1892. Cf. also, *Wahrheits-Freund* (Cincinnati), Sept. 28, 1892; and 37. *General-Versammlung . . . 1892,* pp. 37, 45–46.

37. A delegate to the 1893 CV convention reported this incident to Cardinal Gibbons. Peter Wallrath to Gibbons, Dec. 25, 1893, Archives of the Archdiocese of Baltimore, 95-W-5. The proceedings of the CV's convention do not record Goller's remarks. See 38. *General-Versammlung . . . 1893,* pp. 48, 56. Gibbons forwarded a copy of Wallrath's letter, omitting names, to Monsignor Denis O'Connell in Rome. The copy is in the Archives of the Diocese of Richmond, O'Connell Papers, Box 9.

38. *Northwestern Chronicle* (St. Paul), Aug. 10, 1888; Barry, *op. cit.,* pp. 112, 117.

39. *CV Centennial,* pp. 50, 68.

40. There is much literature on the controversies; the best general summary and guide to the published sources and secondary works is Robert D. Cross, *The Emergence of Liberal Catholicism in America* (Cambridge, 1958).

41. The chief biographical studies are: John Tracy Ellis, *The Life of James Cardinal Gibbons,* 2 vols. (Milwaukee, 1952); James H. Moynihan, *The Life of Archbishop John Ireland* (New York, 1953); Patrick H. Ahern, *The Life of John J. Keane: Educator and Archbishop, 1839–1918* (Milwaukee, 1954); and Zwierlein,

Life and Letters of Bishop McQuaid. Thomas T. McAvoy, C.S.C., *The Great Crisis in American Catholic History, 1895–1900* (Chicago, 1957), also provides much information about the personalities involved as well as a detailed account of the Americanism issue.

42. Barry, *op. cit.,* p. 119.

43. *Ibid.,* p. 10. Barry's work gives the details of German Catholic involvement in the controversies.

44. See Barry, *op. cit.;* John Meng, "Cahenslyism: the First Stage, 1883–1891," *Catholic Historical Review,* XXXI (Jan., 1946), 389–413; Meng, "Cahenslyism: the Second Chapter, 1891–1910," *Catholic Historical Review,* XXXII (Oct., 1946), 302–40. Cross, *op. cit.,* pp. 88–94, is a good brief account. Gleason, *op. cit.,* pp. 29 ff. and 45 ff., discusses the nationality question in the context of the CV's development.

45. See the discussion in A. H. Walburg, *The Question of Nationality* (Cincinnati, 1889); summarized in Barry, *op. cit.,* pp. 82–85.

46. The Buffalo *Volksfreund* wrote on Feb. 17, 1890: "The principal error of Archbishop Ireland lies in his ideas of America, Americans, American Church. America is no nation, no race, no people, like France, Italy, or Germany. . . . We have citizens of a republic, but no nation and, therefore, no national language outside the languages which the races immigrated speak in their families." Quoted in George Zurcher, *Foreign Ideas in the Catholic Church in America* (East Aurora, N.Y., 1896), p. 29. Cf. also John Rothensteiner, *History of the Archdiocese of St. Louis,* 2 vols. (St. Louis, 1928), II, 572–73; Barry, *op. cit.,* pp. 172–73.

47. Barry, *op. cit.,* pp. 62 ff., 72 ff., 289–312. *Relatio De Quaestione Germanica in Statibus Foederatis a Rev. P. M. Abbelen . . . Novembri 1886 . . .* (n.p., n.d.) contains the Memorial and a number of reactions by American prelates.

48. Barry, *op. cit.,* p. 20 ff., and Ch. IV.

49. *Ibid.,* pp. 313–15, gives the text of the Lucerne Memorial.

50. When Monsignor Joseph Schroeder told Bishop Winand Wigger, the president of the American branch of the St. Raphael Society, that Cahensly's enemies had misrepresented the Memorial, Wigger responded "that he had read and studied the memorial both carefully and often, and that he found therein the views ascribed to it by Dr. Schroeder's opponents; indeed, if it did not bear this construction, he declared, he did not see what it meant." Charles G. Herbermann, "Rt. Rev. Winand Wigger, D.D., Third Bishop of Newark," *Historical Records and Studies,* II (1901), 309. H. A. Brann, "Mr. Cahensly and the Church in the United States," *Catholic World,* LIV (Jan., 1892), 568–81, is an attack on Cahenslyism by a priest usually numbered among the conservatives.

51. Daniel F. Reilly, O.P., *The School Controversy (1891–1893)* (Washington, 1943), is the most complete study, but see Barry, *op. cit.,* Ch. V, for more information on the German position. Moynihan, *Ireland,* Ch. V, presents the story from the viewpoint of the most prominent liberal on the school question.

52. For an example of the thinking of the Germans on the role of the school in preserving religion, language, and nationality, see *Verhandlungen der ersten allgemeinen amerikanisch-deutschen Katholiken Versammlung zu Chicago, Ill., am 6. September 1887* (Cincinnati, 1887), pp. 28–29, 40.

53. Ireland and Keane stated in their answer to the Abbelen Memorial: "For

those who are acquainted with their motives, the numerous schools of the Germans prove, among other things, that the new emigrants naturally seek the German language, and that some German priests are a little too much attached to it. . . ." *Relatio*, pp. 20–21; Barry, *op. cit.*, p. 300.

54. On Dec. 3, 1893, the *Katholisches Sonntagsblatt* of Chicago wrote: "We would like to put one question to the Liberal Catholic party, which tries in every way to stamp all secret societies, not Freemason, as innocent and harmless. Is a Catholic allowed in conscience to become a member of the A.P.A.'s? If the one is allowed the other should not be forbidden, especially if people become 'Americanized' thereby." Quoted in Zurcher, *op. cit.*, p. 49. For the general problem, see Fergus McDonald, C.P., *The Catholic Church and Secret Societies in the United States* (New York, 1946). Gleason, *op. cit.*, pp. 50–53, discusses the CV's reaction to the secret society issue.

55. For discussion of the German position in the standard work, see Joan Bland, *Hibernian Crusade; the Story of the Catholic Total Abstinence Union of America* (Washington, 1951), pp. 17, 127, 136, 138–39, 142 ff., 179, 182–83, 191 ff., 203–04, 211 ff., 228, 238 ff. George Zurcher was a priest of German birth whose fanatical devotion to total abstinence made him quite unsympathetic to his ethnic brethren; the German Catholics are the prime targets of his criticism in *Foreign Ideas in the Catholic Church*.

56. Cf., for example, "Bericht über . . . der Dritten General-Versammlung des Amerikanisch-Deutschen-Priester-Vereins," pp. 2, 5. (This report was published as a supplement to *Pastoral-Blatt*, XXIII [Oct., 1889].)

57. Peter M. Abbelen quoted in Buffalo *Volksfreund*, Nov. 29, 1889, as cited in Zurcher, *op. cit.*, pp. 14–15.

58. Cf. "Das Centenarium in Baltimore," *Pastoral-Blatt*, XXIV (Jan., 1890), 1–3.

59. Zurcher, *op. cit.*, p. 16.

60. McAvoy, *Great Crisis in American Catholic History*, the fullest account of Americanism, is especially good on the European ramifications of the story. Cross, *op. cit.*, Ch. X, is an excellent analysis of "The Response of European Catholicism" to the experience of the American Church.

61. Barry, *op. cit.*, p. 237 ff.

62. McAvoy, *op. cit.*, p. 390.

63. *CV Centennial*, p. 70.

64. Typescript, "Playing into the Hands of the Church's Enemies," and "Unwissenheit oder Böswilligkeit? Cahensly-Mär durch Herren Egan und Williams aufgewärmt," Central Bureau Pressbrief, Nov. 1, 1921. Both items in ACV. See also *Herold des Glaubens* (St. Louis), Aug. 13, 1902, Nov. 15, 1911; and Barry, *op. cit.*, pp. 269–71.

65. Frederick P. Kenkel to Joseph Matt, Jan. 14, 1916; Matt to Kenkel, Jan. 15, 1916, AUND.

66. Frederick P. Kenkel to Frederic Siedenburg, June 27, 1913, AUND.

67. Cf. Barry, *op. cit.*, p. 123 ff., Chaps. IV, V; McAvoy, *op. cit.*, esp. pp. 148, 178–79, 338–41; Patrick A. Ahern, *The Catholic University of America, 1887–1896; the Rectorship of John J. Keane* (Washington, 1948), Chaps. IV, V; Patrick E. Hogan, S.S.J., *The Catholic University of America, 1896–1903; the Rectorship of Thomas J. Conaty* (Washington, 1949), Ch. V, and appendices A, B, and C.

68. Rev. David Phelan in the *Western Watchman* (St. Louis), Mar. 9, 1899, as quoted in McAvoy, *op. cit.*, p. 298.

69. *43. General-Versammlung . . . 1898*, p. 11.

70. *41. General-Versammlung . . . 1896*, pp. 47–48, 53–55. Joseph Matt described Schroeder as the "soul of the undertaking" in his essay on the CV in *Das Buch der Deutschen in Amerika*, ed. Max Heinrici (Philadelphia, 1909), p. 713.

71. *42. General-Versammlung . . . 1897*, pp. 12–13.

72. *43. General-Versammlung . . . 1898*, p. 11.

73. Matt remarks on the discouragement in *Buch der Deutschen*, p. 713. For the German reaction to O'Connell's appointment, see *The Review*, X (1903), 12, 180–81. Archbishop Messmer told O'Connell: "Your appointment as rector of the University came as a shock to them [the German-American Catholics], when they had just somewhat recovered from the resentment against the University caused by the treatment of Dr. Schroeder. . . ." Quoted in the Colman J. Barry, O.S.B., *The Catholic University of America, 1903–1909; the Rectorship of Denis J. O'Connell* (Washington, 1950), p. 200.

74. Barry, *The Catholic Church and German Americans*, pp. 249–51; Barry, *Rectorship of O'Connell*, pp. 202–05; *48. General-Versammlung . . . 1903*, pp. 55, 85; *Herold des Glaubens*, June 24, July 15, Oct. 21, 1903. Cf. also, "Germans and the Catholic University," *The Review*, X (1903), 465–68.

75. *57. General-Versammlung . . . 1912*, p. 128.

Chapter III

1. *The Review*, III (Apr. 23, 1896), 1.

2. John A. Hawgood, *The Tragedy of German-America* (New York and London, 1940), p. 287 ff.; Carl Wittke, *The German Language Press in America* (Lexington, Ky., 1957), p. 235; Heinz Kloss, *Um die Einigung des Deutschamerikantertums* (Berlin, 1937), pp. 154–55; Dieter Cunz, *The Maryland Germans; A History* (Princeton, 1948), pp. 320, 382–84, 388; Ludwig Fulda, *Amerikanische Eindrücke* (Stuttgart and Berlin, 1906), pp. 72–104. For a detailed study see G. A. Dobbert, "The Disintegration of an Immigrant Community: The Cincinnati Germans, 1870–1920" (unpublished doctoral dissertation, University of Chicago, 1965).

3. Hawgood, *op. cit.*, p. 57. Mack Walker, *Germany and the Emigration, 1816–1885* (Cambridge, Mass., 1964) is the best study of the background of German emigration.

4. Colman Barry, O.S.B., *The Catholic Church and German Americans* (Milwaukee, 1953), p. 6. Barry's figures are derived from Gerald Shaughnessy, *Has the Immigrant Kept the Faith?* (New York, 1925).

5. *Twelfth Census of the United States . . . Population, part I* (Washington, 1901), p. CXC, Table LXXXVIII; *Reports of the Immigration Commission* (Washington, 1911), vol. XXVIII, 162; E. P. Hutchinson, *Immigrants and their Children, 1850–1950* (New York, 1956), pp. 172–73.

6. Hawgood, *op. cit.*, pp. 289–90; *The Review*, VII (1900–01), 289–90; *57. General-Versammlung . . . 1912*, p. 63.

7. Georg Timpe, "Hundert Jahre katholischer deutscher Presse," in Timpe (ed.), *Katholisches Deutschtum in den Vereinigten Staaten von Amerika* (Freiburg im Breisgau, 1937), p. 7.

8. *Wahrheits-Freund* (Cincinnati), Dec. 26, 1900.

9. *Herold des Glaubens* (St. Louis), Feb. 14 and 21, 1906.

10. E. Heimerschmeid, "Das Deutschthum und der deutsche Unterricht an unseren Pfarrschulen," *Pastoral-Blatt*, XLVI (Jan., 1912), 3–10.

11. *Herold des Glaubens*, Mar. 17, 1909, Sept. 27, 1905. For another example of the literature of exhortation see Ferdinand H. Lohmann, *Die deutsche Sprache. Was können wir beitragen zu ihrer Erhaltung in diesem Lande* (Chicago, 1904), esp. p. 33.

12. *Herold des Glaubens*, Apr. 21, 1909, Nov. 2, 1910, May 13, 1903.

13. *Excelsior*, Nov. 15, 1900, quoted in *The Review*, VII (1900–01), 277. *The Review*, VII (1900–01), 340, 373, for Messmer's order.

14. Quoted in *The Review*, VII (1900–01), 309; see *ibid.*, 340, for Preuss's comments.

15. *Ibid.*, 289, 373. Cf. W. I. Thomas and Florian Znaniecki, *The Polish Peasant in Europe and America*, 1st ed., 5 vols. (Boston, 1920), V, 159. For the ethnic struggles of the Franco-Americans see Mason Wade, "The French Parish and *Survivance* in Nineteenth-Century New England," *Catholic Historical Review*, XXXVI (July, 1950), 163–89.

16. *The Review*, VII (1900–01), 289–90.

17. The interesting role of the German Catholic lay teachers has not been studied. See Georg Timpe, "Karl Adams, Lehrer und Organist," in Timpe (ed.), *op. cit.*, esp. p. 149. *CBSJ*, XXII (Aug., 1929), 143, has a brief item about the Stearns County society.

18. Joseph Matt, "The Catholic Central Union of America," *SJR*, LVII (Sept., 1964) 178; "Das Leo-Haus, der Raphaels-Verein und das Leo-Haus-Blatt," *Pastoral-Blatt*, XXXVI (May, 1902), 74–76; Kloss, *op. cit.*, p. 153.

19. *45. General-Versammlung . . . 1900*, p. 180. The proceedings of the Fund were printed with the Central-Verein's; my discussion of the insurance problem is based on these proceedings for the years of crisis, 1897–1906. Richard DeR. Kip, *Fraternal Insurance in America* (Philadelphia, 1953), Ch. V, is a very helpful treatment of assessment insurance, of which there were a number of varieties and which my description has oversimplified.

20. *44. General-Versammlung . . . 1899*, p. 107. The average age in 1900 is given in *45. General-Versammlung . . . 1900*, p. 187.

21. The executive committee's minutes and the accountant's report are given in *45. General-Versammlung . . . 1900*, pp. 170–73. Joseph J. Wahlen, "Henry J. Spaunhorst, A Catholic Leader," *CBSJ*, XXII (Feb., 1930), 356, exonerates Spaunhorst. It is certain that Spaunhorst reappeared at Fund conventions before his death in 1907, and when he died he was eulogized in the Central-Verein.

22. *45. General-Versammlung . . . 1900*, pp. 26–27.

23. *48. General-Versammlung . . . 1903*, p. 115.

24. *Ibid.*, pp. 109, 119–25.

25. Gonner (b. 1870) was killed in an automobile accident in 1922. His greatest journalistic accomplishment was the founding of the *Catholic Daily Tribune* in

1920. See Daniel Francis Gebhardt, "A History of the *Catholic Daily Tribune*" (unpublished master's thesis, Marquette University, 1953), Chaps. I and II.

26. *55. General-Versammlung . . . 1905*, pp. 41, 101–02.

27. On the state leagues see *CV Centennial*, pp. 80–81, and *Champions of the Catholic Cause; the Central Verein and the Catholic Union of Illinois* (Pamphlet, St. Louis, 1928); on the Bennett Law, Barry, *op. cit.*, pp. 184–85, and "A Historical Pronouncement: Wisconsin Bishops Protest the Bennett Law," *SJR*, XXXIII (Dec., 1940–Jan., 1941), 282–84, 318–20; on the Edwards Law, Daniel W. Kucera, O.S.B., *Church-State Relations in Education in Illinois* (Washington, 1955), p. 111 ff. The Lutherans also opposed these measures. Cf. Walter H. Beck, *Lutheran Elementary Schools in the United States* (St. Louis, 1939), Ch. XI.

28. For the Foresters see *Catholic Encyclopedia* (New York, 1909), VI, 135; for the Western Catholic Union, *Souvenir of the Fiftieth Anniversary of the Western Catholic Union* (Quincy, Ill., 1928), p. 95 ff.; for the Knights of St. George, the jubilee histories in the official organ, *The Knight of St. George*, Apr., 1931, and May, 1956.

29. *Souvenir . . . Western Catholic Union*, pp. 45, 71.

30. See Spaunhorst's talk on "Catholic Societies" in *The World's Columbian Catholic Congresses . . .* (Chicago, 1893), p. 102.

31. *42. General-Versammlung . . . 1897*, pp. 54–55.

32. *47. General-Versammlung . . . 1902*, pp. 74–75. The Illinois league had a very active vigilance, or legislative, committee which attracted favorable comment from non-German Catholics. Cf. the remarks of Francis Cassilly, S.J., in *Catholic Educational Association Bulletin*, IV (Nov., 1907), 100–01.

33. Matt refers to his part in reorganization in *CV Centennial*, p. 80. Joseph Kreuter, " 'Der Wanderer' und sein Redakteur," in Timpe, *op. cit.*, pp. 82–84, is a brief sketch of Matt's career. See also his obituary in *The Wanderer*, Apr. 14, 1966.

34. The reorganization can be followed in detail in the convention proceedings from 1900 to 1905. Compare especially *45. General-Versammlung . . . 1900*, pp. 134–53, and *51. General-Versammlung . . . 1906*, pp. 71–78, for the major constitutional changes. *Catholic Fortnightly Review*, XIII (1906), 422, gives a good summary (Preuss's *Review* changed its title in 1905 to *Catholic Fortnightly Review;* after May, 1912, it was known as *Fortnightly Review*). For examples of the discussion in the German Catholic press see *Herold des Glaubens*, Oct. 22, 1902, Apr. 20, 27, 1904, Mar. 14, 21, and Sept. 19, 26, 1906.

35. *57. General-Versammlung . . . 1907*, part I, p. 29. In states where no *Staatsverband* existed, individual societies still belonged directly to the national federation.

36. *47. General-Versammlung . . . 1902*, p. 105.

37. *48. General-Versammlung . . . 1903*, p. 64.

38. *47. General-Versammlung . . . 1902*, p. 75.

39. *Ibid.*

40. *Ibid.*, p. 77.

41. *Ibid.*, p. 75.

42. *48. General-Versammlung . . . 1903*, pp. 15, 65.

43. Oelkers to "Werter Freund Adelmann," Aug. 10, 1905, AUND. The "German standard" is referred to in *48. General-Versammlung . . . 1903*, p. 66.

44. M. Adele Francis Gorman, O.S.F., "Federation of Catholic Societies in the United States, 1870–1920" (unpublished doctoral dissertation, University of Notre Dame, 1962) rescues the story of the Federation and earlier unification efforts from almost complete oblivion.

45. Francis A. Coghlan, "The Impact of the Spanish-American War on the Catholic Church in the United States of America, 1898–1903" (unpublished master's thesis, University of Notre Dame, 1956), pp. 92–94.

46. Cf. Richard R. Elliott, "Government Secularization of the Education of Catholic Indian Youth," *American Catholic Quarterly Review,* XXV (Jan., 1900), 148–68.

47. Gorman, *op. cit.,* Ch. III, and p. 108 ff.

48. *Wahrheits-Freund,* Dec. 18, 1901; *Die Amerika* (St. Louis), June 14, 1914.

49. *Pastoral Letters, Addresses and Other Writings of the Rt. Rev. James A. McFaul, D.D., LL.D., Bishop of Trenton,* ed. James J. Powers, 2nd ed. (New York, 1916), p. 285.

50. The text of Messmer's address is given in *The Review,* VII (1900–01), 163–64, 170–71.

51. *45. General-Versammlung . . . 1900,* pp. 100–01; *The Review,* VII (1900–01), 265–66, 293, 310, 316.

52. *The Review,* VII (1900–01), 247, 351.

53. *Ibid.,* 281. Cf. also Conde B. Pallen, "Irelandism Exit," *The Review,* IX (1902), 262–63, which asserted the AFCS meant "the beginning of Catholic Emancipation in America."

54. *The Review,* VII (1900–01), 380–81; *The Review,* VIII (1901), 493, 539.

55. *The Review,* IX (1902), 196–203.

56. *46. General-Versammlung . . . 1901,* p. 25.

57. *Ibid.,* 66, 97–101; *The Review,* VIII (1901), 493, 524, 543, 554, 570–71. The German Catholic press lamented the confusion caused by conflicting instructions. See Philadelphia *Nord Amerika* quoted in *Der Patriot* (La Crosse, Wis.), Nov. 28, 1901.

58. *The Review,* IX (1902), 3–6, 170–71, 289–90, provides the most convenient summary of the German position. Gorman, *op. cit.,* pp. 121–22, 123, 129, comments on the organizational difficulties of the AFCS. The CV's stand was epitomized in the slogan *"getrennt marschieren, vereint schlagen"* (march separately; strike as one).

59. The precise changes made at Chicago are obscure, but were hailed as a victory for nationality groups like the CV and the Bohemians. Cf. *Wahrheits-Freund,* Aug. 13, 1902; *Proceedings of the Second National Convention of the American Federation of Catholic Societies, Held at Chicago August 5th, 6th, and 7th, 1902* (Cincinnati, 1902), pp. 17, 25, 28, 37, 65; and *47. General-Versammlung . . . 1902,* pp. 13–14, 26 ff., 86–94, 113, 119–20.

60. *Proceedings of the Third National Convention of the American Federation of Catholic Societies Held at Atlantic City August 1st to 5th, 1903* (Cincinnati, 1903), pp. 121–22; *Bulletin of the American Federation of Catholic Societies,* I (Dec., 1906), 18; *The Review,* XIII (1906), 606.

61. *47. General-Versammlung . . . 1902,* p. 40.

62. The quotation is from a circular on the CV reorganization sent out by Bourscheidt in February, 1906. Cf. *51. General-Versammlung . . . 1906,* pp. 53, 50.

63. *CV Centennial*, pp. 82–83.

64. Hays, *The Response to Industrialism, 1885–1914* (Chicago, 1957).

65. John P. J. Walsh notes that the years 1893–1915 were a time of unification and the end of "segmentation" in Catholic approaches to various matters. "The Catholic Church in Chicago and the Problems of an Urban Society, 1893–1915" (unpublished doctoral dissertation, University of Chicago, 1948), pp. 33–34. Humphrey J. Desmond's *The New Laity and the Old Standards* (Philadelphia, 1914) is slight and disappointing in substance but symptomatic of the new emphasis on the layman's role. See also John T. Murphy, C.S.Sp., "Catholic Secondary Education in the United States," *American Catholic Quarterly Review*, XXII (1897), 455, 462; and *Report of the Second Annual Conference of the Association of Catholic Colleges . . . 1900* (Washington, 1900), pp. 135–36, 139–40.

66. 57. *General-Versammlung . . . 1907*, part I, pp. 34–35, 46; ibid., part II, pp. 19–25, 32–38. For examples of the press discussion see *Herold des Glaubens*, May 9, Oct. 3, 1906, and May 29, Sept. 4, 1907.

67. Rudolph Krueger comments on the changes in the committee's title in "Geschichte des Centralvereins," pp. 102, 104, 106, of the Souvenir Program of the 62nd convention in 1917 (n.p., n.d.).

Chapter IV

1. "Der Clerus und die Einwanderung; Ein Wort zur Lösung der socialen Crisis," *Pastoral-Blatt*, XX (Nov., 1886), 125–28.

2. Cf. *42. General-Versammlung . . . 1897*, p. 85; Joseph J. Wahlen, "Henry J. Spaunhorst, A Catholic Leader," *CBSJ*, XXXII (Dec., 1929), 285; "Labor Bureaus in the C.V.," *CBSJ*, XXIII (Nov., 1930), 274–75; *43. General Versammlung . . . 1898*, pp. 22–23.

3. Aaron I. Abell, *American Catholicism and Social Action* (New York, 1960), pp. 47, 57–60. Cf. also James E. Roohan, "American Catholics and the Social Question, 1865–1900" (unpublished doctoral dissertation, Yale University, 1952), pp. 278–80.

4. Howard H. Quint, *The Forging of American Socialism* (Columbia, S.C., 1953), p. 35 and Ch. I, *passim*. Cf. also Ira Kipnis, *The American Socialist Movement, 1897–1912* (New York, 1952), Ch. II, esp. pp. 19–20.

5. Quint, *op. cit.*, pp. 16 ff., 4.

6. *Catholic World*, XXVII (July, 1878), 433–53; John Tracy Ellis, *The Life of James Cardinal Gibbons*, 2 vols. (Milwaukee, 1952), I, 346–47; Elder to Rev. Charles Hahne, Sept. 21, 1891, in "Bericht über die Verhandlung der fünften General-Versammlung des Deutsch-Amerikanischen Priester-Vereins . . . 1891," which is given as a supplement to *Pastoral-Blatt*, XXVI (Jan., 1892). For the garbled version of Elder's remarks, see *Relatio de Quaestione Germanica in Statibus Foederatis . . .* (n.p., n.d.), p. 46.

7. *Relatio*, p. 28. Cf. also Colman J. Barry, O.S.B., *The Catholic Church and German Americans* (Milwaukee, 1953), p. 306.

8. *Wahrheits-Freund* (Cincinnati), June 19, 1878, gives the resolutions in Ger-

man. The *ICBU* (Irish Catholic Benevolent Union) *Journal* (Philadelphia), Aug., 1878, carried a rather free translation of the resolutions under the heading, "The German Catholic Verein and Socialism."

9. Cf. *32. General-Versammlung . . . 1887*, pp. 12, 35, 37; "Der Central-Verein und die Knights of Labor," *CBSJ*, XIV (Dec., 1921), 297–98; *Wahrheits-Freund*, Sept. 14, 1887; *Northwestern Chronicle* (St. Paul), Sept. 8, 1887; *Catholic Review* (New York), Sept. 17, 1887; Henry J. Browne, *The Catholic Church and the Knights of Labor* (Washington, 1949), p. 291.

10. *Verhandlungen der ersten allgemeinen amerikanisch-deutschen Katholiken-Versammlung zu Chicago, Ill., am 6. September 1887* (Cincinnati, 1887), pp. 51–54.

11. *Ibid.*, pp. 62–63.

12. *36. General-Versammlung . . . 1891*, p. 43; *Pastoral-Blatt*, XXVI (Jan., 1892), 7.

13. *Wahrheits-Freund*, Oct. 5, 1892, gives the text of Herr's speech; quotation from *New York Freeman's Journal*, Oct. 1, 1892.

14. *39. General-Versammlung . . . 1894*, pp. 61–62; *Northwestern Chronicle*, Sept. 21, 1895.

15. M. Liguori Brophy, B.V.M., notes this "somewhat singular" omission in her study, *The Social Thought of the German Roman Catholic Central Verein* (Washington, 1941), p. 78.

16. On Ryan, see the biography of Francis L. Broderick, *Right Reverend New Dealer* (New York, 1963), and Ryan's autobiography, *Social Doctrine in Action* (New York and London, 1941).

17. The quotation is from Shannon's *The Socialist Party of America: A History* (New York, 1955), p. 6. On the growth of socialism, see also Quint, *op. cit.*, Chaps. X and XI; Kipnis, *op. cit.*, Chaps. II–VII; and Marvin Wachman, *History of the Social-Democratic Party of Milwaukee, 1897–1910* (Urbana, Ill., 1945).

18. R. F. Hoxie, " 'The Rising Tide of Socialism,' " *Journal of Political Economy*, XIX (Oct., 1911), 609–31, analyzes the strength of socialism.

19. Cf. Abell, *op. cit.*, Ch. V; M. Harrita Fox, B.V.M., *Peter E. Dietz, Labor Priest* (Notre Dame, Ind., 1953), Ch. II; Marc Karson, *American Labor Unions and Politics, 1900–1918* (Carbondale, Ill., 1958), Ch. IX; and Robert E. Doherty, "The American Socialist Party and the Roman Catholic Church, 1901–1917" (unpublished doctoral dissertation, Teachers College, Columbia University, 1959).

20. *47. General-Versammlung . . . 1902*, p. 120.

21. Wachman, *op. cit.*, pp. 52–53. Bishop James E. Quigley of Buffalo took similar action. Cf. "Bishop Quigley's Attack on Socialism," *Literary Digest*, XXIV (Apr. 12, 1902), 508.

22. *47. General-Versammlung . . . 1902*, pp. 41–42.

23. *Ibid.*, pp. 42–43.

24. *Herold des Glaubens* (St. Louis), Mar. 12, Apr. 2, 1902; Thomas J. McDonagh, C.S.C., "Some Aspects of the Roman Catholic Attitude Toward the American Labor Movement, 1900–1914" (unpublished doctoral dissertation, University of Wisconsin, 1951), Ch. IV; Joan Leonard, "Catholic Attitude Toward American Labor, 1884–1919" (unpublished master's thesis, Columbia University, 1940), pp. 94–95.

25. For the Buffalo society, see the vita of Herman J. Maeckel, S.J., in *American*

Catholic Who's Who (for 1911), ed. Georgina Pell Curtis (St. Louis, 1911); for Dubuque, "Early Workingmen's Societies Had Approval of Archbishop Glennon," *CBSJ*, XXXI (Dec., 1938), 280.

26. *48. General-Versammlung . . . 1903*, p. 15; clipping in ACV from *Katholischer Westen* (Dubuque), Nov. 30, 1899, quoting from *Buffalo Volksfreund*, Nov. 24, 1899; *Herold des Glaubens*, July 22, 1903; *46. General-Versammlung . . . 1901*, p. 20.

27. Cf. Charles J. Plater, S.J., *Catholic Social Work in Germany* (London, 1909); Theodor Brauer, "The Catholic Social Movement in Germany," in *Catholic Social Year Book, 1932* (Oxford, 1932); Edgar Alexander, "Church and Society in Germany (1789–1950)," in *Church and Society*, ed. Joseph N. Moody (New York, 1953); Emil Ritter, *Die katholisch-soziale Bewegung Deutschlands im neunzehnten Jahrhundert und der Volksverein* (Cologne, 1954); and Karl Buchheim, *Ultramontanismus und Demokratie; der Weg der deutschen Katholiken im 19. Jahrhundert* (Munich, 1963).

28. Plater, *op. cit.*, p. 30, and Ch. IV, "The Lessons of German Tactics."

29. *46. General-Versammlung . . . 1901*, p. 20; *43. General-Versammlung . . . 1898*, pp. 161–63. For Preuss's comments, see above Chapter III.

30. On March 29, 1898, Gonner's *Luxemburger Gazette* (Dubuque) said that Keane's article proved the existence of "Americanism," and added: "According to Msgr. Keane, America is a wonderfully free and happy country where we have no problems to speak [of]; we have no racial question, no socialist question, no Jewish question, no labor question. . . ." Quoted in Mary de Paul Faber, O.S.F., "The *Luxemburger Gazette*, A Catholic German Language Paper of the Middle West, 1872–1918" (unpublished master's thesis, Catholic University of America, 1948), p. 38. Joseph Matt, in *Das Buch der Deutschen in Amerika*, ed. Max Heinrici (Philadelphia, 1909), pp. 711–12, says merely that the statement was made by one "very close to the Catholic University in Washington." Keane was the first rector of the Catholic University. In *CV Centennial*, p. 52, Matt attributes it to "a leading Catholic professor." The most specific reference is in August F. Brockland, "Becoming Conscious of the Social Question," *CBSJ*, IV (June, 1911), 51–52. Keane's article is cited here, although he is not named as the author. Brockland says: "The sum and substance of the article . . . is: We have no Social Question." As Brockland's wording indicates, Keane made no such statement explicitly.

31. "The Encyclical *Rerum Novarum*," *American Catholic Quarterly Review*, XVI (July, 1891), 595–611; "The Catholic Church and Economics," *Quarterly Journal of Economics*, VI (Oct., 1891), 25–46. The latter essay was summarized in *Literary Digest*, IV (Nov. 7, 1891), 6–7.

32. Keane, "America as Seen from Abroad," *Catholic World*, LXVI (Mar., 1898), 721–30. For a discussion of the article in the context of the Americanism controversy, see Thomas T. McAvoy, C.S.C., *The Great Crisis in American Catholic History, 1895–1900* (Chicago, 1957), pp. 186–88.

33. The following summary of Heiter's speech is based on the text given in *46. General-Versammlung . . . 1901*, pp. 17–20.

34. See above, Chapter II.

35. *43. General-Versammlung . . . 1898*, pp. 161–63; *44. General-Versammlung . . . 1899*, pp. 21–22.

236/THE CONSERVATIVE REFORMERS

36. Kenkel, "Dem Andenken Franz Brandts," *CBSJ,* VII (Dec., 1914), 259.
37. *58. General-Versammlung . . . 1913,* pp. 66–67.
38. *46. General-Versammlung . . . 1901,* pp. 70, 108.
39. *Ibid.,* pp. 72–76, gives the resolutions in both German and English. The quotation departs somewhat from the translation in the proceedings.
40. *Ibid.,* pp. 22, 67, 96. The bibliography follows p. 178.
41. For Gonner's background, see Daniel F. Gebhardt, "A History of the *Catholic Daily Tribune*" (unpublished master's thesis, Marquette University, 1953), Chaps. II–III.
42. *47. General-Versammlung . . . 1902,* pp. 28–30, 40–41.
43. *Ibid.,* pp. 28–30, 40–43.
44. This description is pieced together from *48. General-Versammlung . . . 1903,* pp. 68–69, 74, and from the following items in ACV: "Verlangt: Männer der That," press release, Nov., 1904; "An die hochwürdige Geistlichkeit," an appeal sent out in 1903; "Vom Volksverein," clipping from *Katholischer Westen,* dated "3-9-5"; "Föderation and Volksverein," clipping from *Katholischer Westen,* Aug. 24, 1905. For the operations of the Volksverein in Germany, see Plater, *op. cit.,* pp. 81–94, and Ritter, *op. cit.,* p. 174 ff.
45. *48. General-Versammlung . . . 1903,* pp. 70, 73–74; "Für den Staatsverband," circular dated Apr. 14, 1902, ACV; *Herold des Glaubens,* Apr. 23, 1902; "Was hat der Volksverein für Amerika gethan," pamphlet report of activities in 1903–04, in ACV; *49. General-Versammlung . . . 1904,* pp. 26–27.
46. *48. General-Versammlung . . . 1903,* p. 70.
47. *Ibid.,* pp. 71–73.
48. All the quotations in the following paragraphs are from this source, which is designated as Volksverein Flugblatt No. 3, May, 1905, in ACV.
49. For studies of Catholic corporatism in Europe, see Ralph H. Bowen, *German Theories of the Corporative State* (New York, 1947), and Matthew H. Elbow, *French Corporative Theory, 1789–1948* (New York, 1953).
50. *48. General-Versammlung . . . 1903,* pp. 68–69; *49. General-Versammlung . . . 1904,* pp. 26–27; *CBSJ,* IV (June, 1911), 62.
51. *49. General-Versammlung . . . 1904,* pp. 26–27; manuscript minutes of the Volksverein executive meeting, Aug. 30, 1903, ACV.
52. Manuscript minutes, Volksverein executive meeting, Jan. 18, 1905, ACV; *Bulletin of the American Federation of Catholic Societies,* I (Dec., 1906), 11, 13–14; *50. General-Versammlung . . . 1905,* p. 40. Cf. M. Adele Francis Gorman, O.S.F., "Federation of Catholic Societies in the United States, 1870–1920" (unpublished doctoral dissertation, University of Notre Dame, 1962), pp. 146–47, 148–49, 150.
53. *55. General-Versammlung . . . 1910,* p. 32.
54. *51. General-Versammlung . . . 1906,* pp. 28, 30, 62; *Bulletin . . . Federation,* I (Dec., 1906), 18; Joseph Matt to Frederick P. Kenkel, July 6, 1913, AUND.

Chapter V

1. *52. General-Versammlung . . . 1907,* p. 46.
2. For Gonner's views see "Vom Centralverein zum Volksverein," reproduced from *Katholischer Westen* in *Central-Blatt,* I (Mar., 1909), 2–3. For Matt's views

and his work in bringing Kenkel to the committee see Matt, "The Central Bureau: Fifty Years of Achievement," *SJR*, LI (Apr., 1959), 392; and Matt, *F. P. Kenkel, Central-Verein Publications: Free Leaflet No.* 104 (St. Louis, 1953).

3. This sketch of Kenkel's life is based on materials contained in the Kenkel papers, AUND. More detailed documentation may be found in my article, "The Early Years of Frederick P. Kenkel: The Background of an American Catholic Social Reformer," *Records of the American Catholic Historical Society of Philadelphia*, LXXIV (Dec., 1963), 195–212.

4. Kenkel to Solanus Hilchenbach, O.S.F., Dec. 20, 1896, PAFF. Photostats of the letters of Kenkel to Father Solanus are in the Kenkel papers, AUND.

5. In an unpublished essay entitled, "F. P. Kenkel–Catholic Social Pioneer (1863–1952)," Mr. Cyril T. Echele, who worked with Kenkel at the Central Bureau, suggests that observation of the miners' depressed conditions stimulated Kenkel's social consciousness.

6. The autobiographical *"Curriculum Vitae"* is in the Kenkel papers, AUND. It was translated for me by Dr. Francis Lazenby, Assistant Director, Notre Dame Memorial Library.

7. Kenkel, *"Curriculum Vitae."*

8. *Ibid.*

9. *Ibid.*

10. The quotations are from the "Curriculum Vitae"; Kenkel's niece, Miss Albertine Schuttler of Milwaukee, recounts the religious history of the family in "Notes on the Early Life of F. P. Kenkel," AUND.

11. Kenkel to Ella von Kamptz, Aug. 6, 1891, AUND, describes his room and his reading. Miss Eleanore Kenkel also provided information on her father's stay at Quincy in an interview. Mary Elizabeth Dye, O.S.U., "F. P. Kenkel, Catholic Social Pioneer" (unpublished master's thesis, St. Louis University, 1951), p. 19 ff., suggests that Kenkel became acquainted with the writings of German social theorists while at Quincy. Since Dye wrote her thesis while Kenkel was still living, this information may have come from him. There is no contemporary evidence indicating any interest in the social question for this period of Kenkel's life. Kenkel's correspondence with Father Solanus Hilchenbach, O.S.F. (discussed below) contains no indication that he had been interested in such matters while at Quincy. Early in their correspondence, Father Solanus wrote that Kenkel would have understood his position better "if we had had more opportunity [while Kenkel was at Quincy] to exchange views on political and social principles." Hilchenbach to Kenkel, Dec. 23, 1892, AUND. The Dye thesis was published under the title *By Their Fruits; A Social Biography of Frederick Kenkel, Catholic Social Pioneer* (New York, 1960).

12. The career of Father Solanus, who died in 1898, is described in *Annals of the Franciscan Province of the Sacred Heart*, No. 14 (n.p., 1935), pp. 884–85. I am indebted to Father Marion Habig, O.F.M., for directing me to this source and for providing me with a copy of the *Annals*. Kenkel to Ella von Kamptz, Aug. 6, 1891, AUND, describes his daily meetings with Father Solanus.

13. Kenkel to Ella von Kamptz, Feb. 20, 1892, AUND. In his letter written Sept. 27–29, 1892, while Ella was in Germany, Kenkel said that ·it displeased (*befremdet*) him that she did not give a direct answer to all his direct questions– "whether you love me, whether you are true to me and were with me in every

thought during the entire separation." "It may be pedantic," he continued, "but I would like a precisely formulated answer to them. I can, indeed, find it in every letter—but not as I should like to read it, almost like a sacred vow." AUND.

14. The Kenkel papers contain accounts of the wedding from the *Saturday Evening Herald* (Chicago), Nov. 19, 1892; the *Daily Inter Ocean* (Chicago), Nov. 16, 1892; and the *Chicago Herald*, Nov. 16, 1892. The *Inter Ocean* described the bride as "a handsome blonde of the true Teutonic type."

15. Kenkel to Hilchenbach, Dec. 19, 1892, PAFF.

16. Kenkel to Hilchenbach, Feb. 17, 1895, PAFF.

17. Kenkel to Hilchenbach, July 11, 1893, and Feb. 17, 1895, PAFF.

18. Kenkel to Hilchenbach, Feb. 17, 1895, PAFF. In an article on "The Parish Church, A True Community Center," published in 1922 (*CBSJ*, XIV, 323–26, 359–60, 396–98), Kenkel incorporated material which he may have gathered during this investigation. In comparing the medieval church to the "closed and silent denominational church of our day" (p. 396), he repeated almost verbatim what he had written to Father Solanus twenty-seven years earlier.

19. Kenkel to Hilchenbach, Aug. 3, 1894; Dec. 20, 1896; Jan. 26, 1897; June 3, 1895; Dec. 21, 1897, PAFF.

20. Kenkel to Hilchenbach, Sept. 18, 1895, PAFF.

21. *Ibid.*

22. Kenkel to Hilchenbach, Dec. 20, 1896, PAFF. In the same letter, Kenkel said that although he was in a much better frame of mind, he had not fully recovered.

23. Kenkel to Hilchenbach, Dec. 21, 1897, PAFF. Matt, *F. P. Kenkel*, CV Leaflet No. 104, mentions Kenkel's "impetuous temperament" and "impatient outbursts" of anger; Echele, "F. P. Kenkel," refers to his pride, impatience and self-assurance.

24. Kenkel to Hilchenbach, Dec. 22, 1895, PAFF.

25. Kenkel to Hilchenbach, Dec. 20, 1896, PAFF.

26. Kenkel to Hilchenbach, June 15, 1898, PAFF. Kenkel also discussed his intention in writing the book in letters of Dec. 22, 1895, and Dec. 20, 1896.

27. The diary of an early German immigrant, which Kenkel edited for the journal, was characterized by a German historian as "by far the most instructive" item in the first two volumes. Cf. *Deutsch-Amerikanische Geschichtsblätter*, III, No. 4 (July, 1903), p. 32.

28. Matt, *F. P. Kenkel*, CV Leaflet No. 104.

29. A. J. Pennartz to Kenkel, Nov. 6, 1905, AUND. Father Joseph Och, himself the editor of a German Catholic newspaper, described *Die Amerika* as the organ which set the tone of educated thinking among German-American Catholics. Cf. Och, *Der Deutschamerikanische Farmer* (Columbus, O., 1913), pp. 191, 198.

30. *The Wanderer* (St. Paul), Feb. 21, 1952; Joan Leonard "Catholic Attitude Toward American Labor, 1884–1919" (unpublished master's thesis, Columbia University, 1940), pp. 75–76, 98. The files of the *Katholisches Wochenblatt* for the period of Kenkel's editorship could not be located.

31. Quoted in J. Christopher Herold, *Mistress to an Age; A Life of Madame de Staël* (Indianapolis, 1958), p. 393. The fondness of the German romantics for the Middle Ages is the theme of Gottfried Salomon's *Das Mittelalter als Ideal in der Romantik* (Munich, 1922).

32. 53. *General-Versammlung . . . 1908*, pp. 17–18, contains the committee

report, which was supplemented by items in *Central-Blatt* (predecessor of *CBSJ*) for April, May, October, November, and December, 1908.

33. *53. General-Versammlung . . . 1908,* pp. 38, 33–34; *57. General Versammlung . . . 1912,* p. 96.

34. *Herold des Glaubens* (St. Louis), Feb. 3, 1909. For earlier installments see *ibid.,* Oct. 21; Nov. 4, 11; Dec. 2, 9, 23, 1908, and Jan. 20, 27, 1909.

35. *54. General-Versammlung . . . 1909,* p. 37; typescript minutes of the Social Propaganda Committee meetings for 1908–1909, ACV.

36. *54. General-Versammlung . . . 1909,* pp. 37–40.

37. *Ibid.,* p. 39, reports that the Central Bureau received 1,700 letters and postcards including 1,100 containing monetary contributions. For Ryan's praise see his article, "Two Important Points in the Social Program of the Central Verein," *Catholic Fortnightly Review,* XVI (1909), 130–32; for activity in the state leagues, *Herold des Glaubens,* Dec. 9, 1908, Mar. 3, 1909, Jan. 19, June 15, 1910.

38. *54. General-Versammlung . . . 1909,* pp. 76–77; Dietz, "The Aftermath of the Indianapolis Convention," *CBSJ,* II (Oct., 1909), 7–9.

39. Krueger, "Altes und Neues über die Finanzlage des Centralvereins," *Central-Blatt,* I (Feb., 1909), 2–3.

40. This plan is outlined in carbon copies of two letters in ACV. The first is dated July 18, 1909, and is directed to Joseph Frey and John B. Oelkers. It is unsigned, but was probably written by Peter J. Bourscheidt of Peoria. The second letter was enclosed with the first and obviously written by the same person, although the signature of Joseph Frey is typed on it. This letter, dated July 31, 1909, contains the details of the proposed change. It is directed to the members of the Committee for Social Propaganda. Frey was a member of the committee, but he is instructed by the writer of the first letter as follows: "Nun Joseph, siehe dazu dass Du dieses Schriftstück zu Anfangs August heraus bekommst. . . ."

41. Typescript minutes of the Social Propaganda Committee meetings for 1908–1909, ACV; Joseph Matt to Kenkel, July 16, 1909, Sept. 5, 1909, Jan. 7, Jan. 14, 1910, AUND; and an unsigned carbon of a letter directed to Rev. Dr. August Breig, and dated Aug. 16, 1910, ACV. The last letter encloses another proposal for reorganizing the Central Bureau.

42. Oelkers to Dietz, Sept. 24, 1911, ACV. Dietz's biographer, M. Harrita Fox, B.V.M., kindly furnished me copies of this letter and the one cited in the following note.

43. Oelkers to Dietz, May 30, 1913, ACV.

44. For examples of Kenkel's thinking see *55. General-Versammlung . . . 1910,* p. 36; "Warum Studienkurse," *CBSJ,* IV (July, 1911), 67–68; "Grundliche Arbeit, gesundes Wachsthum," *CBSJ,* VII (Mar., 1915), 359–60. Kenkel was very conscious of the fact that the leaders could not go faster than the mass of the CV membership. Concerning the "psychology of the men and women who make up the backbone of our societies," he wrote in 1922: "We . . . know how easy it is to give offense to our people. . . ." Kenkel to the members of the Social Propaganda Committee, Sept. 1, 1922, Archives of the Pontifical College Josephinum, Worthington, Ohio.

45. For Dietz's career see Mary Harrita Fox, *Peter E. Dietz, Labor Priest* (Notre Dame, Ind., 1953).

46. Dietz to Kenkel, Oct. 13, 30, 1908, AUND. There is no copy of Kenkel's reply among his letters, but Dietz begins his second letter by saying: "Let me plead guilty to the seeming impatient spirit of my communication. . . ."

47. The letter of the Cleveland group to the Special Committee of the CV was dated Jan. 20, 1909. It was signed by Auxiliary Bishop J. M. Koudelka, F. V. Faulhaber, president of the group, and Charles Reichlin, its secretary. AUND. Fox, *op. cit.*, pp. 29–30, says Dietz was instrumental in organizing the Cleveland group.

48. Kenkel to Joseph Matt, Feb. 17, 1909, letter in possession of Joseph Matt of St. Paul. Nicholas Gonner's letters to Kenkel, Jan. 7?, 26, 1909, AUND, indicate that Kenkel had protested the holding of the Chicago meeting. At about the same time he wrote an article in *Die Amerika* (reprinted in *Central-Blatt*, I [Mar., 1909], 8–9) cautioning that one had to proceed slowly in the matter of social reform.

49. Dietz, "The Dawn of the Indianapolis Convention," *CBSJ*, II (Sept., 1909), 11–12. Fox, *op. cit.*, pp. 31–32, discusses these proposals. On Sept. 21, 1909, Dietz told the Social Propaganda Committee that he had in mind managing the Central Bureau at Oberlin with the help of his sister. Typescript minutes of the Social Propaganda Committee meetings for 1908–1909, ACV.

50. Fox, *op. cit.*, p. 30; Cleveland group to Special Committee of the CV, Jan. 20, 1909, AUND.

51. Dietz, "The Central-Verein and the English Language," *CBSJ*, II (Apr., 1909), 8–9.

52. See, for example, Kenkel's remarks in *60. General-Versammlung . . . 1915*, pp. 118–19.

53. Fox, *op. cit.*, pp. 1–11, reviews Dietz's early life.

54. The quotations are from a letter written by Dietz in 1901, reproduced in *ibid.*, pp. 7–8.

55. Typescript minutes of the Social Propaganda Committee meetings for 1908–1909, ACV; Matt to Kenkel, Jan. 7, 14, 1910, AUND.

56. Dietz's sentiments are scrawled on the back of a letter from Kenkel to Dietz, June 6, 1940 (ACV) in which Kenkel had requested that Dietz deposit some of his papers on Catholic social action at the Central Bureau. Sister Harrita Fox reports that when she began her research on Dietz at the Central Bureau, Kenkel was quite unsympathetic to Dietz's work. When he learned more from Sister Harrita's investigations, his attitude toward Dietz softened. "As he said one day, 'Father Dietz was like a tiny light on the prow of a boat that is traveling through the dark.' This admission was quite a triumph." Letter of Sister Harrita in possession of the author.

Chapter VI

1. My article, "The Social Reform Activities of the Central Bureau, 1909–1917," *SJR*, LIV (Dec., 1961–Jan., 1962), 263–67, 301–04, contains more extensive documentation for the following section. For Ryan's remarks, see *Catholic Citizen*, Jan. 30, 1915.

2. *57. General-Versammlung . . . 1912*, p. 87.

3. *Thätigkeits-Bericht der Central-Stelle . . . 1913–1914* (St. Louis, 1914), pp.

12–13. Ryan commented favorably on the Central Bureau's pamphlet work in the English *Catholic Social Year Book for 1913* (London, 1913), p. 118.

4. *Thätigkeits-Bericht der Central-Stelle . . . 1914–1915* (St. Louis, 1915), p. 13; *Jahresbericht der Centralstelle . . . 1915–1916* (St. Louis, 1916), pp. 6–7.

5. Mary Harrita Fox, *Peter E. Dietz, Labor Priest* (Notre Dame, Ind., 1953), p. 104 ff.

6. *CBSJ*, VII (Sept., 1914), 167–69. The Homestake hearings are in *Industrial Relations; Final Report and Testimony Submitted to Congress by the Commission on Industrial Relations . . .* Senate Document 415, 64th Cong., 1st Sess., 11 vols. (Washington, 1916), IV, 3539–3679. Budenz discusses his association with the Bureau in *This Is My Story* (New York, 1947), p. 32 ff.

7. For Goldstein, see his *Autobiography of a Campaigner for Christ* (Boston, 1936); for Collins, Marc Karson, *American Labor Unions and Politics, 1900–1918* (Carbondale, Ill., 1958), p. 269 ff.

8. *CBSJ*, III (Aug., 1910), 106–07. For further discussion of these courses, see Thomas J. McDonagh, C.S.C., "Some Aspects of the Roman Catholic Attitude Toward the American Labor Movement, 1900–1914" (unpublished doctoral dissertation, University of Wisconsin, 1951), pp. 37–45, 87 ff.

9. Kenkel to Frederic Siedenburg, S.J., June 27, 1913, AUND. See also *CBSJ*, IV (Oct., 1911), 137–38; *CBSJ*, V (Dec., 1912), 206.

10. *58. General-Versammlung . . . 1913*, p. 158.

11. See below, Chapter VII.

12. *Jahresbericht der Centralstelle . . . 1915–1916*, pp. 8–9. For a typical month's report of activities, see "May at St. Elizabeth's Settlement," *CBSJ*, X (June, 1917), 86–87.

13. *58. General-Versammlung . . . 1913*, p. 33.

14. *59. General-Versammlung . . . 1914*, p. 146.

15. Cf. Heinz Kloss, *Um die Einigung des Deutschamerikanertums* (Berlin, 1937), pp. 140–141; *CV Centennial*, pp. 78–79.

16. *CBSJ*, IV (Feb., 1912), 257.

17. The following discussion is based on *59. General-Versammlung . . . 1914*, pp. 163–76.

18. *60. General-Versammlung . . . 1915*, p. 97.

19. *CBSJ*, III (Dec., 1910), 193; *CBSJ*, IV (Nov., 1911), 182. For similar activities on the part of an American group interested in social reform, see Paul S. Boyer, "Boston Book Censorship in the Twenties," *American Quarterly*, XV (Spring, 1963), 3–24.

20. *CBSJ*, IV (Mar., 1912), 276.

21. U. F. Mueller, "Entwicklungsstadien der amerikanischen Sozialdemokratie," *CBSJ*, VIII (July–Oct., 1915), 84–86, 120–23, 156–58, 193–96. On the background of socialism, see P. G. Rohr, "Some Aspects of Socialism," *CBSJ*, III (Nov., 1910), 161–63, and F. J. Eble, "Liberalism and Socialism," *CBSJ*, V (Dec., 1912–Jan., 1913), 191–92, 220–21.

22. "Ein offenes Bekenntniss," *CBSJ*, II (Apr., 1909), 3–4.

23. *57. General-Versammlung . . . 1912*, pp. 96, 149–50. For a more favorable view of the Progressive reform movement, see Kenkel, "Unsere Stellung zur sozialpolitische Bewegung," *CBSJ*, VI (Aug., 1913), 115–16.

24. *61. General-Versammlung . . . 1916*, p. 98. Cf. also, *59. General-Versammlung . . . 1914*, pp. 199, 201; and "The Real Measure of Socialism's Progress," *CBSJ*, VIII (Oct., 1915), 202.

25. *CBSJ*, IV (Mar., 1912), 284; "Making Socialism an Issue in the Chicago Federation of Labor," *CBSJ*, III (Sept., Nov., 1910), 121–22, 177.

26. Kenkel, "Zur Beurtheilung der Arbeiterbewegung," *CBSJ*, II (Jan., 1910), 2–3; and "Die Ausdehnung der Arbeitszeit unter der Freiwirthschaft," *CBSJ*, V (Apr., 1912), 4–5.

27. *CBSJ*, IV (Dec., 1911), 204. Most of this letter is reproduced in M. Liguori Brophy, B.V.M., *The Social Thought of the German Roman Catholic Central Verein* (Washington, 1941), pp. 74–76.

28. *57. General-Versammlung . . . 1912*, p. 99; *CBSJ*, V (Dec., 1912), 201. For Dietz's activities in union affairs, see Fox, *op. cit.*, Chaps. III–IV, and Philip Taft, *The A. F. of L. in the Time of Gompers* (New York, 1957), p. 335 ff.

29. For immigration, see J. Mitchell, "Protect the Workman," *CBSJ*, IV (May-June, 1911), 32–33, 54–55; A. F. Brockland, "The Economic Side of the Immigration Problem," *CBSJ*, V (Dec., 1912), 192–94; L. Budenz, "Some Features of a Constructive Immigration Policy," *CBSJ*, VIII (Sept., 1915), 162–65. For the actions of the Missouri and Wisconsin leagues, *CBSJ*, VII (June, 1914), 83; and *CBSJ*, IX (Aug., 1916), 152–53.

30. Some thirty articles dealing with the subjects mentioned in this paragraph and the following one are cited in my dissertation, "The Central-Verein, 1900–1917: A Chapter in the History of the German-American Catholics" (University of Notre Dame, 1960), pp. 278–81.

31. On these groups, see *CBSJ*, II (Nov., 1909), 8–9, 16; McDonagh, *op. cit.*, Ch. IV; Fox, *op. cit.*, Ch. III; M. Irmtrudis Fiederling, O.S.F., "Adolf Kolping and the Kolping Society of the United States" (unpublished master's thesis, Catholic University of America, 1941); and H. Dexl, "Die Kolpingsvereine in den Vereinigten Staaten," in Georg Timpe (ed.), *Katholisches Deutschtum in den Vereinigten Staaten von Amerika* (Freiburg im Breisgau, 1937), pp. 156–61.

32. The German text of *Singulari Quadam* is given in *CBSJ*, V (Dec., 1912), 185–86. John Courtney Murray, S.J., discusses the matter in "Intercredal Co-operation: Its Theory and Its Organization," *Theological Studies*, IV (1943), 257–86. For a detailed treatment, see Emil Ritter, *Die katholisch-soziale Bewegung Deutschlands im neunzehnten Jahrhundert und der Volksverein* (Cologne, 1954), pp. 313–34.

33. Engelen, "Rome Has Spoken," *CBSJ*, V (Jan.–Mar., 1913), 217–19, 243–45, 269–72. For a mid-century Catholic reaction to Engelen's analysis, see Francis Downing, "Catholic Contribution to the American Labor Movement," in Joseph N. Moody (ed.), *Church and Society* (New York, 1953), pp. 867–68.

34. Budenz, "The Rural Credits Legislation Before Congress,"*CBSJ*, IX (May, 1916), 44–46; E.P., "Die Farmkredit-Akte und der Farmer," *CBSJ*, IX (Sept., 1916), 163–65.

35. On Pesch, see Franz Mueller, *Heinrich Pesch and His Theory of Christian Solidarism* (St. Paul, 1941); Richard E. Mulcahy, S.J., *The Economics of Heinrich Pesch* (New York, 1952); Abram L. Harris, *Economics and Social Reform* (New York, 1958), Ch. VII; and *Social Order*, I (Apr., 1951), *passim*.

36. Engelen's speech is given in *60. General-Versammlung . . . 1915*, pp. 130–37. Except where otherwise indicated, the following exposition of the CV's Solidarism

is based on this source, which will not be cited in detail. Engelen also discussed social theory in fourteen articles in *CBSJ* in the years 1914–16. For citations to these and other articles on social theory, see Gleason, *op. cit.*, p. 287 ff.

37. Engelen in *CBSJ*, VIII (Apr., 1915), 9–10, and *CBSJ*, VII (Mar., 1915), 346.

38. Theodor Brauer, *The Catholic Social Movement in Germany* (Oxford, 1932), p. 5. Brauer adds (p. 7), "Baron von Hügel is not at all wrong when he says that anything which is sufficiently theorized appears to a German to be worthy of a hearing or even of belief."

39. A student of Catholic social theorists in Austria, a group who influenced Kenkel deeply, concludes: "The failure to distinguish between the state as the area of compulsory action and society as the area of voluntary action has emerged as the outstanding feature of Austrian Catholic social thought. This tendency to conceive of human life in unitary or monistic terms can be traced to a view of society as an organic whole, actuated by a single belief system." He further observes: "Fundamentally, then, the inadequacy of Catholic social thought in general, as well as Austrian Catholic thought in particular, lies in its inability to devise a set of concepts applicable to the modern, complex, multigroup society." Alfred Diamant, *Austrian Catholics and the First Republic: Democracy, Capitalism, and the Social Order, 1918–1934* (Princeton, 1960), pp. 286, 287.

40. Engelen, "Capital and Labor Under Solidarism," *CBSJ*, VII (Dec., 1914), 266. Cf. also, E. Prünte, "Volkswirthschaft und Religion," *CBSJ*, V (Sept., 1912), 111–13; and Kenkel, "Über die Nothwendigkeit der Erneurung der öffentlichen Sittlichkeit," *CBSJ*, VII (Aug., 1914), 129–30.

41. *61. General-Versammlung . . . 1916*, pp. 95–96.

42. Walsh's book went through seven printings between 1907 and 1920. Cf. Mary Marcella Smith, "James J. Walsh, American Revivalist of the Middle Ages" (unpublished doctoral dissertation, St. John's University, 1944).

43. *Bulletin of the American Federation of Catholic Societies*, V (Mar.–Apr., 1911), 1–3. Cf. McDonagh, *op. cit.*, p. 33.

44. Ralph H. Bowen, *German Theories of the Corporative State* (New York, 1947), p. 24 ff. Edgar Alexander's discussion of Catholicism and German romanticism is very valuable, although the terminology is at times baffling; see his essay entitled "Church and Society in Germany" in Moody (ed.), *Church and Society*, esp. pp. 366–408.

45. Bowen, *op. cit.*, pp. 98–112, discusses Hitze. See also Alexander, *loc. cit.*, pp. 422–30. Franz H. Mueller, who wrote a biography of Hitze (*Franz Hitze und sein Werk* [Hamburg, Berlin, Leipzig, 1928]), calls him "the John Ryan of Germany." See Mueller's excellent essay, "The Church and the Social Question," in J. N. Moody and J. G. Lawler (eds.), *The Challenge of Mater et Magistra* (New York, 1963), pp. 89–90.

46. Bowen, *op. cit.*, pp. 113–16; Karl Bachem, *Vorgeschichte, Geschichte und Politik der deutschen Zentrumspartei*, 9 vols. (Cologne, 1927–32), IX, 143–50. Alexander, *loc. cit.*, pp. 417–22, is highly critical of Vogelsang; for a more sympathetic discussion, see August M. Knoll, "Karl von Vogelsang und der Ständegedanke," in *Die soziale Frage und der Katholizismus: Festschrift zum 40 jährigen Jubiläum der Enzyklika "Rerum Novarum"* (Paderborn, 1931), pp. 86–98. Diamant, *op. cit.*, which discusses Vogelsang, p. 54 ff., is the best introduction to the whole subject in English and is an excellent analysis throughout.

47. Cf. Ritter, *Die katholisch-soziale Bewegung*, Ch. XIV; Bachem, *op. cit.*, VII, Ch. III; Ernst Deuerlein, "Verlauf und Ergebnis des 'Zentrumsstreit' (1906–09)," *Stimmen der Zeit*, CLVI (May, 1955), 103–26; "Die sozialpolitischen Richtungen unter den deutschen Katholiken seit 1870," *SJR*, XXXIII (May, June, 1940), 67, 104–06; M. Johannella Fiecke, O.S.F., *The Revival of Catholic Literature in Twentieth-Century Germany* (Milwaukee, 1948), pp. 114–58.

48. Bachem, *op. cit.*, VII, 164 ff.; Deuerlein, *loc. cit.*, p. 111 ff.

49. Bachem, *op. cit.*, VII, 156 ff., 175, 179 ff., 191.

50. Ritter, *op. cit.*, p. 338.

51. *Die Amerika* (St. Louis), Feb. 20, 1914. John Ireland was the American prelate Kenkel had in mind; for his role in the school controversy, see James H. Moynihan, *The Life of Archbishop John Ireland* (New York, 1953), Ch. 5.

52. Kenkel, "Dem Andenken Franz Brandts," *CBSJ*, VII (Dec., 1914), 257–59.

53. G. Rybrook, "The Christian State of the Future," *CBSJ*, III (Oct., 1910), 143–44. For discussions of Pesch, see Alexander, *loc. cit.*, pp. 418–19, 514–24; Joseph Dobretsberger, *Katholische Sozialpolitik am Scheideweg* (Vienna, 1947), p. 67 ff.; and Diamant, *op. cit.*, p. 159 ff.

54. *Die Amerika*, Nov. 24, 1914; Engelen to Kenkel, Oct. 18, 1915, AUND.

55. Engelen to Kenkel, Dec. 16, 1915, AUND.

56. Cf. Alexander, *loc. cit.*, pp. 417–22, and Dobretsberger, *op. cit.*, p. 74 ff. For two early samples of Kenkel's esteem for Vogelsang, see *CBSJ*, II (Mar., 1910), 6, and *CBSJ*, III (Sept., 1910), 115–16.

57. Cf. Alexander, *loc. cit.*, pp. 421, 475–76, 489–90; Bachem, *op. cit.*, VII, 168, 202–05.

Chapter VII

1. *61. General-Versammlung . . . 1916*, pp. 108–10. Cf. also *53. General-Versammlung . . . 1908*, p. 11.

2. Morton Grodzins, *The Loyal and the Disloyal; Social Boundaries of Patriotism and Treason* (Chicago, 1956), Chaps. I–IV.

3. *53. General-Versammlung . . . 1908*, p. 33; *54. General-Versammlung . . . 1909*, pp. 42–44.

4. *Bulletin of the American Federation of Catholic Societies*, V (Mar.–Apr., 1911), 1–3.

5. *57. General-Versammlung . . . 1912*, pp. 90–91; *59. General-Versammlung . . . 1914*, pp. 121–22. Cf. also, Frey to Kenkel, Nov. 14, 1913, AUND; F. W. Heckenkamp to Rev. Joseph Wubbe, June 23, 1913; Heckenkamp to J. W. Freund, Sept. 3, 1913; Freund to Heckenkamp, Sept. 8, 1913, all in ACV.

6. *57. General-Versammlung . . . 1912*, pp. 31–32, 35–36; *60. General Versammlung . . . 1915*, pp. 37–39. Cf. also *Darum Central-Verein und Staatsverband*, Central Bureau Flugblatt, No. 14 (St. Louis, 1916).

7. F. W. Heckenkamp to J. W. Freund, Sept. 2, 1913, ACV.

8. *59. General-Versammlung . . . 1914*, pp. 211, 120–22.

9. There is a copy of the agreement, entitled "Central-Verein und Federation," in ACV. Cf. also *CBSJ*, VII (Nov., 1914), 240.

245/NOTES TO CHAPTER SEVEN

10. *CBSJ*, IX (June, 1916), 78–79; Engelen to Kenkel, Feb. 21, May 10, 1916, AUND. On the Catholic Week, see *Literary Digest*, LIII (Sept. 2, 1916), 562–63.

11. Mary Harrita Fox, *Peter E. Dietz, Labor Priest* (Notre Dame, Ind., 1953), p. 98.

12. *Ibid.*, pp. 126–27; Kenkel to Muldoon, Sept. 25, 1912, ACV. I am indebted to Sister Mary Harrita Fox for a copy of this letter.

13. Joseph Frey to Kenkel, June 15, 1913; J. Meckel to Kenkel, May 20, 27, 1913. AUND. For the Study House, see above, Chapter VI.

14. Siedenburg to Kenkel, June 25, 1913, AUND. For Dietz' position, see Frey to Kenkel, June 12, 1913, AUND.

15. The following quotations are from the letter, Kenkel to Siedenburg, June 27, 1913, AUND.

16. Siedenburg to Kenkel, July 5, 1913, AUND.

17. Frey to Kenkel, July 2, 1913; Matt to Kenkel, July 6, 1913, AUND.

18. The quotations are from a statement, written in English, accompanying a cover letter in German, Meckel to Kenkel, June 30, 1913, AUND.

19. All quotations from the letter, Frey to Kenkel, July 3, 1913, AUND.

20. *58. General-Versammlung . . . 1913*, pp. 97, 121–22; Frey to Kenkel, Aug. 13, 1914, AUND.

21. *58. General-Versammlung . . . 1913*, pp. 7–8, 29.

22. Cf. the unsigned report of a conference of Catholic social agencies held in Baltimore, dated Oct. 8, 1914, ACV; Dietz to Kenkel, Mar. 1, 1915; Kenkel to George W. Heer, Mar. 6, 1916; Dietz to Kenkel, Mar. 18, 1915, AUND. The Kenkel to Heer letter is a fragment.

23. *61. General-Versammlung . . . 1916*, p. 32; *New York Times*, Aug. 20, 1916.

24. Cf. M. Adele Francis Gorman, O.S.F., "Peter E. Dietz and the N.C.W.C.," *Records of the American Catholic Historical Society of Philadelphia*, LXXIV (Dec., 1963), 213–26; Fox, *op. cit.*, p. 139 ff.

25. Most useful for the Alliance are: Clifton J. Child, *The German-Americans in Politics, 1914–1917* (Madison, Wis., 1939); Heinz Kloss, *Um die Einigung des Deutschamerikanertums* (Berlin, 1937), pp. 254–74; Max Heinrici (ed.), *Das Buch der Deutschen in Amerika* (Philadelphia, 1909), pp. 781–876; Ralph F. Bischoff, *Nazi Conquest through German Culture* (Cambridge, Mass., 1942), pp. 155–64. Two invaluable sources are: *National German-American Alliance,* Hearings before the Subcommittee on the Judiciary, United States Senate, 65th Cong., 2nd Sess. (Washington, 1918); and *Brewing and Liquor Interests and German Propaganda,* Hearings before a Subcommittee of the Committee on the Judiciary, United States Senate, 65th Cong., 2nd Sess. (Washington, 1919). Hereafter cited as *Hearings, German-American Alliance* and *Hearings, Brewing Interests.*

26. Child, *op. cit.*, pp. 10–21. By June, 1915, the brewer's group had given the DANB $39,033.41 for antiprohibition work. *Hearings, German-American Alliance,* p. 239.

27. Heinrici (ed.), *op. cit.*, p. 782.

28. Kloss, *op. cit.*, pp. 259, 260–61. Cf. also Child, *op. cit.*, p. 176; *Hearings, German-American Alliance,* p. 70.

29. *50. General-Versammlung . . . 1905*, p. 22; *51. General-Versammlung . . .*

1906, p. 63. Arthur Preuss, in *The Review*, VIII (1901), 503, sounded an early critical note in discussing the Alliance.

30. *52. General-Versammlung . . . 1907*, pp. 38, 47.

31. *Herold des Glaubens* (St. Louis), Nov. 27, 1907, and Oct. 14, 21, 1908; for earlier friendly items in this paper, see *ibid.*, Oct. 3, 1906, and Sept. 11, 1907. *Der Wanderer*, Apr. 2, 1908, reprinted in *Central-Blatt*, I (May, 1908), 6–8; Kloss, *op. cit.*, pp. 266–67, quotes several paragraphs of Matt's attack.

32. George Sylvester Viereck said of the DANB leaders: "They appealed exclusively to *Deutschtum*, but the Golden Grail of their idealism was filled to the brim with lager beer." Viereck, *Spreading Germs of Hate* (New York, 1930), p. 236.

33. *Central-Blatt*, I (July, 1908), 5.

34. Matt to Kenkel, July 16, 1909, AUND; Kloss, *op. cit.*, p. 266; *54. General-Versammlung . . . 1909*, p. 63.

35. This was the recollection of a participant, written long after the event. Francis S. Betten, S.J., to the Central Bureau, Sept. 3, 1931, ACV.

36. *54. General-Versammlung . . . 1909*, pp. 34, 67, 81–82.

37. John B. Oelkers to Kenkel, Nov. 13, 1909, AUND. On the Ferrer case and Catholic reaction, see "The American Catholics and the Ferrer Trial," *McClure's Magazine*, XXXV (Oct., 1910), 697–711.

38. *55. General-Versammlung . . . 1910*, pp. 54–56. *Herold des Glaubens*, Aug. 31, 1910, also criticized the DANB's conduct in St. Louis.

39. There was a lively debate on this point. *57. General-Versammlung . . . 1912*, pp. 55–58.

40. Kloss, *op. cit.*, pp. 267–68.

41. *Hearings, German-American Alliance*, p. 224.

42. *59. General-Versammlung . . . 1914*, p. 117.

43. For evidence of the DANB's interest in organizing German Catholics with brewing funds, see *Hearings, Brewing Interests*, pp. 841, 842, 847, 874–75, 1280–81, 1283–84, 1291–99. In 1915, the DANB sent an organizer to the CV convention "to get in touch with the heads of that great organization." *Ibid.*, p. 880.

44. Cf. *Hearings, German-American Alliance*, pp. 645–48. A DANB officer testified in 1918 that this agreement "has practically been a dead letter." *Ibid.*, p. 443.

45. *Ibid.*, pp. 547–51. For the anti-German hysteria of the war years, see Carl Wittke, *German-Americans and the World War* (Columbus, O., 1936), Ch. VI. On Bartholdt, who retired from Congress in 1915, see his autobiography, *From Steerage to Congress* (Philadelphia, 1931).

46. *Die Amerika* (St. Louis), July 25, 1913. For the Senate subcommittee's difficulties with the elusive term *Deutschtum*, see *Hearings, German-American Alliance*, pp. 464–66, 468–69.

47. Rev. Cl. Bellmann to Kenkel, July 26, 1913, AUND.

48. *59. General-Versammlung . . . 1914*, pp. 31, 32, 123. For the mass meeting in St. Louis, see A. F. Brockland to Kenkel, Aug. 7, 10, 1914, AUND; and John C. Crighton, *Missouri and the World War, 1914–1917: A Study in Public Opinion* (Columbia, Mo., 1947), pp. 28–29, 30–31 n.

49. *59. General-Versammlung . . . 1914*, p. 197. CBSJ, IX (Mar., 1917), 353, gives the total for the relief fund.

50. Engelen to Kenkel, Oct. 17, 1914, AUND. See *Catholic World*, C (Oct., 1914), 125–33, for the discussion in question.

51. Francis Markert, S.V.D., to Kenkel, Oct. 3, 1914, AUND; 60. *General-Versammlung . . . 1915*, p. 159.

52. The English-language editions of these depressing works are: Alfred Baudrillart (ed.), *The German War and Catholicism* (Paris, 1915); *The German War and Catholicism: German Defense Against French Attacks*, Authorized American Edition (St. Paul, 1916); and *German Culture, Catholicism, and the World War*, published by George Pfeilschrifter, *et al.*, Authorized American Edition (St. Paul, 1916).

53. Och to Kenkel, Jan. 21, 1915, AUND.

54. 59. *General-Versammlung . . . 1914*, pp. 4–5, 72. For *Amerika's* analysis of the causes of the war, see Crighton, *op. cit.*, p. 34.

55. 60. *General-Versammlung . . . 1915*, pp. 16, 18.

56. "Eigenartige Feier," *CBSJ*, IX (Mar., 1917), 349.

57. 60. *General-Versammlung . . . 1915*, pp. 159–60.

58. *CBSJ*, VIII (Sept., 1915), 168; 60. *General-Versammlung . . . 1915*, p. 24.

59. "Ein vernüftiger Standpunkt in der Tauchbootfrage," *CBSJ*, IX (May, 1916), 56.

60. Engelen to Kenkel, Oct. 18, 1915, AUND.

61. Cedric C. Cummins, *Indiana Public Opinion and the World War (1914–1917)* (Indianapolis, 1945), pp. 13–15; Arthur S. Link, *Woodrow Wilson and the Progressive Era, 1910–1917* (New York, 1954), pp. 145–48. Link, *Wilson: the Struggle for Neutrality, 1914–1915* (Princeton, 1960), Ch. I, is a discriminating account of initial American reactions to the war. Mark Sullivan, *Our Times: The United States, 1900–1925*, 6 vols. (New York, 1926–33), V, 1–32, describes how the war appeared to the reader of American newspapers. For the general question of hyphenation, see Louis L. Gerson, *The Hyphenate in Recent American Politics and Diplomacy* (Lawrence, Kan., 1964), esp. Chaps. III–IV.

62. James M. Read, *Atrocity Propaganda, 1914–1919* (New Haven, 1941), pp. 200–08; H. C. Peterson, *Propaganda for War: The Campaign Against American Neutrality, 1914–1917* (Norman, Okla., 1939), p. 53 ff.; Cummins, *op. cit.*, pp. 117–19.

63. Cummins, *op. cit.*, p. 105 ff.; Sullivan, *op. cit.*, pp. 107–32; Ernest R. May, *The World War and American Isolation, 1914–1917* (Cambridge, Mass., 1959), pp. 133–36, 148 ff.

64. Sullivan, *op. cit.*, pp. 184–96; Viereck, *op. cit.*, pp. 43–118. Cf. David W. Hirst, "German Propaganda in the United States, 1914–1917" (unpublished doctoral dissertation, Northwestern University, 1962).

65. Franz von Rintelen, *The Dark Invader: Wartime Reminiscences of a German Naval Intelligence Officer* (New York, 1933), pp. 96 ff., 122.

66. Child, *op. cit.*, Ch. V. Cf. also, John Higham, *Strangers in the Land; Patterns of American Nativism, 1860–1925* (New Brunswick, N.J., 1955), p. 195 ff.

67. The distinction between American patriotism and ethnic nationalism is developed in J. Albert Foisy, *The Sentinellist Agitation in New England, 1925–1928* (Providence, R.I., 1930), Chaps. XIV–XV.

68. Quoted in Child, *op. cit.*, p. 90.

69. *61. General-Versammlung . . . 1916*, p. 201; *New York Times*, Aug. 24, 26, 1916. See *New York Times*, Sept. 4, 1916, for a letter from "A Belgian Catholic" on the CV's resolution. The CV was highly critical of Wilson's Mexican policy, as were most American Catholics, and this added to their displeasure with the administration.

70. *New York Times*, Oct. 24, 1916. On the American Truth Society, see Viereck, *op. cit.*, pp. 97–98, 227–28; and *Hearings, Brewing Interests*, pp. 1411, 1541–43. O'Leary's *My Political Trial and Experiences* (New York, 1919), gives an account of some of his activities. Professor Kuno Francke of Harvard and Father Peter E. Dietz warned against the danger of "self-isolation" arising from German-American pressure-group tactics. See Francke, *Deutsche Arbeit in Amerika* (Leipzig, 1930), pp. 67–70; Fox, *op. cit.*, p. 128.

71. Child, *op. cit.*, Ch. III; *Literary Digest*, L (Feb. 13, 1915), 299–301.

72. Richard Bartholdt to Kenkel, Jan. 21, 1915; Kenkel to Bartholdt, Jan. 26, 1915; Frey to Kenkel, Feb. 14, 1915; Bartholdt to Kenkel, Feb. 28, 1915. All in AUND.

73. *60. General-Versammlung . . . 1915*, p. 43. Cf. Child, *op. cit.*, pp. 76–78; *Hearings, Brewing Interests*, pp. 2697–99.

74. *60. General-Versammlung . . . 1915*, pp. 108, 9, 43–44, 47–48; *CBSJ*, VII (Sept., 1915), 171; Child, *op. cit.*, pp. 81–83; J. P. Jones and P. M. Hollister, *The German Secret Service in America, 1914–1918* (Boston, 1918), illustration facing p. 250.

75. Kloss, *op. cit.*, pp. 277–78; Kenkel to Frey, May 6, 1916, AUND.

76. This is the caption of a picture of Koelble that appeared in the St. Louis *Post-Dispatch*, Mar. 8, 1916, clipping, ACV. For a discussion of the affair, see Child, *op. cit.*, p. 90 ff.; *Literary Digest*, LII (Mar. 18, 1916), 699.

77. There are two such telegrams, dated Apr. 7 and Apr. 19, 1916, in AUND. Cf. also, Wittke, *op. cit.*, pp. 80–81.

78. *CBSJ*, IX (Apr., 1916), 18–19.

79. Crighton, *op. cit.*, p. 153; *CBSJ*, IX (Aug., 1916), 155.

80. Matt to Kenkel, Jan. 11, Feb. 1, [May] 6, 1916, AUND. For evidences of dissatisfaction with Hexamer's Chicago meeting among DANB leaders, see *Hearings, German-American Alliance*, pp. 289, 414, 418.

81. Frey to Kenkel, May 3, 1916; Kenkel to Frey, May 6, 1916, AUND.

82. *61. General-Versammlung . . . 1916*, pp. 29, 31. Cf. also, Child, *op. cit.*, p. 122 ff.; Kloss, *op. cit.*, pp. 278–84; *CBSJ*, IX (July, 1916), 120–21; *New York Times*, Aug. 21, 1916.

83. Child, *op. cit.*, pp. 135–36. Arthur S. Link, *Wilson; Campaigns for Progressivism and Peace, 1916–1917* (Princeton, 1965), pp. 135–40, 161, discusses the role of the German-Americans in the election of 1916.

84. Frey to Kenkel, Sept. 26, 1916, AUND. Stone also talked to Kenkel in St. Louis; see Crighton, *op. cit.*, pp. 152–53. For Stone's work in the East, see *New York Times*, Oct. 12, 13, 1916.

85. Frey to Kenkel, Sept. 26, Oct. 30, 1916, AUND; *New York Times*, Oct. 24, 1916.

86. Viereck, *op. cit.*, pp. 245–47; *Hearings, German-American Alliance*, pp. 295–96; *Hearings, Brewing Interests*, pp. 1381–85, 1484–1502, 1508–13; *New York Times*, Oct. 23, 24, 25, 1916.

87. *New York Times,* Oct. 24, 26, 27, 1916; *Die Amerika* (weekly ed.), Oct. 31, 1916.
88. *Die Amerika* (weekly ed.), Oct. 31, 1916; *New York Times,* Oct. 24, 1916.
89. Seyfried to Kenkel, Oct. 12, 20, 23, 1916, AUND; *Die Amerika* (weekly ed.), Oct. 31, 1916.
90. Frey to Kenkel, Sept. 26, 1916, AUND.
91. *New York Times,* Oct. 23, 24, 25, 1916. Cf. Link, *Wilson: Campaigns for Progressivism and Peace,* pp. 138–39.
92. The copy of this letter in AUND is dated simply Oct., 1916.
93. Frey to Kenkel, Oct. 30, 1916, AUND. *Die Amerika* (weekly ed.), Oct. 27, 1916.
94. *Die Amerika* (weekly ed.), Oct. 27, 1916; Seyfried to Kenkel (telegram), Oct. 23, 1916; Matt to Kenkel, Nov. 12, 1916, AUND. Paul Prodoehl to Joseph Frey, Oct. 28, 1916, in *New York Times,* Nov. 4, 1916.
95. Wittke, *op. cit.,* p. 106; Crighton, *op. cit.,* pp. 150–51.
96. Seyfried to Kenkel, Oct. 27, 1916, AUND.
97. Frey to Kenkel, Feb. 5, 1917, ACV.
98. Peterson, *op. cit.,* p. 173.

Chapter VIII

1. Xaver Geyer, *Bei den Deutschamerikanern* (Godesberg am Rhein, n.d.), p. 141 ff.; Kenkel to Geheimrath Hermann Herder, Mar. 14, 1925 (copy), AUND.
2. "One who knows" to Kenkel, Apr. 9, 1917, AUND.
3. *The Menace,* May 4, 1918, clipping ACV. On the suspension of mailing privileges see William J. Stone to Mr. Sartorius (manager of *Amerika*), Mar. 19, 1918, AUND; *CBSJ,* XI (May, 1918), 60; *CBSJ,* XXIV (Dec., 1931), 288; *SJR,* XXXV (June, 1942), 96.
4. Sebastian G. Messmer to Kenkel, Apr. 22, 1918, AUND; *63. General-Versammlung . . . 1919,* pp. 40, 47; *64. General-Versammlung . . . 1920,* pp. 60, 104.
5. "How Cardinal Gibbons Fought Pan Germans," *New York Times Magazine,* June 3, 1917; Maurice Francis Egan, *Ten Years Near the German Frontier* (New York, 1919), p. 166 ff. Cf. Colman J. Barry, O.S.B., *The Catholic Church and German Americans* (Milwaukee, 1953), pp. 269–70, and "Dokumente zum Cahensly-Streit," *CBSJ,* XVI (June, 1923), 91–92.
6. *Protokoll über die Vorstandsversammlung des D. R. K. Central-Vereins . . . 1918,* p. 10.
7. *Amerika* (St. Louis), Apr. 24, 1917 (semiweekly ed.). The text of the archbishops' letter is given in Michael Williams, *American Catholics in the War* (New York, 1921), pp. 3–5; pledges of support for the war by the three American cardinals are given in *Catholic Mind,* XV (May 22, 1917), 234–37.
8. Two of Kenkel's sons, for example, served in the U.S. Marines; one was hospitalized after being gassed in the last days of the war. *CBSJ* published lists of German Catholic servicemen during the war years.
9. Kenkel touched on these points in two editorials, *Amerika,* Apr. 10, 1917

(weekly ed.). A correspondent wrote to him on the same day: "And it has sadly drifted to this, that Wall Street dominates the American people with a more disastrous despotism than perhaps any autocratic Russian Monarch ever oppressed his own people. Will the American people finally awaken to this calamitous degeneration of the Republic? Hail to you for your manly American Stand!" Rev. Fred Beuckman to Kenkel, Apr. 10, 1917, AUND.

10. See Carl Wittke, *German-Americans and the World War* (Columbus, O., 1936), p. 132; Clifton J. Child, *The German-Americans in Politics, 1914–1917* (Madison, Wis., 1939), Ch. III; H. C. Peterson and Gilbert C. Fite, *Opponents of War, 1917–1918* (Madison, Wis., 1957), p. 84. On the revisionist interpretation see Richard W. Leopold, "The Problem of American Intervention, 1917: An Historical Retrospect," *World Politics,* II (1949–50), 405–25.

11. Max Wurst to Kenkel, Nov. 29, 1917, AUND; *63. General-Versammlung . . . 1919*, p. 3. Cf. also H.A.F., "American Catholics in War and Peace," *Fortnightly Review*, XXX (Feb. 15, 1923), 75. (*Fortnightly Review*, edited by Arthur Preuss, was formerly called *Catholic Fortnightly Review*.)

12. F. J. Eble to Kenkel, May 30, 1917, AUND.

13. F. J. Eble to Kenkel, Nov. 18, 1918, AUND.

14. Georg Timpe, "Hundert Jahre katholischer deutscher Presse," in Timpe (ed.), *Katholisches Deutschtum in den Vereinigten Staaten von Amerika* (Freiburg im Breisgau, 1937), pp. 29–31. Cf. also Geyer, *op. cit.*, pp. 156–85.

15. Kenkel to Social Propaganda Committee, Nov. 11, 1921, ACV; Kenkel to Geheimrath Hermann Herder, Mar. 14, 1925 (copy) AUND.

16. *72nd General Convention . . . 1928*, pp. 73–74. There were still several passages of German in this convention report, just as English had been used in earlier ones; however, the secretary regarded it as a departure from the former use of German as the official language.

17. Kenkel to Social Propaganda Committee, Sept. 1, 1922, Archives of the Pontifical College Josephinum, Worthington, Ohio; *64. General-Versammlung . . . 1920*, p. 64; *67. General-Versammlung . . . 1923*, p. 55; *68. General-Versammlung . . . 1924*, pp. 58–59; *CBSJ*, XVII (May, 1924), 65.

18. This investigation is briefly reported in *CBSJ*, XXIV (July–Aug., 1931, Jan., 1932), 139, 328. The replies to the inquiry were forwarded to the Central Bureau and are preserved in ACV.

19. *CBSJ*, XXIII (Feb., 1931), 396; cf. also *CBSJ*, XXIV (Apr., 1931), 32–33; *CBSJ*, XXIV (Jan., 1932), 337.

20. Cf. *The Review*, VII (1900–1901), 277; *CBSJ*, II (Apr., 1909), 8–9.

21. *68. General-Versammlung . . . 1924*, pp. 62–67.

22. Muench to Kenkel, Apr. 3, 1927, AUND. See also Muench to Kenkel, Mar. 22, 1927, AUND; and *71. General-Versammlung . . . 1927*, pp. 13–18.

23. In 1925 CV president Korz wrote: "I am born and educated in Germany and nobody can love his mothertongue more than I do. But when it comes to the point of usefulness for Church and Country, I admit that we must begin to conduct our business in the language of the country. By doing this we preserve our societies, our traditions, our German character far more than by clinging to the German tongue, because, we will be able to fill our ranks with young blood and educate our posterity to those ideals we of German extract [sic] prize so highly. . . ." Korz to

H. J. Bellarts, Feb. 18, 1925 (unsigned copy), ACV. Several replies to the language inquiry referred to above in note 18 express similar views.

24. *Protokoll über die Vorstandsversammlung* . . . *1918,* pp. 22–23.

25. *61. General-Versammlung* . . . *1916,* pp. 69–71; *Diamond Jubilee Convention* . . . *1930,* pp. 44–45.

26. *63. General-Versammlung* . . . *1919,* pp. 11–15; *CBSJ,* XII (Oct., 1919), 197, 218–19; *CV Centennial,* pp. 92–93.

27. *63. General-Versammlung* . . . *1919,* pp. 47, 54.

28. Placidus Oechsle, O.S.B., to Kenkel, Oct. 3, 1919; Joseph Matt to Kenkel, Dec. 29, 1919, AUND.

29. By 1924, the Bureau had received $520,127.31 for European relief; by 1930, the total reached $597,472.94. Compare *68. General-Versammlung* . . . *1924,* p. 101, and *Diamond Jubilee Convention* . . . *1930,* p. 118. Matt, *CV Centennial,* p. 93, estimates the total collected by all the agencies of the German-American Catholics at one and a half million dollars.

30. Kenkel to Social Propaganda Committee, Nov. 1, 1922, Archives of the Josephinum. It seemed to Kenkel a year earlier that the German-American Catholics had done about all they could to help their brethren in Germany. See Kenkel to Ignatius Conrad, O.S.B., Nov. 3, 1921, Archives of New Subiaco Abbey, Arkansas.

31. *68. General-Versammlung* . . . *1924,* pp. 32, 59.

32. Charles Korz to Kenkel, Sept. 10, 1925, AUND; *69. General-Versammlung* . . . *1925,* p. 20.

33. *Diamond Jubilee Convention* . . . *1930,* p. 121; *68. General-Versammlung* . . . *1924,* p. 99.

34. The Central Bureau's report in the depression year of 1932 begins as follows: "To the wisdom and generosity of those . . . who agitated for and contributed to the Foundation Fund, the achievements of the Central Bureau during its past fiscal year are largely due. Although some retrenchment was necessary, on the whole it was possible to continue every activity inaugurated in the past, since income was not greatly affected by the depression." *77th General Convention* . . . *1932,* p. 104.

35. *70. General-Versammlung* . . . *1926,* pp. 63–65.

36. *68. General-Versammlung* . . . *1924,* pp. 52–54; *69. General-Versammlung* . . . *1925,* pp. 39–41, 45, 109; *70. General-Versammlung* . . . *1926,* p. 63.

37. *68. General-Versammlung* . . . *1924,* p. 14.

38. The text of the new constitution is given in *70. General-Versammlung* . . . *1926,* pp. 58–60. Korz explained the membership features in *Aurora und Christliche Woche* (Buffalo), clipping dated only 1926, ACV.

39. *72nd General Convention* . . . *1928,* p. 82; *73rd General Convention* . . . *1929,* p. 34.

40. *71. General-Versammlung* . . . *1927,* pp. 105–06; *Diamond Jubilee Convention* . . . *1930,* p. 40.

41. *73rd General Convention* . . . *1929,* pp. 87, 84.

42. *72nd General Convention* . . . *1928,* p. 37; *69. General-Versammlung* . . . *1925,* p. 115.

43. In Illinois, the old guard's watchwords were "Die liebe deutsche Sprache"

and "Die Frau gehört in's Haus." Louis Scheuermann to Kenkel, Jan. 21, 1931, ACV.

44. *73rd General Convention . . . 1929*, pp. 129–33.

45. *Ibid.*, p. 131.

46. *71. General-Versammlung . . . 1927*, p. 121.

47. W. Lloyd Warner and Associates, *Democracy in Jonesville* (New York: Harper Torchbook ed., 1964), p. 125 ff., discusses the continuing vitality of women's auxiliaries despite the general decline of the men's lodges of which they are adjuncts. Lodges lost ground throughout the country beginning in the 1920's.

48. *Diamond Jubilee Convention . . . 1930*, p. 121.

49. *76th General Convention . . . 1931*, p. 128.

50. For evidence of concern even among businessmen, see my article, "The Attitude of the Business Community toward Agriculture during the McNary-Haugen Period," *Agricultural History*, XXXII (Apr., 1958), 127–38.

51. *68. General-Versammlung . . . 1924*, p. 40; *72nd General Convention . . . 1928*, pp. 64–70; Bishop Wehrle's speech, *67. General-Versammlung . . . 1923*, pp. 29–31. Joseph Matt to Kenkel, Dec. 29, 1919, AUND, discusses Wehrle's concern over the Non-Partisan League.

52. Nicholas Gonner to Kenkel, Aug. 31, 1917, AUND; *67. General-Versammlung . . . 1923*, p. 54; *CBSJ*, XXII (Aug., 1929), 135–36.

53. Robert D. Cross, "The Changing Image of the City among American Catholics," *Catholic Historical Review*, XLVIII (Apr., 1962), 33–52, is an excellent brief treatment. For O'Hara and the Rural Life Conference see Raymond Philip Witte, S.M., *Twenty-five Years of Crusading; A History of the National Catholic Rural Life Conference* (Des Moines, 1948).

54. Witte, *op. cit.*, p. 45 ff.

55. H. A. Frommelt, "The Modern City: An Ogre," *CBSJ*, XVI (Apr., 1923), 7–8.

56. Witte, *op. cit.*, pp. 62–63. Cf. also *CBSJ*, XVI (Dec., 1923–Feb., 1924), 318–20, 356–57, 392–93.

57. Kenkel's articles ran all through volumes XIV (1921–22) and XV (1922–23) of *CBSJ*. Engelen, "A Modern Middle Class Society," *CBSJ*, XVIII (Oct., 1925–Jan., 1926), 219–21, 255–57, 291–93, 327–29.

58. Kenkel, " 'Farm Relief' According to the Chairman of the Federal Farm Board," *CBSJ*, XXII (Aug., 1929), 129–31.

59. In addition to the Kenkel and Engelen series see Carl Bruehl, "Die einzelnen Punkte des bishöflichen Programms sozialer Reconstruction," *CBSJ*, XII (May, 1919), 31–33; A. F. Brockland, "Initiative, Self-Help and Mutual Help Far Preferable to Dependence on Government," *CBSJ*, XVIII (July, 1925), 131–32. For rejection of the American dream see *CBSJ*, XVI (July, 1923), 117. For business opposition to farm relief see Gleason, "Attitude of the Business Community," *loc. cit.*

60. *65. General-Versammlung . . . 1921*, p. 85. The CV's interest in credit unions is reviewed in *CBSJ*, XXIV (Apr., 1931), 21–22. On the general enthusiasm for cooperatives in the early 1920's see Wilson Gee, *The Social Economics of Agriculture*, rev. ed. (New York, 1942), pp. 335–37; Murray R. Benedict, *Farm Policies of the United States, 1790–1950* (New York, 1953), pp. 194–98.

61. Kenkel, "Das Genossenschaftswesen als Wegbereiter," *CBSJ*, XII (Nov., 1919), 239–41; Kenkel, "Es Mangelt das geistige Band," *CBSJ*, XII (Dec., 1919), 273–74.

62. Paul Marx, O.S.B., *Virgil Michel and the Liturgical Movement* (Collegeville, Minn., 1957), p. 86 ff. On the preservation of religious folkways, cf. also Mary Eloise Johannes, C.S.J., *A Study of the Russian-German Settlements in Ellis County, Kansas* (Washington, 1946), p. 63 ff.; Ronald G. Klietsch, "Social Change, Ethnicity and the Religious System in a Rural Community," *American Catholic Sociological Review*, XXIV (Fall, 1963), 226 n.; and Klietsch, "The Religious Social System of the German-Catholics of the Sauk" (unpublished master's thesis, University of Minnesota, 1958).

63. *CBSJ*, XIV (Jan.–Mar., 1922), 323–26, 259–60, 396–98. Cf. also "Social Blessings of the Catholic Liturgy," *CBSJ*, XVIII (May, 1925), 58–59.

64. J.u.H., "Der Schlüssel zur Lösung der soziale Frage," *CBSJ*, XVIII (July–Aug., 1925), 122–24, 158–60. The authors were Fathers Anthony Jasper and Martin Hellriegel of O'Fallon, Missouri. Translated into English and published as a pamphlet by the Central Bureau, the essay "sold thousands of copies." See the discussion in Marx, *op. cit.*, pp. 110, 131 n. *Ibid.* Chaps. IX and X deal with Michel's social thought.

65. The word "Conference" replaced "Council" in the NCWC in 1923; to avoid confusion, I have called it National Catholic Welfare Conference throughout. There is no history of the organization. Michael Williams, *American Catholics in the War; National Catholic War Council, 1917–1919* (New York, 1921), is helpful, and M. Adele Francis Gorman, O.S.F., "Federation of Catholic Societies in United States, 1870–1920" (unpublished doctoral dissertation, University of Notre Dame, 1962), Ch. VII, discusses the transition from the AFCS to the War Council. For brief general treatments of the NCWC see John Tracy Ellis, *American Catholicism* (Chicago, 1956), p. 136 ff.; Aaron I. Abell, *American Catholicism and Social Action* (New York, 1960), Ch. VI; and Austin Dowling, "The National Catholic Welfare Conference," *Ecclesiastical Review*, LXXIX (Oct., 1928), 337–54. Several of the documents that led to the founding of the NCWC are printed in *Ecclesiastical Review*, LXI (July, 1919), 1–19.

66. Charles Korz to Bishop Schrembs, Nov. 1, 1921 (copy); Schrembs to Korz, Nov. 2, 1921, ACV. Williams, *op. cit.*, pp. 78–83, discusses Cahenslyism; on pp. 364–65 he omitted the CV from the list of organizations supporting the Catholic War Council. *Amerika*, Oct. 16, 1921; *Wanderer*, Oct. 20, 1921; and *The Echo* (Buffalo), Nov. 17, 1921, all discuss Korz's criticisms, which originally appeared in *Aurora und Christliche Woche* (Buffalo). Cf. also Central Bureau Pressbrief No. 16, Nov. 1, 1921, ACV.

67. Charles Korz criticized the NCWC Education Bureau in *Aurora und Christliche Woche*, June 24, 1921; so also did Kenkel in a confidential letter to the Social Propaganda Committee, Dec. 1, 1921, ACV. An undated clipping from the *St. Joseph Blatt* (Mt. Angel, Oregon) in ACV criticized the NCWC's civic catechism. Justin McGrath to John J. Burke, C.S.P., Apr. 23, 1923 (copy), ACV, responds to Kenkel's criticism of the NCWC's treatment of the Ruhr question.

68. Engelen to Kenkel, Dec. 27, 1918, AUND.

69. Engelen to Kenkel, Apr. 4, 1921, AUND. Joseph Husslein, S.J., was on the staff of the Jesuit magazine *America* and was the author of several books on social problems.

70. Husslein, for example, told Kenkel that he recommended the *Central-Blatt and Social Justice* often and had heard it spoken of very highly by other reform-

minded Catholics. He urged dropping German from the CV's social reform organ so as to broaden its appeal. Husslein to Kenkel, Nov. 6, 1918, Nov. 14, 1921, AUND.

71. Otto Kreuzberger to Kenkel, June 13, 1921, ACV.

72. Brock [August F. Brockland] to Kenkel, Mar. 30, 1921, ACV.

73. Kenkel to Brockland, May 21, 1921, ACV.

74. Kenkel to "Sehr verehrter hochw'ster Herr Bischof," Apr. 19, 1921 (copy), ACV. This five-page, single-space typed letter is really a short essay on the defects of the NCWC's structure owing to its unorganic character.

75. Engelen to Kenkel, Feb. 24, 1920; Nov. 29, 1922; Jan. 15, 1923; Nov. 8, 1925, AUND. In his letter of Nov. 8, 1925, Engelen wrote: "I had already given up all hope against the Ryan Faction." Cf. also C. Bruehl, "Auf dem Wege des Paternalismus," *CBSJ*, XVIII (July, 1925), 139. Franz H. Mueller brings out clearly the differences between Kenkel and Ryan; see his long essay, "The Church and the Social Question" in *The Challenge of Mater et Magistra*, ed. Joseph N. Moody and Justus George Lawler (New York, 1963), esp. pp. 96–97, 103 ff.

76. Kenkel, "Der Staatssozialismus gefährdet die Erneurung der Gesellschaft," *CBSJ*, XI (Mar., 1919), 378.

77. The text is given in John Tracy Ellis (ed.), *Documents of American Catholic History* (Milwaukee, 1956), pp. 611–29. See the discussion in John A. Ryan, *Social Doctrine in Action: A Personal History* (New York and London, 1941), p. 143 ff., and Francis L. Broderick, *Right Reverend New Dealer; John A. Ryan* (New York and London, 1963), pp. 104–11.

78. Bruehl, "Die einzelnen Punkte des bishöflichen Programms sozialer Reconstruktion," *CBSJ*, XII (May, 1919), 21–33.

79. Bruehl, "Eine wichtige Kundgebung," *CBSJ*, XII (Apr., 1919), 2–3.

80. Cf. Stanley Coben, "A Study in Nativism, The American Red Scare of 1919–20," *Political Science Quarterly*, LXXIX (Mar., 1964), 52–75; Robert K. Murray, *Red Scare; A Study of National Hysteria* (Minneapolis, 1955).

81. Wallace Henry Moore, "The Conflict Concerning the German Language and Propaganda in the Public Secondary Schools of the United States, 1917–1919" (unpublished doctoral dissertation, Stanford University, 1937), p. 92 ff.; Kenneth B. O'Brien, Jr., "Education, Americanization and the Supreme Court: The 1920's," *American Quarterly*, XIII (Summer, 1961), 161–71.

82. Walter Lippmann, "The Setting for John W. Davis," *Atlantic Monthly*, CXXXIV (Oct., 1924), 533.

83. For examples of the CV's stand on educational issues see *64. General-Versammlung . . . 1920*, pp. 60, 93–94, 101–02; *65. General-Versammlung . . . 1921*, pp. 38, 52–53, 56, 83–84. For the general Catholic reaction see M. Gabrieline Wagener, I.H.M., "A Study of Catholic Opinion on Federal Aid to Education, 1870–1945" (unpublished doctoral dissertation, University of Notre Dame, 1963), pp. 69–123.

84. *71. General-Versammlung . . . 1927*, p. 104.

85. Vincent A. McQuade, O.S.A., *The American Catholic Attitude on Child Labor since 1891* (Washington, 1938), p. 82 ff.

86. *Third Annual Meeting of the Catholic Conference on Industrial Problems . . . 1925* (Washington, n.d.), pp. 5–16.

87. Ryan to editor, *Daily American Tribune*, Nov. 25, 1927, AUND.

88. H. S. Spalding to Kenkel, Feb. 27, 1923, AUND.

89. Engelen to Kenkel, Feb. 24, 1920, AUND.

90. Cf. George Marshall Dill, Jr., "The Christian Trade Unions and Catholic Corporatism in Germany, 1914–1924" (unpublished doctoral dissertation, Harvard University, 1949), esp. Ch. VII; Ralph Bowen, *German Theories of the Corporative State* (New York, 1947), p. 118; Alfred Diamant, *Austrian Catholics and the Social Question, 1918–1933* (Gainesville, Fla., 1959); Diamant, *Austrian Catholics and the First Republic; Democracy, Capitalism, and Social Order* (Princeton, 1960).

91. *CBSJ*, XIII (Mar., 1921), 362–63; *CBSJ*, XIV (Mar., 1922), 390.

92. "Staatssozialistische Tendenzen des deutschen Centrums," *CBSJ*, XIV (May, 1921), 39–40; Engelen to Kenkel, Jan. 24, 1921, AUND. For items of a similar tenor, see "Warum die christlich-soziale Partei Oesterreichs versagte; Eine Lehre für die Katholiken unseres Landes," *CBSJ*, XVI (Aug., 1923), 165–66, and "Die sozialpolitischen Richtungen unter den deutschen Katholiken seit 1870," *CBSJ*, XXXIII (Apr.–Aug., 1940), 31–33, 67–68, 104–06, 140–41.

93. E. K. Winter, "Die katholische Aktion," *CBSJ*, XVII (Jan., 1925), 340–41, 359. Cf. also Winter, "Der Meister der katholischen Kultur- und Sozial-Reform," *CBSJ*, XIV (Aug., 1921), 137–39.

94. *CBSJ*, XXIII (July–Aug., 1930), 130. For a typical set of resolutions see 69. *General-Versammlung . . . 1925*, pp. 72–80.

95. Engelen to Kenkel, Nov. 13, 1921, AUND.

96. This phrase is used in *72nd General Convention . . . 1928*, p. 28.

97. Cf. Joseph Edward Clark, "The American Critique of the Democratic Idea, 1919–1929" (unpublished doctoral dissertation, Stanford University, 1958), esp. p. 434 ff.

98. Ralph Adams Cram, *The Nemesis of Mediocrity* (Boston, 1917); Cram, *The Great Thousand Years* (Boston, 1918). See the discussion in David Spitz, *Patterns of Anti-Democratic Thought* (New York: Free Press paperback, 1965), pp. 132–35.

99. Milwaukee *Excelsior*, Sept. 30, 1923, quoted in Geyer, *Bei den Deutsch-amerikanern*, p. 174.

100. Engelen, "Reconstruction by Force," *CBSJ*, XII (Dec., 1919), 280. See also Engelen, "Social Observations," *CBSJ*, XVI (July, 1923), 111–13. Novalis' essay begins: "Those were fine, magnificent times when Europe was a Christian country, when one Christendom inhabited this civilized continent and one great common interest linked the most distant provinces of this vast spiritual empire." The text in English is given in *The Political Thought of the German Romantics, 1793–1815*, ed. H. S. Reiss (New York, 1955), p. 126 ff. Ludwig W. Kahn, *Social Ideals in German Literature, 1770–1830* (New York, 1938), p. 57 ff., contains a discussion of the romantic notion of community that is relevant here. Cf. also Gottfried Salomon, *Das Mittelalter als Ideal in der Romantik* (Munich, 1922); Mary Magdalita Scheiber, C.S.C., *Ludwig Tieck and the Medieval Church* (Washington, 1939); and Karl Mannheim, *Essays on Sociology and Social Psychology* (New York, 1953), pp. 89 ff., 123 ff. Alfred Cobban discusses the relationship between romanticism, medievalism, and social reform in *Edmund Burke and the Revolt Against the Eighteenth Century*, 2nd ed. (London, 1960), Ch. VII, esp. p. 197 ff.

101. Reinhold Aris, *History of Political Thought in Germany from 1789 to 1815* (London, 1936), p. 335.

Chapter IX

1. *Diamond Jubilee Convention . . . 1930*, p. 13.
2. *Ibid.*, pp. 57–58; *CV Centennial*, pp. 96–97.
3. Cf. *87th General Convention . . . 1942*, pp. 75, 88–89, for the 1942 membership and affiliation of the fraternals. Within two years the fraternals added some 50,000 nominal members to the CV, but the move was disappointing as a means of strengthening the organization. See the complaints voiced in *93rd General Convention . . . 1948*, pp. 56–58. For the situation in 1966 see, *111th General Convention . . . 1966*, pp. 95–109.
4. *78th General Convention . . . 1933*, p. 87.
5. *Ibid.*
6. Cf. *SJR*, XXXIII (Apr., 1940), 25–26; *SJR*, XXXIX (Apr., 1946), 32.
7. *78th General Convention . . . 1933*, pp. 35, 41, 44, 72.
8. *Ibid.*, pp. 91–92; *CBSJ*, XXVI (June–Dec., 1933), 80–81, 117, 170, 301. David J. O'Brien, "American Catholic Social Thought in the 1930's" (unpublished doctoral dissertation, University of Rochester, 1965) is a good comprehensive treatment, but it does not provide details on the position of the CV. O'Brien notes, p. 387, that "Catholic social thought in the 1930's was characterized by unanimous acceptance of official [Catholic] teachings and wide and bitter disagreement as to their meaning and application." See also O'Brien's article, "American Catholics and Organized Labor in the 1930's," *Catholic Historical Review*, LII (Oct., 1966), 323–49.
9. *CBSJ*, XXVIII (Mar., 1936), 381–84; *CBSJ*, XXXI (Apr., Oct., 1938), 7–10, 194; *SJR*, XXXV (Nov., 1942), 223–25; *SJR*, XL (Sept., Dec., 1949), 154–55, 262–63.
10. See, for example, *SJR*, LV (Dec., 1962), 259–61; *SJR*, LII (Feb., 1960), 330–34.
11. *SJR*, XXXIV (Jan., 1942), 301–02. Kenkel was still citing Vogelsang very favorably in 1949. Cf. *SJR*, XL (May, 1949), 42.
12. Cf. *CBSJ*, XXXI (Oct., 1938), 193–94, 206–07; *CBSJ*, XXV (June, 1932), 104; *SJR*, XXXIX (Nov., 1946), 236–37.
13. *CBSJ*, XXXI (Mar., 1939), 372–75; an adaptation of this article is included in F. A. Hermens, *The Representative Republic* (Notre Dame, Ind., 1958), p. 193 ff.
14. Nathan Glazer, "Ethnic Groups in America: From National Culture to Ideology," in *Freedom and Control in Modern Society*, ed. Morroe Berger, *et al.* (New York, 1954).
15. Another Catholic ethnic organization that attempted the same kind of adaptation to the shifting nationality consciousness of its clientele was the American Lithuanian Roman Catholic Federation. This society made dedication to "Catholic Action" its mission in an effort to retain the loyalty of the Americanized second generation. See M. Timothy Audyaitis, S.S.C., "Catholic Action of the Lithuanians in the United States: A History of the American Lithuanian Roman Catholic Federation, 1906–1956" (unpublished master's thesis, Loyola University, [Chicago], 1958), pp. 84–95, 424 ff.
16. See John E. Smith, *Royce's Social Infinite; the Community of Interpretation* (New York, 1950).

17. Robert A. Nisbet, *The Quest for Community* (New York, 1953); reissued in paperback under the title, *Community and Power* (New York, 1962).

18. Free Press paperback edition (New York, 1964), pp. 1–31.

19. Milton M. Gordon, *Assimilation in American Life* (New York, 1964), p. 23 ff.

BIBLIOGRAPHICAL NOTE

Since this is an organizational and ideological analysis of the evolution of the German-American Catholic group the most important sources were those which dealt with the associational life of the group and revealed the thinking and the attitudes of its leaders. The two most important collections of materials of this sort are at the Central Bureau in St. Louis and at the University of Notre Dame.

The Kenkel Papers in the Archives at Notre Dame include thirteen boxes of family letters and fourteen boxes of general letters. The latter are principally letters received by Kenkel as editor of *Die Amerika* and as director of the Central Bureau, but there are some letters, or copies of letters, written by Kenkel to various correspondents. The collection also includes clippings, speeches by Kenkel, reports of Central Bureau activities, and copies of pamphlets published by the Bureau. The family letters likewise include clippings, photographs, and other miscellaneous materials. Taken together these papers are indispensable both for an insight into Kenkel's personality and thinking, and also for an understanding of the organizational development of the Central-Verein after 1907.

The Central Bureau houses both the Archives of the Central-Verein and an extensive collection of German Catholic newspapers, records of societies, parish histories, and related published sources. In addition, the papers of Peter E. Dietz are at the Central Bureau, as are the papers of the following significant figures in the German-American Catholic community: Edward Preuss, Arthur Preuss, and John E. Rothensteiner. Correspondence and records of the Central-Verein are spotty for the period before 1909, when the Bureau began its work under Kenkel's direction, but enough has been preserved on the Volksverein für Amerika to piece together the story of that organization. The most useful of the letters for this study were those dealing with the setting up and operation of the Central Bureau and with the relationship of the Central-Verein to the American Federation of Catholic Societies and the National German-American Alliance.

Except for the Provincial Archives of the Franciscan Fathers in St. Louis, which had the letters of Kenkel to Father Solanus Hilchenbach, no other archival collection consulted yielded much relevant material. The Archives of the Pontifical College Josephinum, Worthington, Ohio, had a few letters of interest; and the late Mr. Joseph Matt of St. Paul, who was a close friend of Kenkel, allowed me to examine a number of letters in his possession. Nothing could be found in the Archives of the Diocese of Cleveland on the activities of the group from that city whose initiative led to the establishment of the Central Bureau in 1909. The papers of Herman J. Heuser at the American Catholic Historical Society of Philadelphia, which Colman J. Barry found a rich source for his study of *The Catholic Church and German Americans*, had nothing of value for this investigation. Nothing could be found in the Archives of the Archdiocese of Milwaukee to elucidate the relationship of Sebastian G. Messmer either to the Central-Verein or to the American Federation of Catholic Societies.

First in importance among the published sources were the proceedings of the annual conventions of the Central-Verein and its official magazine *Central-Blatt and Social Justice* (called *Social Justice Review* after 1940). The most complete collection of the convention proceedings is at the Central Bureau and is now available on microfilm. The *Central-Blatt's* articles are of course the most substantial source for the social reform attitudes; but the magazine also contains a wealth of information about organizational activities of the Central-Verein. The annual reports of the Central Bureau were regularly carried in the *Central-Blatt* and in the convention proceedings, but the Kenkel papers and the Central Bureau also contain separate printed reports. The Central Bureau also has a file of the Press Letters which Kenkel began soon after the Bureau was established. Reports from the state leagues are given each year in the Central-Verein's convention proceedings; and both the Central Bureau and the Notre Dame Library have some published convention proceedings from various state leagues.

Souvenir programs, parish anniversary histories, and records of societies are included in the collection of Catholic German-Americana at the library of the Central Bureau. This library also has a large collection of German Catholic newspapers which are now available on microfilm. The libraries of the University of Notre Dame and of the St. Francis Seminary in Milwaukee also have a number of microfilms of German Catholic newspapers. Georg Timpe, "Hundert Jahre katholischer deutscher Presse," in Timpe (ed.), *Katholisches Deutschtum in den Vereinigten Staaten von Amerika* (Freiburg im Breisgau, 1937), is a good general guide to the German Catholic press. Individual newspapers are dealt with fully in Eugene P. Willging and Herta Hatzfeld, *Catholic Serials in the Nineteenth Century in the United States: A Descriptive Bibliography and Union List*, which appeared in installments in the *Records of the American Catholic Historical Society of Philadelphia*, beginning with Volume LXV (Sept., 1954), and which has been published in separate mimeograph installments by the Catholic University of America Press since 1959.

Arthur Preuss's *Review* (called *The Review* from 1893 to 1905; *Catholic Fortnightly Review* from 1905 to 1912; and *Fortnightly Review* from 1912 until its demise in 1934) is of special value as an English-language publication that reflected the thinking of a well-informed, conservative German-

American Catholic and because it often reported the views of the German Catholic press. Of somewhat similar character, although less useful, is the *Josephinum Review*, published after 1914 in Columbus, Ohio. The historical articles published regularly in *Central-Blatt and Social Justice* cover many aspects of German-American Catholic development. The *Pastoral-Blatt*, also published in St. Louis, likewise carried many historical articles, especially biographical sketches of important clerical leaders of the German Catholics. Another journal containing many historical articles is *The Salesianum*, published at St. Francis Seminary in Milwaukee.

Among secondary studies of the German-American Catholics, Colman J. Barry, O.S.B., *The Catholic Church and German Americans* (Milwaukee, 1953) is outstanding for the latter half of the nineteenth century. Less adequate for earlier periods are Lambert Schrott, O.S.B., *Pioneer German Catholics in the American Colonies (1734–1784)* (New York, 1933), and Emmet H. Rothan, O.F.M., *The German Catholic Immigrant in the United States (1830–1860)* (Washington, 1946). Georg Timpe (ed.), *Katholisches Deutschtum in den Vereinigten Staaten von Amerika* (Freiburg im Breisgau, 1937) is a collection of essays of uneven value. Mary Liguori Bropy, B.V.M., *The Social Thought of the German Roman Catholic Central Verein* (Washington, 1941) is sketchy and neglects the historical dimension.

Diocesan histories of areas settled by German Catholics, like John E. Rothensteiner's *History of the Archdiocese of St. Louis*, 2 vols. (St. Louis, 1928), can be useful. There are also some studies of German Catholics in certain cities, such as J. C. Bürgler, *Geschichte der kathol. Kirche Chicagos* (Chicago, 1889); Theod. Brüner, *Katholische Kirchengeschichte Quincy's . . .* (Quincy, Ill., 1887); and Thomas W. Mullaney, C.SS.R., *Four-Score Years: A Contribution to the History of the German Catholics in Rochester* (Rochester, N.Y., 1916). Mary Eloise Johannes, C.S.J., *A Study of the Russian-German Settlements in Ellis County, Kansas* (Washington, 1946) is a competent work. Bonaventura Hammer, *Die Katholische Kirche in den Vereinigten Staaten Nordamerikas* (New York, 1897) is an older general history that gives special attention to German Catholics, but it is of limited value. Ludwig Hertling, S.J., *Geschichte der katholischen Kirche in den Vereinigten Staaten* (Berlin, 1954), is more recent but adds nothing particular to what is known about the German Catholics.

Among histories of religious orders, the following were particularly useful: A School Sister of Notre Dame, *Mother Caroline and the School Sisters of Notre Dame in North America*, 2 vols. (St. Louis, 1928); Colman J. Barry, O.S.B., *Worship and Work: A History of St. John's Abbey and University* (Collegeville, Minn., 195?); *Four Historical Booklets Regarding the American Province of the Most Precious Blood Written by Francis DeSales Brunner* (Carthagena, O., 1957); Michael J. Curley, C.SS.R., *The Provincial Story* (New York, 1963); Francis X. Curran, S.J., "The Buffalo Mission of the

German Jesuits, 1869–1907," *Historical Records and Studies*, XLIII (1955); Gilbert J. Garraghan, S.J., *The Jesuits of the Middle United States*, 3 vols. (New York, 1938); and Marion A. Habig, O.F.M., *Heralds of the King; the Franciscans of the St. Louis-Chicago Province, 1858–1958* (Chicago, 1958). Another valuable study of a religious institution important to the German Catholics is Peter Leo Johnson, *Halcyon Days: Story of St. Francis Seminary Milwaukee, 1856–1956* (Milwaukee, 1956).

There are many histories of German Catholic parishes. Many are little better than chronicles, but two studies deserve special mention. Albert Kleber, O.S.B., *Ferdinand, Indiana, 1840–1940* (St. Meinrad, Ind., 1940) is a competent and interesting account of a rural German Catholic settlement in southern Indiana. Francis J. Hertkorn, *A Retrospect of Holy Trinity Parish* (Philadelphia, 1914), recounts the story of the first German national parish in the country and reproduces many documents. The early years of Holy Trinity are examined in detail in Vincent J. Fecher, S.V.D., *A Study of the Movement for German National Parishes in Philadelphia and Baltimore (1787–1802)* (Rome, 1955), an excellent study that sheds much light on trusteeism in the early years of American Catholicism.

Among biographical treatments of German Catholic figures are: Benjamin J. Blied, *Three Archbishops of Milwaukee* (Milwaukee, 1955); Michael J. Curley, C.SS.R., *Venerable John Neumann, C.SS.R., Fourth Bishop of Philadelphia* (Washington, 1952); Mary Harrita Fox, *Peter E. Dietz, Labor Priest* (Notre Dame, Ind., 1953); Peter Leo Johnson, *Crosier on the Frontier; A Life of John Martin Henni, Archbishop of Milwaukee* (Madison, Wis., 1959); Paul Marx, O.S.B., *Virgil Michel and the Liturgical Movement* (St. Paul, 1957); and Leo F. Miller *et al.*, *Monsignor Joseph Jessing (1836–1899), Founder of the Pontifical College Josephinum* (Columbus, O., 1936). Mary Elizabeth Dye, O.S.U., *By Their Fruits; A Social Biography of Frederick Kenkel, Catholic Social Pioneer* (New York, 1960), a modified master's thesis, is quite unsatisfactory.

Three biographical directories of German-speaking priests that also provide some information on newspapers and societies are: Ernst A. Reiter, S.J., *Schematismus der Katholischen Geistlichkeit in den Ver. Staaten Nord-Amerika's* . . . (New York, 1869); W. Bonenkamp, J. Jessing, and J. B. Müller, *Schematismus der deutschen und der deutsch-sprechenden Priester* . . . (St. Louis, 1882); and Johannes N. Enzlberger, *Schematismus der katholischen Geistlichkeit deutscher Zunge in den Vereinigten Staaten Amerikas* . . . (Milwaukee, 1892).

Joseph Salzbacher, *Meine Reise nach Nord-Amerika im Jahre 1842* (Vienna, 1845) is an account of conditions in the United States by a traveling German cleric who was especially interested in the situation of the German-American Catholics. Similar travel reports by visiting German churchmen in the twentieth century are: Xaver Geyer, *Bei den Deutschamerikanern*

(Godesberg am Rhein, n.d.), and Engelbert Krebs, *Um die Erde* (Paderborn, 1928). Beda Kleinschmidt, O.F.M., *Auslanddeutschtum und Kirche,* 2 vols. (Münster, 1930), which constitutes Vols. XXI and XXII in the series *Deutschtum und Ausland,* ed. Georg Schreiber, furnishes an account of German-American Catholicism as it appeared to a Catholic in Germany in the 1920's. Charles Plater, S.J., *Catholic Social Work in Germany* (London, 1909) is a good brief introduction to the social reform background of German Catholics in the homeland. Franz H. Mueller's lengthy essay, "The Church and the Social Question," in *The Challenge of Mater et Magistra,* ed. Joseph N. Moody and Justus George Lawler (New York, 1963), is especially useful for the comparisons it draws between Catholic social action in the United States and Germany. Mueller's *Heinrich Pesch and His Theory of Christian Solidarism* (St. Paul, 1941) is likewise helpful. The emphasis of Richard E. Mulcahy, S.J., *The Economics of Heinrich Pesch* (New York, 1952) is suggested by the title. Edgar Alexander's "Church and Society in Germany (1789–1950)" in *Church and Society,* ed. Joseph N. Moody (New York, 1953), is of book length and is extremely valuable. Ralph H. Bowen, *German Theories of the Corporative State* (New York, 1947) includes a section on German Social Catholicism. Alfred Diamant, *Austrian Catholics and the Social Question, 1918–1933* (Gainesville, Fla., 1959), and Diamant, *Austrian Catholics and the First Republic; Democracy, Capitalism, and the Social Order, 1918–1934* (Princeton, 1960) are excellent for German as well as Austrian social Catholicism and for a longer period than indicated in the titles. Relevant works in German are: Karl Bachem, *Vorgeschichte, Geschichte und Politik der deutschen Zentrumspartei,* 9 vols. (Cologne, 1927–32); Karl Buchheim, *Ultramontanismus und Demokratie; der Weg der deutschen Katholiken im 19. Jahrhundert* (Munich, 1963); Franz Mueller, *Franz Hitze und sein Werke* (Hamburg, Berlin, Leipzig, 1928); Emil Ritter, *Die katholisch-soziale Bewegung Deutschlands im neunzehnten Jahrhundert und der Volksverein* (Cologne, 1954); and the essays in the volume *Die soziale Frage und der Katholizismus: Festschrift zum 40 jährigen Jubiläum der Enzyklika "Rerum Novarum"* (Paderborn, 1931).

Among general studies of German immigration the most useful for my purposes was Heinz Kloss, *Um die Einigung des Deutschamerikanertums* (Berlin, 1937), which includes discussions of both the Central-Verein and the National German-American Alliance. Clifton J. Child, *The German-Americans in Politics, 1914–1917* (Madison, Wis., 1939) is the fullest treatment of the Alliance, but *Das Buch der Deutschen in Amerika,* ed. Max Heinrici (Philadelphia, 1909) contains much information on personalities. Carl Wittke, *German-Americans and the World War* (Columbus, O., 1936) covers much of the same material as Child but concentrates on public opinion more than political action. Among Wittke's numerous other works in the field of German immigration the most helpful were *The German Language Press in America*

(Lexington, Ky., 1957), and *Refugees of Revolution* (Philadelphia, 1952). The older standard work by Albert B. Faust, *The German Element in the United States*, 2 vols. (New York, 1909), was of little relevance to this study, but John A. Hawgood, *The Tragedy of German-America* (New York and London, 1940) has a good analysis of German immigration statistics in the nineteenth century. Dieter Cunz, *The Maryland Germans; A History* (Princeton, 1948) is a thorough study of German-American development in one state. Herman E. Hagedorn, *The Hyphenated Family* (New York, 1960) is an interesting reminiscence by a German-American; and Ludwig Fulda, *Amerikanische Eindrücke* (Stuttgart and Berlin, 1906) is a German traveler's report at the turn of the century. Mack Walker, *Germany and the Emigration, 1816–1885* (Cambridge, Mass., 1964) is the best treatment of the German background to immigration.

Maldwyn Allen Jones, *American Immigration* (Chicago, 1960) is a superlative brief synthesis of the subject, and its bibliographical essay is a fine guide to the literature on immigration. The classic work of W. I. Thomas and Florian Znaniecki, *The Polish Peasant in Europe and America*, 5 vols. (Boston, 1918–1920), is particularly enlightening on the nature and functions of immigrant organizations, as is William C. Smith, *Americans in the Making* (New York and London, 1939) on the process of immigrant assimilation. Other works that I found especially helpful on the same topic were Robert A. Park and Herbert A. Miller, *Old World Traits Transplanted* (New York and London, 1921); W. D. Borrie (ed.) *The Cultural Integration of Immigrants* (UNESCO, 1959); and Milton M. Gordon, *Assimilation in American Life* (New York, 1964). Joshua A. Fishman *et al.*, *Language Loyalty in the United States*, which I read in the form of a dittoed report to the U.S. Office of Education (1964), was published in the Hague in 1966. Studies of other immigrant groups that are particularly relevant because of the comparisons they offer in respect to organizational matters or the growth of immigrant self-consciousness are: Thomas N. Brown, *Irish American Nationalism* (Philadelphia and New York, 1966); Joseph Cada, *The Catholic Central Union* (Chicago, 1952), a study of a Czech Catholic society comparable to the Central-Verein; Nathan Glazer, "Ethnic Groups in America: From National Culture to Ideology," in *Freedom and Control in Modern Society*, ed. Morroe Berger, *et al.* (New York, 1954); Victor R. Greene, "For God and Country: The Origins of Slavic Catholic Self-Consciousness in America," *Church History*, XXXV (Dec., 1966); Timothy L. Smith, "Religious Denominations as Ethnic Communities: A Regional Case Study," *Church History*, XXXV (June, 1966); and Mason Wade, "The French Parish and *Survivance* in Nineteenth-Century New England," *Catholic Historical Review*, XXXVI (July, 1950).

Robert D. Cross, *The Emergence of Liberal Catholicism in America* (Cambridge, Mass., 1958) is a good synthesis of American Catholic history in the late nineteenth century, and the notes provide a guide to all but the most recent secondary literature. Thomas T. McAvoy, C.S.C., *The Great Crisis in American Catholic History, 1895–1900* (Chicago, 1957) is authoritative on Americanism. John Tracy Ellis, *The Life of James Cardinal Gibbons*, 2 vols. (Milwaukee, 1952) provides detailed coverage of the principal issues in the American Church during the years of Gibbons' leadership. Other important biographical studies are: Patrick H. Ahern, *The Life of John J. Keane: Educator and Archbishop, 1839–1918* (Milwaukee, 1954); James H. Moynihan, *The Life of Archbishop John Ireland* (New York, 1953); David F. Sweeney, O.F.M., *The Life of John Lancaster Spalding, First Bishop of Peoria, 1840–1916* (New York, 1966); Frederick J. Zwierlein, *The Life and Letters of Bishop McQuaid*, 3 vols. (Rochester, N.Y., 1925–27). Francis G. McManamin, "Peter J. Muldoon, First Bishop of Rockford, 1862–1927," *Catholic Historical Review*, XLVIII (Oct., 1962) is a useful brief sketch.

The period after 1900 has received very little attention from historians of American Catholicism. Thomas T. McAvoy, C.S.C., offers a stimulating interpretive survey of the Progressive period in "The Catholic Minority after the Americanist Controversy, 1899–1917: A Survey," *Review of Politics*, XXI (Jan., 1959). John A. Ryan's *Social Doctrine in Action: A Personal History* (New York and London, 1941) is the autobiography of the foremost Catholic champion of social reform; Francis L. Broderick, *Right Reverend New Dealer; John A. Ryan* (New York and London, 1963) is a scholarly biography. Fox's biography of Dietz (listed earlier) is also relevant to this period and subject. Marc Karson, *American Labor Unions and Politics, 1900–1918* (Carbondale, Ill., 1958) has a good deal of information on Catholic anti-socialist work. Aaron I. Abell, *American Catholicism and Social Action* (New York, 1960), both broad and thorough in coverage, is the indispensable work on American Catholic social thought and action from the mid-nineteenth to the mid-twentieth century.

A number of unpublished doctoral dissertations and master's theses proved very helpful for this study; since they are obscure and difficult to locate, it will be worthwhile to list them here. The most useful for my purposes was M. Adele Francis Gorman, O.S.F., "Federation of Catholic Societies in the United States, 1870–1920" (Ph.D., Notre Dame, 1962). Francis A. Coghlan, "The Impact of the Spanish-American War on the Catholic Church in the United States of America, 1898–1903" (M.A., Notre Dame, 1956) is useful for some of the same material covered by Gorman. The following Ph.D. dissertations dealing with various aspects of general American Catholic history were also helpful: Anthony H. Deye, "Archbishop John Baptist Purcell of Cincinnati: Pre-Civil War Years" (Notre Dame, 1959); Carl D. Hinrichsen, "The History of the Diocese of Newark, 1873–1901" (Catholic University, 1962); Mary Marcella Smith, "James J. Walsh, American Revivalist of the Middle Ages" (St. John's [Brooklyn], 1944); John P. J. Walsh, "The Catholic Church in Chicago and the Problems of an Urban Society, 1893–1915"

(University of Chicago, 1948); M. Gabrieline Wagener, I.H.M., "A Study of Catholic Opinion on Federal Aid to Education, 1870–1945" (Notre Dame, 1963); and James A. White, "The Era of Good Intentions; A Survey of American Catholics' Writing Between the Years 1880–1915" (Notre Dame, 1956). Robert E. Doherty, "The American Socialist Party and the Roman Catholic Church, 1901–1917" (Ed.D., Teachers College [Columbia] 1959), is based primarily on socialist sources and deals with the Church's crusade against socialism as it appeared to those in the socialist camp. Three studies concentrate on the relations of Catholics to the labor movement: Joan Leonard, "Catholic Attitude Toward American Labor, 1884–1919" (M.A., Columbia, 1940); Thomas J. McDonagh, C.S.C., "Some Aspects of the Roman Catholic Attitudes toward the American Labor Movement, 1900–1914" (Ph.D., Wisconsin, 1951); and Edward G. Roddy, "The Catholic Newspaper Press and the Quest for Social Justice, 1912–1920" (Ph.D., Georgetown, 1961). James E. Roohan, "American Catholics and the Social Question, 1865–1900" (Ph.D., Yale, 1952) is comprehensive and detailed. David J. O'Brien, "American Catholic Social Thought in the 1930's" (Ph.D., Rochester, 1965) is more limited in scope but equally thorough and valuable. Thomas O. Wood, "The Catholic Attitude Toward the Social Settlement Movement: 1886–1914" (M.A., Notre Dame, 1958) is a good treatment of a special aspect of the social reform movement. James Edward Clark, "The American Critique of the Democratic Idea, 1919–1929" (Ph.D., Stanford, 1958), is an excellent study of American social and political attitudes in the 1920's.

The following theses dealing with various aspects of German-American Catholic history proved useful: Mary de Paul Faber, O.S.F., "*The Luxemburger Gazette*, A Catholic German Language Paper of the Middle West, 1872–1918" (M.S., Catholic University, 1948); Charles E. Fehrenbach, C.SS.R., "German Literary Activities of the Redemptorists in the United States" (M.A., Catholic University, 1937); M. Irmtrudis Fiederling, O.S.F., "Adolf Kolping and the Kolping Society of the United States" (M.A., Catholic University, 1941); Daniel Francis Gebhardt, "A History of the *Catholic Daily Tribune*" (M.A., Marquette, 1953); Ronald G. Klietsch, "The Religious Social System of the German-Catholics of the Sauk" (M.A., Minnesota, 1958); M. Hedwigis Overmoehle, F.S.P.A., "The Anti-Clerical Activities of the Forty-Eighters in Wisconsin, 1848–1860" (Ph.D., St. Louis, 1941); Anthony L. Saletel, S.M., "Damian Litz and the Catholic German-American Press" (M.A., Catholic University, 1939); Georg F. Sperl, "Die Vereinigten Staaten von Amerika und der deutsche Kulturkampf" (Ph.D., Ludwig-Maximilians Universität [Munich], 1953).

Especially helpful on the background of social reform ideas in Germany is George Marshall Dill, Jr., "The Christian Trade Unions and Catholic Corporatism in Germany, 1914–1924" (Ph.D., Harvard, 1949).

G. A. Dobbert, "The Disintegration of an Immigrant Community: The

Cincinnati Germans, 1870–1920" (Ph.D., University of Chicago, 1965) is an excellent case study of German immigrant life. Noel Iverson, Jr., "Germania, USA: The Dynamics of Change of an Ethnic Community into a Status Community" (Ph.D., Minnesota, 1963) is a sociological study of less value. David W. Hirst, "German Propaganda in the United States, 1914–1917" (Ph.D., Northwestern, 1962) is based on materials in the National Archives and supplies a needed corrective to traditional views on the subject of German propaganda. Wallace Henry Moore, "The Conflict Concerning the German Language and Propaganda in the Public Secondary Schools of the United States, 1917–1919" (Ph.D., Stanford, 1937) is pedestrian, but brings together much useful information.

Several studies of immigrant groups other than Germans provided information or insights that were helpful. Helena Znaniecki Lopata, "The Function of Voluntary Associations in an Ethnic Community: 'Polonia' " (Ph.D., University of Chicago, 1954) is a sociological treatment of the general subject of immigrant organizations. M. Timothy Audyaitis, S.S.C., "Catholic Action of the Lithuanians in the United States: A History of the American Lithuanian Roman Catholic Federation, 1906–1956" (M.A., Loyola [Chicago], 1958) is a lengthy and detailed account of an immigrant organization whose evolution offers some interesting parallels to that of the Central-Verein. Russell Barta, "The Concept of Secularization as a Social Process" (Ph.D., Notre Dame, 1959) is a sociological study that focusses on changes among French-Canadian and Polish-American groups as indicators of the process of secularization. Two theses that examine these groups in more detail are: George F. Theriault, "The Franco-Americans in a New England Community: An Experiment in Survival" (Ph.D., Harvard, 1951), which is sociological in orientation, and Frank A. Renkiewicz, "The Polish Settlement of St. Joseph County, Indiana: 1855–1935" (Ph.D., Notre Dame, 1967), a detailed historical account of one Polish-American community. James J. Zatko, "A Social History of the Slovak Immigrants in America, 1873–1914" (M.A., Notre Dame, n.d.) discusses more generally another largely Catholic immigrant group from Central Europe.

INDEX